Christ over All Things

Christ over All Things

Cosmic Christ in Colossians and Ephesians in the Context of Ancient Judaism

JAMES P. CROCKETT JR.

WIPF & STOCK · Eugene, Oregon

CHRIST OVER ALL THINGS
Cosmic Christ in Colossians and Ephesians in the Context of Ancient Judaism

Copyright © 2024 James P. Crockett Jr. All rights reserved. Except for brief quotations in critical publications or reviews, no part of this book may be reproduced in any manner without prior written permission from the publisher. Write: Permissions, Wipf and Stock Publishers, 199 W. 8th Ave., Suite 3, Eugene, OR 97401.

Wipf & Stock
An Imprint of Wipf and Stock Publishers
199 W. 8th Ave., Suite 3
Eugene, OR 97401

www.wipfandstock.com

PAPERBACK ISBN: 979-8-3852-2941-3
HARDCOVER ISBN: 979-8-3852-2942-0
EBOOK ISBN: 979-8-3852-2943-7

VERSION NUMBER 10/21/24

Dedicated to:
my parents
Jim and Joy Crockett

my sons
Owen and Landon

and

my dearest wife Abby,
whom I love and adore.

Contents

Acknowledgments | ix
List of Abbreviations | xi

1 Introduction | 1
    What Is Cosmic Christology? | 2
    Thesis | 3
    History of Scholarship | 4
    Scholarly Gap | 15
    Methodology and Scope | 17

2 The Root of Cosmic Christ in the Old Testament and Early Judaism | 20
    The Adamic Tradition | 21
    The Messianic King from David | 31
    Summary and Conclusions | 50

3 Cosmic Christ in the New Testament | 52
    Cosmic Christ in the Gospels | 53
    Cosmic Christ in the Undisputed Letters of Paul | 64
    Other Key NT Texts on Cosmic Christ | 88
    Summary and Conclusions | 92

4 Cosmic Christ in Colossians | 95
    Colossians 1:12–20 | 96
    Colossians 2:6–15 | 118
    Colossians 3:1–11 | 128
    Summary and Conclusion | 133

5 Cosmic Christ in Ephesians | 135
   The Relationship between Colossians and Ephesians | 136
   Ephesians 1:3–14 | 139
   Ephesians 1:20–23 | 144
   Ephesians 2:1–22 | 150
   Ephesians 3:8–11 | 156
   Ephesians 4:7–16; 5:5 | 159
   Summary and Conclusion | 165

6 Conclusion | 168
   The Royal Backdrop | 168
   The Cosmic King in Colossians and Ephesians | 170
   Implications and Further Points of Study | 174

Bibliography | 179

Acknowledgments

WHILE WORKING ON SUCH an extensive study can often feel like a lonely process, the reality is that it is a group effort. So many people have walked alongside me as I have taken this difficult yet rewarding journey, and words fall short in expressing the gratitude I feel toward them. Here is my best attempt to give thanks to these people.

I express my deepest gratitude to my PhD supervisor, Dr. S. Aaron Son. Dr. Son took an interest in me before I entered the PhD program at Southwestern Baptist Theological Seminary. In my first semester, I was a part of his NT reading seminar and his class on Colossians. Dr. Son's passion gave me a love for Pauline studies, and I am grateful that he invited me to study under his guidance. He pushed me and continually encouraged me to pursue excellence in my work. At the same time, he showed great patience and kindness throughout the course of this project. His comments, advice, and insights have been invaluable to the completion of this study. I have come to consider him not only as my supervisor but as my mentor and dear friend. I am also grateful to Dr. Terry Wilder, who taught a course on Ephesians of which I was fortunate to be a part. His class only grew my desire to deepen my understanding of Ephesians. I am also grateful for Dr. Paul Hoskins, whose seminar on the NT use of the OT piqued my interest in how Paul used the OT to articulate his Christology and brought clarity to how I would approach my research. I am also grateful to Dr. Mark Taylor and Dr. Andrew Streett, who provided me with invaluable feedback on this study.

I must also acknowledge the members and staff at Hillcrest Baptist Church in Cedar Hill, Texas. Throughout the course of this project, I had the wonderful privilege of serving as their minister to college students and young adults. I am thankful for a church that both valued and financially supported my academic pursuits. At various points, they willingly gave me time away from my ministry responsibilities to allow me to complete this study. Hillcrest was truly the best place I could have served during this time.

I am grateful for my parents, Jim and Joy Crockett. Their love of Scripture throughout my life sparked a passion in me to pursue a deeper understanding of the biblical text. They encouraged me as I expressed my desire to pursue PhD studies and believed in me on every step of this journey. They have also provided tremendous financial support as I spent many years as a "poor seminary student." I am grateful for their unconditional love. I am also thankful for my siblings Heather and Katie, as they have always supported me in my academic pursuits. I am thankful for my sons, Owen and Landon. During this study, I was blessed to become their father, and they have brought me untold joy. Becoming their father has truly been one of the greatest highlights of my life and has lightened the load of this work. Owen and Landon, I am extremely proud that you call me Dad. I love you both very much.

Most of all, I am grateful for my wife, Abby, who is my greatest supporter. She married me while I was researching and writing this study and willingly made many sacrifices so that I could complete this academic pursuit. Her words of encouragement and unconditional love were sometimes the only thing that kept me going. Abby, I cannot thank you enough for your love and support. I love you more than words can express.

List of Abbreviations

JOURNALS

ABR	*Australian Biblical Review*
AUSS	*Andrews University Seminary Studies*
BBR	*Bulletin of Biblical Research*
BET	*Bulletin of Ecclesial Theology*
Bib	*Biblica*
BibInt	*Biblical Interpretation*
BSac	*Bibliotheca Sacra*
BZ	*Biblische Zeitschrift*
CurBR	*Currents in Biblical Research*
CBQ	*Catholic Biblical Quarterly*
CTR	*Criswell Theological Review*
CTQ	*Concordia Theological Quarterly*
Di	*Dialog*
DSD	*Dead Sea Discoveries*
EvQ	*Evangelical Quarterly*
ExAud	*Ex Auditu*
ExpTim	*Expository Times*
FilNeot	*Filologia Neotestamentaria*
HTR	*Harvard Theological Review*
HvTSt	*Hervormde teologiese studies*
Int	*Interpretation*
JANER	*Journal of Ancient Near Eastern Religions*
JBL	*Journal of Biblical Literature*
JESOT	*Journal for the Evangelical Study of the Old Testament*
JETS	*Journal of the Evangelical Theological Society*

JSNT	Journal for the Study of the New Testament
JTS	Journal of Theological Studies
LTP	Laval théologique et philosophique
Neot	Neotestamentica
NovT	Novum Testamentum
NRTh	La nouvelle revue théologique
NTS	New Testament Studies
OtSt	Oudtestamentische Studien
Phron	Phronema
RB	Revue biblique
R&T	Religion and Theology
RevExp	Review and Expositor
RevScRel	Revue des sciences religieuses
ScEs	Science et esprit
SCJ	Stone-Campbell Journal
SEÅ	Svensk exegetisk årsbok
SJOT	Scandinavian Journal of the Old Testament
SJT	Scottish Journal of Theology
SPhilo	Studia Philonica
SwJT	Southwestern Journal of Theology
TrinJ	Trinity Journal
TynBul	Tyndale Bulletin
TZ	Theologische Zeitschrift
VE	Vox Evangelica
VV	Verbum Vitae
WTJ	Westminster Theological Journal
ZAW	Zeitschrift für die alttestamentliche Wissenschaft
ZNW	Zeitschrift für die neutestamentliche Wissenschaft und die Kunde der älteren Kirche
ZST	Zeitschrift für wissenschaftliche Theologie

COMMENTARIES

AB	Anchor Bible Commentary
BNTC	Black's New Testament Commentaries
BECNT	Baker Exegetical Commentary on the New Testament
CBC	Cambridge Bible Commentary
CC	Continental Commentaries

CGTC	Cambridge Greek Testament Commentary
EEC	Evangelical Exegetical Commentary
EGGNT	Exegetical Guide to the Greek New Testament
IBC	Interpretation: A Bible Commentary for Teaching and Preaching
ICC	International Critical Commentary
NCBC	New Century Bible Commentary
NCCS	New Covenant Commentary Series
NIBCNT	New International Biblical Commentary on the New Testament
NICNT	New International Commentary on the New Testament
NICOT	New International Commentary on the Old Testament
NIGTC	New International Greek Testament Commentary
NTL	New Testament Library
NTR	New Testament Readings
PNTC	Pillar New Testament Commentary
SHBC	Smith & Helwys Bible Commentary
SP	Sacra Pagina
TNTC	Tyndale New Testament Commentaries
WBC	Word Biblical Commentary
ZECNT	Zondervan Exegetical Commentary on the New Testament

OTHERS

ANRW	*Aufstieg und Niedergang der römischen Welt: Geschichte und Kultur Roms im Spiegel der neueren Forschung* Part 2
AOTS	Augsburg Old Testament Studies
BDAG	Danker, Frederick W., Walter Bauer, William F. Arndt, and F. Wilbur Gingrich. *Greek-English Lexicon of the New Testament and Other Early Christian Literature*. 3rd ed. Chicago: University of Chicago Press, 2000.
ETS	Evangelical Theological Society
LXX	Septuagint
MT	Masoretic Text
NT	New Testament
OT	Old Testament
SBL	Society of Biblical Literature
TLG	Thesaurus Linguae Graecae

APOCRYPHA AND PSEUDEPIGRAPHA

2 Bar.	2 Baruch
1 En.	1 Enoch
2 En.	2 Enoch (Slavonic Apocalypse)
4 Ezra	4 Ezra
Jub.	Jubilees
Pss. Sol.	Psalms of Solomon
Sir	Sirach
Wis	Wisdom of Solomon

PHILO

Agr.	*De agricultura*
Conf.	*De confusione linguarum*
Det.	*Quod deterius potiori insidiari soleat*
Leg. 1	*Legum allegoriae* I
Opif.	*De opificio mundi*
QG	*Quaestiones et solutiones in Genesin* IV
Somn. 1	*De somniis* I

QUMRAN

4Q161	Pesher Isaiah A
4Q174	Florilegium (Midrash on Eschatology)
4Q246	Apocryphon of Daniel
4Q252	Pesher on Genesis A
4Q285	Sefer Hamilhamah
4Q504	Dibre Hame'orot (Words of the Luminaries)
4Q521	Messianic Apocalypse
4Q534	Elect of God
1QH[a]	Hodayot[a] or Thanksgiving Hymns[a]
1QS	Serek Hayaḥad or Rule of the Community
CD	Cairo Genizah copy of the Damascus Document

1

Introduction

A CLOSER LOOK AT Paul reveals a vital cosmic dimension to his Christology. Paul's writings contain several explicit references to cosmic Christology both in his undisputed letters (for example, Rom 8:18–23, 38–39; 1 Cor 15:20–28; Phil 2:6–11) and disputed letters (for example, Col 1:15–20; Eph 1:20–23). Unfortunately, Pauline scholarship often treats Paul's cosmic Christology as a subsidiary issue.[1] Scholarship has given more attention to issues like the origins of Paul's Christology,[2] whether Hellenism or Judaism influenced his Christology,[3] or his view of Christ's divinity.[4] While these concerns are certainly vital to understanding Paul's Christology, an exclusive focus on these concerns fails to cover the full scope of Christ's person and work within Paul's writings. Perhaps no two Pauline

---

1. Larry Hurtado points out the cosmic dimension of Christ's rule and exaltation as a "noteworthy feature" of Paul's messianic Christology, but he does not provide a detailed exploration of this cosmic dimension. Hurtado gives an example of what many scholars have done—that is, they will note the cosmic aspects of Christ as a significant feature in Paul but then say little more about the significance of this idea in Paul's thought (Hurtado, *Ancient Jewish Monotheism*, 547).

2. For example, see Hahn, *Christologische Hoheitstitel*; Marshall, *Origins of New Testament Christology*; Dunn, *Christology in the Making*; Juel and Dahl, *Jesus the Christ*; Collins, "Psalms, Philippians 2:6–11," 361–72; Bird, *How God Became Jesus*.

3. For example, see Hengel, *Son of God*; Newman et al., *Jewish Roots*; Talbert, *Development of Christology*; Hurtado, *One God*.

4. For example, see Dunn, *Christology in the Making*; Bauckham, *God of Israel*; Tilling, *Paul's Divine Christology*; Capes, *Divine Christ*.

letters emphasize Christ's relationship to the cosmos more than Ephesians and Colossians. Scholarship has pointed to passages like Col 1:15–20 and Eph 1:20–23 as pinnacle texts for cosmic Christology. However, extensive study focused on the cosmic Christology of the letters is surprisingly lacking. Scholarship has done little work on how Paul incorporates cosmic Christology as an ongoing theme in the letters.[5] In some cases, scholars focus on Colossians while giving little consideration to Ephesians.[6] Given the similarity between the two letters, a study that does not incorporate both letters is incomplete. Therefore, this study seeks to examine the cosmic Christology of the two letters together to provide a deeper understanding of their cosmic christological insights.

WHAT IS COSMIC CHRISTOLOGY?

Some may be unsure of what is meant by Paul's "cosmic Christology" or, more specifically, the term "cosmic/cosmos." Scholars who discuss cosmic Christology generally do not provide a clear definition of the term, but there seems to be an unspoken yet understood definition among scholars who work in this area. While this lack of definition does not discredit studies on cosmic Christology, it can cause a couple issues. First, people who do not work primarily in the field of cosmic Christology may not fully understand what is meant by "cosmic Christology" and are forced to assume their own definition. Second, one cannot definitively determine whether scholars who use the terms "cosmic Christology" or "cosmic/cosmos" all mean the same thing. The lack of a uniform definition for "cosmic Christology" may also be due to the vague nature of Paul's own cosmology. Paul does not explicitly provide a systematic layout of his own cosmology in any of his letters.

Given these difficulties, the best recourse for defining "cosmic Christology" is to use Paul's own language. In Phil 2:9–11, Paul declares that God has exalted Christ and given him authority over every being "in heaven and on earth and under the earth" (Phil 2:10).[7] In Col 1:16, Paul claims that everything "in heaven and on earth, visible and invisible,"

---

5. When the subject is addressed, it typically appears as merely a portion of a larger work, an essay in a collection of essays, or possibly a journal article. For some examples, see Helyer, "Cosmic Christology," 235–46; Martin, "Prison Epistles," 201–17; Lioy, "Apocalyptic Interpretation," 27–64.

6. For example, see Ibrahim, *Gesu Cristo*; Jackson, *New Creation*; and Leese, *Christ*.

7. All translations of the NT text are the author's own translation.

Ulrich Mell argues that "new creation" in pre-Pauline Judaism and in Paul's thought was almost exclusively cosmological in focus.[12] J. L. Martyn also champions this cosmological approach by describing the in-breaking of Christ as "the cosmic apocalyptic event," which pivots from the old order of the cosmos to God's new cosmic order.[13] Moyer Hubbard downplays the cosmological approach in favor of the anthropological-soteriological approach, suggesting that "new creation" (specifically in 2 Cor 5:17 and Gal 6:15) was simply an aspect of Paul's pneumatology and has in view spiritual transformation of the heart, which gives life to the individual.[14]

Seeking a more balanced approach to Paul's understanding of "new creation," Martinus de Boer argues that both cosmological and anthropological aspects were present in Paul's thought.[15] T. R. Jackson argues that scholars have seen a "false dichotomy" between anthropological and cosmological aspects of Paul's creation language. He argues that new creation in Paul is "an expression of his eschatologically infused soteriology which involves the individual, the community, and the cosmos."[16] J. Johnson Leese concurs with Jackson in arguing that Paul uses "new creation" as a comprehensive theological term meant to encompass the cosmic scope of Christ's work.[17] This more balanced approach better explains Paul's use of creation language. The same Christ who brings about new creation in the individual and the church also brings about the new creation of the cosmos.

One cannot speak of Paul's understanding of creation without connecting it to his understanding of redemption. Both creation and redemption appear in Colossians and Ephesians as aspects of Christ's cosmic work. John Gibbs was one of the first scholars in the twentieth century to give extended treatment to these themes in Paul. Gibbs argues that creation and redemption are held in "coordination" within the mind of Paul.[18] Through an examination of selected texts from the undisputed letters of Paul and the post-Pauline tradition, Gibbs concludes that Paul

12. Mell, *Neue Schöpfung*.
13. Martyn, *Theological Issues*, 90, 121.
14. Hubbard, *New Creation*, 17–25, 234–35.
15. De Boer, "Apocalyptic Eschatology," 169–90.
16. Jackson, *New Creation*, 4–6.
17. Leese, *Christ*, 60–62.

18. Gibbs, *Creation and Redemption*, 1–10. Gibbs argues that previous approaches failed to understand cosmic Christology because they either (1) set creation and redemption against one another or (2) subsumed creation under redemption.

presupposes the lordship of Christ as the lens through which he views the relationship between creation and redemption. Paul did not attempt to universalize one's inner experience of conversion nor did he deduce cosmic Christology from the church's experience of redemption. Rather, creation and redemption meet under Christ's position as Lord and mediator.[19]

Since Gibbs, scholars have continued to explore Paul's writings on Christ's role in redeeming the whole cosmos, but many studies on cosmic redemption focus primarily on ecological redemption. Jürgen Moltmann argues for a development of a new cosmic Christology that addresses ecological concerns (what he calls a "Christology of nature").[20] Recent scholarship has pursued this ecological focus, as illustrated by numerous recently published journal articles on the subject.[21] Leese also suggests that one might use Paul's theological categories concerning the redemption of creation to enhance ecological discussions.[22] While this study acknowledges that there may be some ecological implications to cosmic redemption, one should question whether these concerns were present in Paul's mind as he constructed his own understanding of cosmic redemption.

Christ's Position within the Cosmos

Scholars have sought to understand how Paul would have reconciled Christ's divinity within his own Jewish monotheism. These questions are of importance to the present study because Christ's role as cosmic Creator, Redeemer, and Lord is predicated on his identity as the divine Son of God. James Dunn's seismic work on Christology begins with the question of how the doctrine of Christ's incarnation developed within early Christianity. In particular, he explores whether Christ's divine preexistence was a belief within the early NT church that arose from pre-Christian Jewish

---

19. Gibbs, *Creation and Redemption*, 134–45.
20. Moltmann, *Way of Jesus Christ*, 274–79.
21. One can see this emphasis simply from the titles of many recently published journal articles. For examples, see McCarthy, "Christ cosmique," 27–47; Santmire, "Fill All Things," 257–78; Trainor, "Cosmic Christology," 54–69; Horrell, "New Perspective on Paul?," 3–30.
22. Leese, *Christ*, 194–203. Leese presents these theological categories as a hermeneutical lens that can advance ecological discussions, but she does not present an ecotheology informed by these categories.

monotheism or whether it was a development of the post-NT world.²³ Dunn makes the following conclusions: First, Dunn argues that Christ's exalted status was appointed to him at his resurrection, not one that he had in some preexistent state. This status includes his appointment to divine sonship²⁴ and as the last Adam.²⁵ Second, Dunn argues that the concept of the preexistent Christ among first century Christians is only found in the application of Jewish Wisdom categories.²⁶ He argues that pre-Christian Judaism viewed Wisdom as nothing more than a personification of a function of YHWH and a way of describing YHWH's wise creation and purpose.²⁷ He suggests that Paul does not identify Christ as a preexistent being but views Christ as simply embodying and expressing God's power and action in creation, revelation, and redemption.²⁸ Therefore, Dunn argues that Christ "is the instrument of, rather than an unqualified partaker in, God's unique sovereignty."²⁹

Other scholars have challenged Dunn's christological conclusions by challenging his understanding of Jewish monotheism. Richard Bauckham suggests that one can conceive of the "divine identity" by determining the unique distinguishing marks that make God distinct from all other reality.³⁰ He argues that "high Christology was possible within a Jewish monotheistic context, not by applying to Jesus a Jewish category of semidivine intermediary status, but by identifying Jesus directly with the one God of Israel, including Jesus in the unique identity of this one God."³¹ Bauckham states that the NT writers, including Paul, included Jesus in the divine identity in the following ways: (1) inclusion in divine sovereignty, (2) inclusion in divine creation, (3) identification by divine names, and (4) worship that accords with the divine identity.³² Christ

---

23. Dunn, *Christology in the Making*, 1–11.
24. Dunn, *Christology in the Making*, 35–36, 64.
25. Dunn, *Christology in the Making*, 98–128.
26. Dunn, *Christology in the Making*, 167, 210.
27. Dunn, *Christology in the Making*, 174–76.
28. Dunn, *Christology in the Making*, 176–96. See also Dunn, "Human Face of God," 77–79. Concerning the Colossian hymn, Dunn admits that it "at first reads as a straight-forward assertion of Christ's pre-existent activity in creation" (Dunn, *Christology in the Making*, 194), but he attributes this reading to later traditions of Christ's preexistence and incarnation.
29. Dunn, *Theology of Paul*, 253.
30. Bauckham, *God Crucified*, 2–4.
31. Bauckham, *God of Israel*, 182.
32. Bauckham, *God Crucified*, 26–44.

shared this divine identity with the Father from the beginning.[33] Larry Hurtado argues that Paul's veneration of the exalted Jesus, whom he identified as Lord alongside YHWH, represented an innovation in his Jewish monotheism, not a rejection of it.[34] Whereas Bauckham views "chief-agent" categories in Second Temple Judaism as incompatible with the conception of the "divine identity,"[35] Hurtado argues that "Jesus is included within the 'divine identity' specifically as God's unique chief-agent."[36] Therefore, Hurtado argues that the divine agency categories of early Judaism reflect a fundamental idea that God might have a chief-agent who exercises his rule and is closely associated with him[37] and proposes that Paul's Christology represented a "mutation" of the Jewish conception of divine agency.[38]

Gordon Fee gives a heavy emphasis to the preexistence of Christ. Fee suggests that Paul does not need to argue for Christ's preexistence and incarnation because he holds the common belief in Christ as the divine, preexistent Savior.[39] Fee argues that the presuppositional nature of Pauline material allows scholars like Dunn to argue for non-incarnational views of given texts. Fee points to three aspects of Christ's saving activity in Paul's writings that presuppose Christ's preexistence: Christ as agent of creation and redemption (1 Cor 8:6; 10:4, 9; Col 1:15–20; Eph 2:9), Christ as "impoverished" redeemer (2 Cor 8:9; Phil 2:6–8; 2 Tim 1:9–10), and the Son as the "sent one" (Gal 4:4–7; Rom 8:3–4; 1 Tim 1:15, 2:5, 3:16).[40] As a result, Fee concludes that Paul's view of Christ's divinity served as the "constant presupposition of everything that he says about Christ as Savior."[41]

While other scholars have contributed to discussions regarding Jesus' divinity,[42] the preceding scholars provide a good representation of

33. Bauckham, *God of Israel*, 184–85.

34. Hurtado, *One God*, 1–2. Hurtado calls this practice the "binitarian shape of early Christian devotion" (Hurtado, *One God*, 1).

35. Bauckham, *God of Israel*, 221–32.

36. Hurtado, *Ancient Jewish Monotheism*, 105.

37. Hurtado, *One God*, 17–96.

38. Hurtado, *One God*, 97–131. While Hurtado does suggest that Jesus' resurrection initiates his exaltation to the status as God's chief agent, he does not clarify whether Christ may have possessed this identity as preexistent Lord.

39. Fee, *Pauline Christology*, 500–501.

40. Fee, *Pauline Christology*, 502–11.

41. Fee, *Pauline Christology*, 511.

42. For example, see Tilling, *Paul's Divine Christology* and Capes, *Divine Christ*.

the major points and contentions. The questions regarding Jesus' identity can be summarized as follows: Did Paul ascribe divinity to Jesus equal with the one God of Israel, or did he merely view Christ as a subordinate agent through whom God exercises his rule? Did Christ possess his unique lordship over all things at his resurrection, or was it something he possessed in a preexistent state? Would a preexistent view of Jesus' lordship represent a radical break from Jewish monotheism, or would it fit the Jewish conception of YHWH's unique identity? Despite numerous conversations, these questions remain in contention. A careful study of how Ephesians and Colossians portray Jesus' relationship with the cosmos could contribute toward answering these questions.

Origins of Paul's Cosmic Christ

Previous studies of the origins of Paul's conception of cosmic Christ have had a profound effect on how scholars have framed the Christology of Ephesians and Colossians. Early in the twentieth century, many mainstream NT scholars, including Wilhelm Bousset[43] and Bultmann,[44] attributed the cosmic aspects of Paul's Christology as an adoption of Hellenistic traditions, which represented a break from his Jewish roots. However, scholarship began to find Hellenism as an unsatisfactory solution to the formation of Paul's Christology and developed interest in the Jewish origins of Paul's cosmic Christ. W. D. Davies' work provides an early example of this shift. Davies suggests that Paul introduces the conception of Christ as the last Adam, which may have arisen from Jewish speculation regarding the cosmic significance of Adam.[45] Second, Davies argues that the Jewish idea of the messianic age conceived a messiah of cosmic significance, and the ascription of messiahship to Jesus by the early Christians implied Jesus' cosmic significance.[46]

Subsequent studies pursued other Jewish motifs to explain Paul's Christology. Specifically, NT scholars began to look to the Jewish conception of Wisdom as a key influencer of Paul's Christology. Dunn argues

---

43. Bousset, *Kyrios Christos*, 153–210. Bousset argues Paul adopted the ascription of the title κύριος for Jesus from the believers in Antioch, who adopted it from their pagan religions.

44. Bultmann argues that many of the cosmic aspects of Paul's Christology were adopted from the gnostic-redeemer myth. See Bultmann, *New Testament*, 6–10, 130–32.

45. Davies, *Paul*, 38, 44–55.

46. Davies, *Paul*, 38–41.

extensively that Paul's cosmic conception of Christ is best understood as originating with the Jewish conception of personified Wisdom.⁴⁷ As a result, Dunn's conclusions regarding Paul's Christology become almost wholly dependent on Jewish Wisdom. Though not all scholars go to the same extreme as Dunn nor follow his christological conclusions, some scholars still suggest that personified Wisdom significantly influences Paul's conception of cosmic Christ. Seyoon Kim holds that Paul's prior knowledge of personified Wisdom serves as the key to his Christology.⁴⁸ Bauckham suggests that Wisdom is viewed as an aspect of YHWH's unique identity and that Paul identifies Jesus with Wisdom as a way of relating him to YHWH's unique identity.⁴⁹ Moltmann explicitly equates Wisdom Christology with cosmic Christology.⁵⁰ Others have argued that Wisdom serves as a key influencer of the Colossian hymn (the pinnacle of Paul's cosmic christological thought).⁵¹

Despite its seeming popularity, some scholars call into question Paul's supposed dependence on Wisdom traditions in formulating his ideas on Christ's cosmic identity. Herman Ridderbos argues that, at best, Colossians reflects "vague reminiscences" of Wisdom, and Wisdom falls short in explaining Paul's radical pronouncements concerning the cosmic Christ.⁵² Fee argues that the idea that Paul depends on Wisdom has arisen from a need to find a background for Paul's idea of a preexistent Christ who is the agent of creation, but it does not arise from sound exegetical work.⁵³ Fee argues that Jesus is identified as the agent of creation in a way that Judaism never identifies personified Wisdom.⁵⁴ Instead, Fee

47. Before Dunn, Wisdom Christology appeared in the twentieth century first with the work of Hans Windisch (Windisch, "Die göttliche Weisheit," 220–34). This view received further notoriety from Martin Hengel, who argued that Paul was the originator of Wisdom Christology (Hengel, *Early Christology*, 73–119).

48. Kim, *Paul's Gospel*, 100–136. To be fair, one must note the Kim does not come from the same school of christological thought as Dunn. While Kim does see personified Wisdom as the key to his Christology, he does not necessarily equate Jesus with divine Wisdom in the same way as Dunn.

49. Bauckham, *God Crucified*, 21–22. Bauckham does not suggest that personified Wisdom is the foundation of Paul's conception of Christ's divine identity, but he does still view it as a part of Paul's formation of his Christology.

50. Moltmann, *Way of Jesus Christ*, 282.

51. For example, see Lohse, *Colossians and Philemon*, 48; Helyer, "Cosmic Christology"; Bevere, *Inheritance*, 124–34; and Beetham, *Echoes*, 113–42.

52. Ridderbos, *Paul*, 78–80.

53. Fee, *Pauline Christology*, 597–98.

54. Fee, *Pauline Christology*, 317–25, 599–619. See also Fee, "Wisdom Christology,"

suggests that, at least in the case of the Colossian hymn, Paul utilizes imagery from Genesis and the Davidic kingship.[55]

Recent scholarship has demonstrated increased interest in royal ideology as a potential background for Paul's high Christology. William Horbury argues that kingship is central to understanding Jewish messianism and that Jewish regal messianism helped originate early high Christology.[56] Adela Yarbro Collins argues that Paul's abundant use of Christ language suggests that the identification of Christ with Israel's royal messiah was fundamental to the formation of his communities.[57] Matthew Novenson demonstrates that Paul's use of Χριστός aligns with other uses of royal honorifics in the ancient world. He suggests that Jewish royal ideology, as represented in Israel's Scriptures, provided Paul with the necessary conceptual and linguistic resources by which Paul could understand and communicate Christ's royal status to his hearers.[58] Joshua Jipp extends the arguments of Novenson by suggesting that Jewish, Hellenistic, and Roman regal language provide linguistic and conceptual resources through which Paul could articulate Christ's regal status.[59]

Van Kooten's Cosmic Christ in Ephesians and Colossians

Since this study focuses on the cosmic Christology of Colossians and Ephesians, it is necessary to address the work of George van Kooten, who provides the only book-length study that focuses exclusively on the cosmic Christology of Colossians and Ephesians. Kooten argues that the Colossians author understands σῶμα as referring to a cosmological body, a meaning which, he argues, disappears in Ephesians.[60] He derives this meaning from the contemporary physics of Stoicism and Middle Platonism, which views physics and theology as identical since the cosmos

---

351–75.

55. Fee, *Pauline Christology*, 325.

56. Horbury, *Jewish Messianism*.

57. A. Y. Collins and J. J. Collins, *King and Messiah*, 122. See also Schreiber, *Gesalbter und König*.

58. Novenson, *Christ among the Messiahs*. Novenson does suggest that Paul's use of this language does not necessarily mean that Paul intends to conform Christ to the Jewish messianic ideal. Novenson, *Christ among the Messiahs*, 47.

59. Jipp, *Christ Is King*.

60. Kooten, *Cosmic Christology*, 9–10.

is God's body,[61] and interprets the usages of σῶμα in Col 2:9, 17, and 19 as referring to Christ's cosmic body.[62] Kooten then positions Christ as the head of this cosmic body.[63] This interpretation differs from the typical ecclesiological interpretations, which, he argues, arise from a dependency on a correlation between Ephesians and Colossians. Kooten proposes that if one takes Colossians by itself, one can make a plausible case for a "physical, cosmological" understanding that sets Colossians in line with Middle Platonic-Stoic ideas.[64] After examining the cosmology of Paul's undisputed letters (specifically Gal 4:3–10 and 1 Cor 15:23–28),[65] Kooten suggests that Colossians departs from Paul in two ways. First, Colossians presents the principles, powers, and elements of the present cosmos as harmonized in Christ's cosmic body, whereas Paul views these forces as being annihilated.[66] Second, Paul views his Christ-centered cosmos as a future reality, whereas Colossians views the harmony of Christ's cosmic body as a present reality. Kooten concludes that Colossians presents a further hellenization of Paul's cosmology in order "to overcome the invalidation of Paul's imminent eschatology and to save what the author of Colossians regards as the core of Paul's theology: Christ's submission of the cosmological principles, powers, and elements."[67]

Kooten argues that the Ephesians author seeks to correct and "re-Paulinize" the cosmology and cosmic Christology of Colossians.[68] Therefore, the Ephesians author deliberately rearranges the structure of Colossians to correct its view of Christ's body. Rather than promoting the cosmos as Christ's body, Ephesians presents only the church as Christ's

---

61. Kooten, *Cosmic Christology*, 18.

62. Kooten, *Cosmic Christology*, 17–52.

63. Kooten, *Cosmic Christology*, 18–19. Kooten sees Christ as parallel with the Stoic concept of the ηγεμονικον, which served as the commanding faculty that regulated the functions of the body of the cosmos. The Stoics then adjusted to Platonic thought in viewing the head as the site of the ηγεμονικον. He then concludes that "it is highly likely that the author of Col situated the ηγεμονικον of the body of the cosmos in Christ's head which thus became a metaphor for the governing part of the universe" (Kooten, *Cosmic Christology*, 19). It should be noted that the term ηγεμονικον is never used in Colossians.

64. Kooten, *Cosmic Christology*, 56–59.

65. Kooten, *Cosmic Christology*, 60–80.

66. Kooten, *Cosmic Christology*, 130–31.

67. Kooten, *Cosmic Christology*, 146.

68. Kooten, *Cosmic Christology*, 165–66.

body.⁶⁹ Kooten argues that the Ephesians author has replaced this notion so skillfully that readers of Colossians are unable to discern the cosmological body because their minds are saturated with the views of Ephesians.⁷⁰ Additionally, he suggests that Ephesians views the filling of all things as a gradual process rather than a finished work (contra Colossians).⁷¹

Kooten's work attempts what previous scholars have failed to do by offering an approach that integrates studies on the cosmic Christology of both Colossians and Ephesians.⁷² Though Kooten certainly offers a unique and noteworthy study, he fails to provide a satisfactory analysis of the letters for a few reasons. Some of Kooten's basic presuppositions concerning the letters hinder his study from the start. First, Kooten assumes non-Pauline authorship as practically a fact. However, Pauline authorship remains a contested issue, with a growing number of scholars willing to accept Pauline authorship of the letters. Kooten gives almost no attempt to interact with arguments that suggest that these letters are indeed Pauline.⁷³ His conclusion that Colossians presents a less Pauline cosmic Christology than Ephesians is particularly surprising given that more scholars seem willing to accept Pauline authorship of Colossians than Ephesians. Even if one did not hold to Pauline authorship of the letters, Kooten's scenario for when these letters were written is questionable. He proposes that Colossians was written in AD 80 and Ephesians between AD 80 and 140. Such a late date for Ephesians seems unlikely given its probable attestation by multiple early church fathers in the late first century and early second century AD.⁷⁴ This brings into question whether the relationship he sees between Colossians and Ephesians is probable.

Second, while Kooten certainly provides some interesting possible parallels between the letters and Greco-Roman thought, he seemingly

69. Kooten, *Cosmic Christology*, 149–201.

70. Kooten, *Cosmic Christology*, 204.

71. Kooten, *Cosmic Christology*, 160–68.

72. Kooten notes the studies of others upon which he has built his research have failed to offer an approach that integrates both letters. For examples, see Dupont, *Gnosis*; Demaris, *Colossian Controversy*; and Schwindt, *Weltbild des Epheserbriefes*.

73. See Bockmuehl, Review of *Cosmic Christology*, 443–44.

74. For an extended discussion of the early church fathers' use of Ephesians, see Hoehner, *Ephesians*, 2–6. Clement of Rome possibly alludes to Eph 1:17–18; 4:4–6, 18; and 5:21. Ignatius of Antioch possibly alludes to Eph 5:1–2 and 6:11–17. Polycarp alludes to Eph 4:26. Kooten suggests that it is unlikely that Clement or Ignatius had knowledge of Ephesians but fails to give any justification for this assertion (Kooten, *Cosmic Christology*, 2). Further, he does not interact with any scholars who would challenge such an assertion.

approaches the study with the assumption of a Greco-Roman background and subsequently projects that background onto the text. He gives very little consideration to any possible Jewish source (with the exception of Philo, 2 Maccabees, and 4 Maccabees in his study of Paul's cosmology). Kooten's method is even more surprising considering the abundant use of the OT in Ephesians.[75] Recent studies have also demonstrated that, though Colossians may not have any direct quotations from the OT, it contains many possible allusions to the OT.[76] However, Kooten seems to ignore any possible Jewish influence on the text.

Third, some of Kooten's own exegetical work is very questionable. For example, Kooten's understanding of the cosmology in Colossians begins with the assumption that σῶμα speaks of the whole cosmos as Christ's body. This interpretation leads him to argue that when Ephesians presents the church as Christ's σῶμα, it represents a divergent cosmology from Colossians. However, Kooten begins his exegesis in Col 2 when Col 1:18 clearly identifies Christ's σῶμα as the church (a verse that Kooten virtually ignores). Therefore, it seems doubtful that Colossians changes its conception of Christ's σῶμα from chapter 1 to chapter 2. Kooten's conclusion regarding Christ's σῶμα seems more driven by his own presupposition of the Hellenistic nature of Colossians than by sound exegetical analysis.

The present study will differ from Kooten's work in two major ways: First, this work will assume Pauline authorship of the two letters. As a result, rather than finding conflicting conceptions of cosmic Christ, this study hopes to provide a synthesized cosmic Christology of both letters while noting the distinct aspects of each letter's presentation of cosmic Christ. Additionally, rather than viewing the letters as moving away from Pauline thought, this study will suggest that the cosmic Christology of these letters merely represents further developments of Pauline thought. Second, rather than looking primarily to Greco-Roman cosmology, this work will look to the OT and works in Second Temple Judaism to discover possible backgrounds to the cosmic Christology of the two letters. This approach does not suggest that there is no Greco-Roman influence. Rather, this approach suggests that there is plenty of evidence for Jewish influence in the letters and that Judaism may give clearer answers to how Paul formulated his ideas of cosmic Christ. As a result, this study hopes

---

75. For a study on the use of the OT in Ephesians, see Moritz, *Profound Mystery*.

76. For an extended study on the use of the OT in Colossians, see Beetham, *Echoes*.

of these two approaches do not suggest that Greco-Roman thought or Wisdom traditions could have no influence on Colossians and Ephesians, but they do indicate that one may need an alternative approach to fully understand the cosmic Christology of the letters.

A survey of Colossians and Ephesians reveals other Jewish themes that have received very little attention. First, the letters contain probable references to the Genesis creation narrative and Adamic motifs in their description of cosmic Christ. Jesus is explicitly described as the one (1) who possesses the image of God (Col 1:15), (2) under whose feet all things are placed (Eph 1:22), and (3) in whom the church is being created into one new man (Col 3:9–11; Eph 2:10, 15).[85] Second, the letters consistently portray Jesus as the cosmic Lord using regal motifs. That is, the letters view Jesus as God's appointed King who (1) conquers all his enemies, (2) under whom God subordinates all things, and (3) through whom God rules over all things (Col 1:12–20; 2:6, 9–10, 15; 3:1; Eph 1:10, 20–23; 2:6; 3:10–11; 4:7–10; 5:5).[86] The increased interest in Paul's use of Jewish royal ideology among NT scholars suggests a reexamination of Colossians and Ephesians in light of this background. If both letters do contain references to both Adamic and regal motifs, it seems necessary to examine how they utilize the relationship of the two themes in their portrayal of cosmic Christ.

METHODOLOGY AND SCOPE

One can characterize the approaches of this study under three separate categories: exegetical, intertextual, and theological. First, the largest portions of the study will focus on careful exegesis of relevant passages in Colossians and Ephesians pertaining to cosmic Christology. The goal is to understand the cosmic Christ as he is presented in these letters. Second, intertextuality[87] will serve as a helpful tool to bolster the exegesis of

---

85. Fee has acknowledged the potential appearance of Adamic Christology in the letters. See Fee, *Pauline Christology*, 521–22. Leese also advocates for Adamic Christology in Colossians. See Leese, *Christ*, 108–13, 119–21.

86. For example, John Anthony Dunne suggests regal motifs play a much more significant role in the Colossians hymn than wisdom traditions (Dunne, "Regal Status," 3–18). Both Ephesians and Colossians explicitly cite the language of Ps 110:1, which is a primary text describing the ideal Davidic king, in their descriptions of Christ's enthronement (Col 3:1, Eph 1:20).

87. The intertextual method was popularized in NT studies by Richard Hays' seminal work on Paul's interpretation of the OT, though we should note the Hays' work was

Colossians and Ephesians. Third, since one of the primary goals of this study is to obtain a clearer understanding of cosmic Christology in these letters, it is necessary to present theological conclusions and advance certain theological arguments.

Chapter 2 will examine the OT and Second Temple Jewish texts that discuss the significance and function of Adam and the ideal Davidic king in God's cosmic order.[88] Specifically, this chapter considers passages that suggest that the Adamic figure or Davidic king function as God's royal agent through whom he enacts his rule over the nations and, at times, over the physical and spiritual realms.[89] Chapter 3 will briefly examine NT passages (primarily in the Gospels and Paul's undisputed letters) that utilize Adamic and Davidic royal language to portray Christ's position and function in the cosmos.[90] While these passages are not the focus of the current project, these passages reveal that the cosmic Christology of Colossians and Ephesians remains consistent with Paul's Christology in his other letters and with other christological statements in the NT. As a result, chapter 2 and chapter 3 will endeavor to provide a meaningful royal backdrop upon which Paul could have plausibly constructed his cosmic christological portrait in Colossians and Ephesians.

Chapters 4 and 5 will focus on texts from Colossians and Ephesians that are related to cosmic Christology. Cosmic Christology / cosmic Christ

---

preceded by Michael Fishbane's work on intertextuality in the OT (see Fishbane, *Biblical Interpretation*; Hays, *Echoes of Scripture*).

88. Relevant passages include (but are not limited to) Gen 1:26–28; 2:7–20; 2 Sam 7:11–17 (cf. 1 Chr 17:10–14); Pss 2, 8, 45, 89, 110; 132; Isa 11:1–10; 42:1–17; 52:13—53:12; 59:14—63:6; and Dan 7. Relevant Second Temple Jewish texts include 1 En. 38:2, 39:6, 42:1–3, 45:3–5, 46:1–6, 48:1–7, 48:10—49:4, 51, 52:4–9, 53:6, 55:4, 61:5–13, 62:1–16, 69:26–27, 90:37–38; Jub. 3:1–31; Pss. Sol. 17–18; 2 Bar. 40:1–3, 72–74; 4 Ezra 7:26–44; 12:32–33; and 13:25–53. These motifs also appear in some Qumran texts, including 4Q246, 4Q174, 4Q504, 4Q521, 4Q534, 4Q252, and 4Q161, and in the works of Philo, including *Conf.* 60–63, *Opif.* 84–89, 136–51, and *Leg.* 1:31–38. These works speak on God's anointed King whom he enthrones to rule over the whole cosmos. This study does not suggest a "straight-line" development of messianic expectations in early Judaism. A close study of Jewish messianism reveals a diversity of tradition. However, this study will suggest that the cosmic significance of the messiah was a common thought in Second Temple Judaism.

89. This study then does not consider passages that focus on how God enacts his rule through his king specifically over Israel.

90. Relevant passages include (but are not limited to) Mark 12:35–37; 13:24–27; 14:61–65; Matt 22:41–46; 24:29–31; 26:63–65; Luke 1:26–35; 21:25–28; 22:67–71; John 1:1–14, 49–51; 18:33–38; Rom 1:3–3; 5:12–21; 8:18–23, 38–39; 1 Cor 8:6; 15:21–28, 44–49; Gal 6:12–15; Phil 2:6–11. Outside of the Gospels and Paul's letters, ch. 3 will also address Acts 2:25–36 and Heb 1:1–13 and 2:5–9.

will serve as all-encompassing terms referring to Christ's unique person, position, and function as he relates to the cosmos. The cosmos extends to all areas of creation, whether the physical realm or the spiritual realm. With this understanding of cosmic Christology in mind, it is necessary to focus on passages in these letters that discuss the following aspects of Paul's Christology: (1) Jesus' identity as Lord and Christ, (2) Christ's creative work, (3) Christ's redemptive work, (4) Christ's enthronement, and (5) Christ as the fullness of God.[91] These passages demonstrate the ways in which Paul utilizes Jewish royal language and concepts (specifically through the lens of the Adamic and Davidic king) to articulate his cosmic Christology in these letters. This study will also bring Colossians and Ephesians into dialogue with each other to discover the similarities and differences in their cosmic christological portraits.

Third, Paul's articulation of Christ's place and function in the cosmos in Colossians and Ephesians has broader theological implications. The way Paul utilizes Jewish royal ideology in Colossians and Ephesians has significant implications for Christology, specifically its cosmic components. These christological implications have significant impact on how Paul constructs the identity of the church. However, theological conclusions must be derived from sound exegesis of the relevant texts. Therefore, the completion of the exegetical task provides the necessary foundation upon which one can build a coherent summary of cosmic Christology in Colossians and Ephesians and can advance certain theological arguments.

---

91. The passages that meet this criterion are Col 1:12–20; 2:6–15; 3:1–11; Eph 1:3–14, 20–23; 2:1–22; 3:8–11; 4:7–16; 5:5.

2

The Root of Cosmic Christ in the Old Testament and Early Judaism

IN DISCUSSING HOW PAUL framed his view of Jesus' place within the cosmos, Jipp argues that "significant portions of Paul's Christ discourse [are] kingship discourse in which Paul creatively transforms the responsibilities, traits, and titles commonly understood to belong to kings and applies them to Jesus."[1] If this assertion is true, one may ask the following questions: What linguistic and conceptual markers of Jewish royal ideology would lead Paul to view Christ as a cosmic ruler? What are the characteristics of God's ideal king in the OT and early Jewish literature? What role, if any, does Judaism grant God's ideal king in bringing about cosmic harmony? A brief survey of the OT and early Jewish literature reveals the enthronement of the royal messiah as a key component of the Jewish hope. While the Jewish people are most often the primary beneficiary of this king's reign, his enthronement also bears significance for the nations and, at times, for the cosmos. To understand what Jewish royal motifs may have led Paul to portray Jesus as a cosmic ruler in Colossians and Ephesians, one should begin by surveying the conceptions of God's ideal king in the OT and early Judaism. Specifically, one should focus on texts that portray a royal figure through whom God enacts his rule over the earth, creation, and/or the cosmos.

1. Jipp, *Christ Is King*, 7.

THE ADAMIC TRADITION

When examining the royal ideology of the OT, one's first inclination may be to examine the idealized Davidic king, but any examination of OT royal ideology should begin with Adam. Scholarship has attested to the use of royal language in the account of Adam's creation.[2] In the field of OT scholarship, the royal interpretation of Gen 1–2 might be the most influential view of the text today.[3] For this reason, this chapter will begin by revisiting the Genesis creation narrative to identify God's royal appointment of Adam over creation and the functions that accompanied his position.

Adam in Genesis 1–2

At the climax of the creation story, God creates and appoints humanity to rule over his creation. Genesis 2 provides a more specific account on the creation of Adam and the responsibilities given to him by God.[4] More than an etiology of humanity, this narrative contains numerous elements that suggest a narrative of enthronement.[5] Several aspects of the Genesis narrative point to Adam's initial royal status.

Genesis 1:26–27 declares that God created Adam in his "image" (צלם) according to his "likeness" (דמות).[6] Scholars and theologians have

---

2. See the discussion on preceding scholarship from Westermann, *Genesis 1–11*, 147–54, 159; and Hamilton, *Genesis 1–17*, 137–38.

3. Middleton, *Liberating Image*, 25–26. For a history on how OT scholarship came to this consensus, see Jonsson, *Image of God*, 219–25. Even though he did not necessarily agree with this interpretation, James Barr acknowledged this point in the early 1990s (Barr, *Biblical Faith*, 158). Current studies continue to illustrate that the royal interpretation remains the prominent view in OT scholarship. For examples, see Schüle, "Made in the 'Image,'" 1–20; Crouch, "Image of God," 1–21; and LeFebvre, "Adam Reigns in Eden," 25–57.

4. The composition of and relationship between Gen 1 and 2 has been thoroughly argued. Regardless of the exact nature of the creation narrative's composition, this study simply makes the point that both accounts contribute to the picture of Adam as God's first universal king.

5. LeFebvre, "Adam Reigns in Eden," 26–27. LeFebvre argues that Adam's kingship (rather than human origins) is the primary message of Genesis. For the purposes of this study, one need not determine whether etiology of kingship or human origins has priority in the Genesis narrative. It will simply be enough to say that royal enthronement is a significant motif within the creation story.

6. All Scripture references are taken from the Hebrew MT.

long debated the exact meaning of צלם in this account.[7] However, a few key points indicate that this term is primarily a royal term. First, this terminology has several parallels with other ancient Near Eastern conceptions of divine kingship. Several studies have highlighted the Mesopotamian and Egyptian traditions, which view the king (or Pharaoh) as being the visible representative of the gods.[8] In some sense, these kings were considered to have divine status as a result of this royal relationship with the divine. To be an "image" of the gods meant that the king not only had an exalted position over his people but also within the whole cosmos.[9] Additionally, the "image" of the divine in many ancient Near Eastern contexts refers to "a localized, visible, corporeal representation of the divine."[10] For example, Pharaoh, in his bodily form, was declared to be the living image of the gods on earth.[11] That is, the king's bodily form was vital to his exercising the rule of the gods on the earth. In relation to Gen 1, such an understanding of צלם indicates that Adam,[12] as the

---

7. Gordon Wenham outlines five different proposed meanings for צלם: (1) "image" as distinct from "likeness," (2) mental and spiritual factors humanity shares with the Creator, (3) physical resemblance, (4) God's royal representative on earth, and (5) relational (Wenham, *Genesis 1–15*, 29–32). For a brief history on the interpretation of this term, see McDowell, *Image of God*, 126–31.

8. Johannes Hehn is credited as the first scholar to take these parallels into account. (Hehn, "Bild Gottes," 36–52). Some significant studies include Wildberger, "Abbild Gottes," 245–59; Schmidt, *Schöpfungsgeschichte*; Otto, "Mensch als Geschöpf," 334–48; Bird, "Male and Female," 129–59; Curtis, "Man as the Image"; Batto, "Divine Sovereign," 143–86; Middleton, *Liberating Image*, 93–146; and McDowell, *Image of God*.

9. Schüle, "Made in the 'Image,'" 5.

10. Middleton, *Liberating Image*, 25. In his application to the Genesis text, Middleton makes the important distinction that this point does not mean that humanity has a bodily resemblance with God. Rather, "the invisible God is imaged by bodily humanity" (Middleton, *Liberating Image*, 25).

11. Schmidt, *Schöpfungsgeschichtle*, 137. See also the discussion in Ruppert, *Genesis*, 90–92.

12. There has been considerable debate over whether אדם refers to Adam as an individual or to corporate humanity as a whole. Westermann argues that the creation narrative is concerned with humanity as a collective, not the individual (Westermann, *Creation*, 56). This view is also argued by Clines (Clines, "Humanity as the Image of God," 476–80). Crouch pushes back against this approach. She argues that the language of royal ideology utilized in the narrative typically points to one kingly representative (Crouch, "Image of God," 9–11). The difficulty seems to suggest that both Adam as an individual and corporate humanity are in view. Paul Niskanen suggests that the use of both the singular and plural pronouns for אדם in v. 27 highlight that both the individual human being and humanity in its differentiation ("male and female") are connected to the image of God (Niskanen, "Poetics of Adam," 430–35). For the present study, it is sufficient to say that while the image of God may be applied to corporate humanity, it

first human, in his bodily form possessed an exalted position within the cosmos as the one who exercised God's rule over the creation.[13]

The use of דמות with צלם may indicate a filial relationship between God and Adam.[14] Genesis 5:3 uses both nouns to describe the father-son relationship between Adam and Seth. Seth bore Adam's likeness because he was Adam's son. Thus, one could argue that Gen 1 utilizes sonship language to describe Adam's relationship with God. To be clear, Genesis is not suggesting that Adam is God's actual son. The creation language differs from language that describes human procreation. Rather, as Meredith G. Kline argues, Gen 1 may present "a kind of divine-authoring analogous to human procreation."[15] Kline suggests that "the father-son imagery in the record of creational origins becomes virtually explicit in the record of the birth of Seth in Gen 5:1–3."[16] As a result, one could plausibly speak of Adam as God's royal son.[17] This God-given status results in God commissioning Adam to exercise divine rule over the creation.

The expressed function of the original Adam also indicates his position of royalty. God states that his initial purpose for endowing his צלם on Adam is so that Adam might rule over the earth and all the creatures in the earth (Gen 1:26b). Upon his creation of Adam, God commissions Adam to "subdue" (כבש) and "rule" (רדה) over the creation and all its inhabitants (Gen 1:28). Previous scholarship has demonstrated that these two verbs convey royal ideology.[18] In many ancient Near Eastern parallels, the king who was ascribed the divine image was "charged with perfecting the divine sovereign's work of creation by promoting right

---

also has definite royal implications for Adam as an individual.

13. One should note that the parallels drawn between Gen 1–2 and other ancient Near Eastern enthronement traditions do not necessitate the view that these traditions directly influenced the Gen 1–2 narrative. Rather, these traditions provide contemporary linguistic and conceptual precedents that illuminate the potentially regal nature of the creation narrative.

14. Wilfong, "Human Creation," 43. The term דמות is a broad term referring to resemblance. In the OT, it can speak of literal or metaphorical resemblance. It would be a stretch to suggest that דמות is indicating something distinct from צלם in Gen 1. Rather, the terms bring mutual clarity to one another (Wenham, *Genesis 1–15*, 29; J. C. Collins, *Genesis 1–4*, 65; and McDowell, *Image of God*, 124–25).

15. Kline, *Kingdom Prologue*, 46.

16. Kline, *Kingdom Prologue*, 45.

17. Vriezen, "Creation," 104; and Schüle, *Prolog*, 81.

18. Westermann, *Genesis 1–11*, 158–59; Rad, *Old Testament Theology*, 146; and Crouch, "Image of God," 12–13.

order, justice, and the human weal."[19] Additionally, the Hebrew verb רדה is used several times in the OT to describe the rule of the king (1 Kgs 4:24; Pss 72:8; 110:2; Isa 14:6; Ezek 34:4). The Hebrew verb כבש in the most general sense refers to bringing something under control by use of authority or power.[20] At various points, the OT associates the verb with a royal figure (2 Sam 8:11; 1 Chr 22:18; Jer 34:11). In the context of the Gen 1 narrative, Adam's dominion over multiple spheres of the cosmos is ontologically based on his possession of God's image.[21] At the same time, the commission to rule and subdue further implies that "the image of God" is indeed meant as a royal designation.[22] As a result of his royal appointment, Adam was responsible for maintaining God's established order and for exercising God's right and just rule.

Genesis 2 provides further evidence for Adam's royal appointment. None of the following elements on their own prove the royal ideology of Gen 2. Rather, it is the combination of the elements within the text that at least makes it highly probable that a royal ideology underlies the narrative. First, Adam's creation out of the dust reflects a royal ideological motif in which a king is brought from obscurity to kingship (Gen 2:7). This dust motif is utilized in other OT passages to describe the exaltation of a person of obscurity to a position of royalty (1 Sam 2:6–8; 1 Kgs 16:2; Ps 113:7). Walter Brueggemann argues that the appearance of this motif points to the creation of man as being an enthronement event.[23] Thus, he

---

19. Batto, "Divine Sovereign," 163.

20. Middleton, *Liberating Image*, 51–52. Middleton does note that the word often has violent connotations in other instances in the OT. However, he rightly points out that the word itself is not inherently violent. Crouch suggests that the use of the verb in this passage may carry a military emphasis. That is, Adam is commissioned to join God in his battle against chaos (Crouch, "Image of God," 13).

21. Schüle, "Made in the 'Image,'" 4. In reviewing the differing views regarding the meaning of the image of God, C. John Collins groups these views into three broad categories: resemblance (or ontological), representative, and relational views. One may be tempted to draw a sharp distinction between these views. However, Collins rightly notes that this distinction seems to be an unnecessary contradiction. Adam's function as a royal figure is in some way based on his ontological relationship to God (J. C. Collins, *Genesis 1–4*, 62–67).

22. Bird, "Male and Female," 140.

23. Brueggemann, "Dust to Kingship," 1–18. Brueggemann also argues the language of "returning to dust" indicate a king's fall to obscurity, which often indicates the fracturing of a covenant relationship with YHWH. One should note that the assertion that Adam being formed from dust represents an enthronement ritual does not necessarily negate a literal reading of Gen 2:7. It is certainly possible to read the text as a literal account of God's creation of Adam while also recognizing it as a story of enthronement.

concludes that "Adam, in Gen 2, is really being crowned as king over the garden with all the power and authority with which it implies."[24]

Second, God's placement of Adam in the Garden of Eden alludes to royal appointment.[25] Genesis 2:15 utilizes the second Hiphil form of נוח to describe the installation of Adam in the garden. Catherine McDowell notes other instances in the OT where the second Hiphil form of this verb describes the installation of a divine image (2 Kg 17:29; Isa 46:7; Zech 5:5–11).[26] Although the evidence for this particular interpretation of the verb is inconclusive on its own, the overall context of Gen 2 makes it possible that the passage utilizes this verb form "to indicate that Adam was not simply placed in the Garden of Eden but that Yahweh installed him there in the office of royal caretaker or watchman."[27] Furthermore, the location of the garden as Adam's dwelling reflects a common royal trope in the OT that views the garden as part of the king's dwelling place (1 Kgs 21:2; 2 Kgs 21:8, 26; Eccl 2:4–5; Jer 39:4, 52:7).[28]

---

24. Brueggemann, "Dust to Kingship," 12. See also LeFevbvre, "Adam Reigns," 33. Alternatively, John Soden argues that the dust motif primarily points to the fragility of human life and its dependence upon the Creator (Soden, "From the Dust," 45–66). This argument may be more plausible if the dust motif were the only evidence of enthronement in the text. However, given the other enthronement elements in the story, the royal interpretation of the dust motif seems to better represent the context of Gen 2.

25. Some scholars understand the garden as associated with God's temple. Gordan Wenham argues the garden represented an "archetypal sanctuary" where God dwells. Adam is then placed in this garden to dwell with God. Adam's dwelling in the garden could point to his priestly status (Wenham, "Sanctuary Symbolism," 19–25). G. K. Beale argues that by placing Adam in the God, God installed him in a royal temple to begin his reign as a "priest-king" (Beale, *Temple*, 66–80). While such an interpretation may be appealing, it seems rather difficult in the immediate context of Gen 2 to identify the garden as a temple. For the present, it is sufficient to identify the garden simply as a royal dwelling place, especially as it fits within the other royal themes in the passage.

26. McDowell, *Image of God*, 157–58.

27. McDowell, *Image of God*, 158.

28. LeFebvre, "Adam Reigns," 30. The placing of Adam in the garden also parallels Mesopotamian ritual texts where the created divine image is placed in a garden to be brought to completion. The gods come and spend time with the newly formed divine image, preparing to receive it into their celestial home. While such texts provide a precedent for the placement of a divine image in a garden, one must be cautious in asserting that the Genesis author either borrowed or reworked such traditions. For the present study, one should note that while these Mesopotamian texts refer to the creation of statues/idols, the Genesis account refers to the creation and royal appointment of a living human being. For further discussion on the relation of these Mesopotamian parallels with Gen 2, see McDowell, *Image of God*, 142–77 and Schüle, "Made in the 'Image,'" 12–14.

Third, Adam's responsibility within the garden reflects the function of royalty. Adam is tasked with maintaining the garden (Gen 2:15). This responsibility parallels ancient Near Eastern royal ideologies that view the king as a gardener. In this role, the king's ability to maintain and cultivate the garden was symbolic of his dominion and ability to maintain the order of his realm.[29] Thus, Adam's responsibility to care for the garden illustrates his larger responsibility of caring for God's created order. God also tasks Adam with naming the animals (Gen 2:19–20a). The act of naming indicates either ownership or power over something. In Gen 2, Adam's naming of the animals demonstrates his God-given authority over them.[30] In naming the animals, Adam begins to fulfill the mandate given in Gen 1 to subdue the earth.

In summary, both Gen 1 and 2 provide several allusions that make it highly probable that Adam was meant to be God's universal king who would exercise God's rule over the whole creation. The creation of Adam in God's צלם suggests that Adam was God's royal representative. God's commission to Adam to rule and subdue the earth further affirms his royal function. Genesis 2 gives more evidence that Adam's creation was also his enthronement. His creation out of dust, his installation in the garden, and his responsibility to maintain the garden and name the animals together give a probable picture of his kingship. For these reasons, Jipp rightly concludes, "Adam is God's royal ruler, imbued as God's chosen kingly son, who is commissioned to act as God's sovereign, subduing and ruling the earth for God."[31] As God's king, Adam was to be the channel through whom all creation would experience the benefits of God's rule.

Ultimately, Adam failed to fulfill the responsibilities of his royal appointment. His disobedience in Gen 3 leads to his removal from the garden and his "dethronement" from his royal position. Upon Adam and Eve's expulsion from the garden, Gen 3:15 provides a possible allusion to the restoration of God's king by promising that the woman's seed would have victory over the serpent.[32] Genesis 49:10 provides a clearer allusion

---

29. Wyatt, "Royal Garden," 1–35. Wyatt cites Mesopotamian and Egyptian parallels that convey the king's role as a gardener. See also the discussion from Hutter, "Adam als Gartner," 258–62.

30. Reichenbach, "Genesis 1," 62–63.

31. Jipp, *Christ Is King*, 105–6.

32. At the risk of overstating the evidence in Gen 3:15, one cannot say with absolute certainty that this verse previews the restoration of God's king. OT scholars have vigorously debated whether this verse can be considered a "protoevangelium." Westermann adamantly denies this interpretation of Gen 3:15 on the grounds that (1) seed should

to God's plan to appoint for himself a new king. This verse previews the installation of a king who will exercise rule over the nations.[33] By the end of Genesis, it seems clear that God desires once again to appoint a king through whom he will mediate his rule over the earth.

Adam in Psalm 8

Outside of Gen 1, Ps 8 provides the only explicit reference to Adam's initial kingship at creation in the OT canon. This Psalm has creation as its primary theme and reflects upon Adam's initial position at creation.[34] The Psalm begins by giving praise to the Lord's name for his power displayed in his creative work (Ps 8:2–4). In praising YHWH as Creator, the psalmist also exalts him as Lord over the whole universe. As Lord, YHWH may distribute his authority to whom he wills. The psalmist continues by asking the question, "What is man?" (Ps 8:5). The question primarily reflects upon Adam's position within the created order. This reflection reiterates important royal characteristics of the creation narrative.[35]

First, the Psalmist's declaration that man is made a little less than divine (מעט מאלהים) seems to be an interpretation of the *imago Dei* from

---

be understood as referring to humanity as a whole rather than an individual king and that (2) the verse appears as part of a pronouncement of a curse (Westermann, *Genesis 1–11*, 260). If one only considers this verse in its immediate context, it would be difficult to disagree with Westermann. However, T. Desmond Alexander argues that when Gen 3:15 is considered in light of Genesis as a whole, the messianic interpretation becomes highly probable (Alexander, "Messianic Ideology," 32). He suggests that this interpretation becomes more probable when considering Gen 3:15 within Genesis–Kings as a redactional unity (Alexander, "Royal Expectations," 204). Walter Wifall argues that Gen 3:15 owes its present form to the Yahwist's adoption of a Davidic or messianic framework (Wifall "Gen 3:15," 365).

33. As will be seen later in the chapter, many OT passages interpret this verse as referring to the ideal Davidic king.

34. One can find a full discussion on creation as the central theme of the Psalm in Kraus, *Theology of the Psalms*, 62–64, and Brueggemann, *Message of the Psalms*, 28–38. Alternatively, Peter Craigie argues that while Ps 8 reflects upon the created order and even refers to it as "a psalm of creation," the majesty of the Lord's name is the central theme (Craigie, *Psalms 1–50*, 106–9). In either case, scholars view creation as an important theme in the Psalm.

35. Whether the Psalm drew upon a tradition related to Gen 1 or Gen 1 itself is irrelevant to the argument of this study. While arguing that it is likely that the Psalmist drew upon a condensed account of Gen 1, Hubert Keener readily admits that such studies "are interesting, but inconclusive" (Keener, *Eighth Psalm*, 99–100). In either case, the argument is that Ps 8 draws upon royal traditions related to Gen 1. See also Childs, "Psalm 8," 21–22 and Craigie, *Psalms 1–50*, 106.

Gen 1:26–28 (Ps 8:5).³⁶ While the phrase distinguishes man from the divine, he stands closer to the divine than any other creature within the created order.³⁷ Man's royal status arises from his unique relationship with the divine Lord of the cosmos. This unique relationship manifests itself in the universal Lord's crowning of man and anticipates man's exalted position within the created order and his responsibility to exercise dominion over creation.

Second, the Psalm portrays man in an initially obscure position yet then views him as immediately being elevated to a position of royalty, which parallels the "dust to kingship" motif in Gen 2. The Psalmist comments on the inferiority of man in comparison to the heavenly bodies (Ps 8:3–4) but reverses his tone in the latter half of the Psalm. He states that God has set man in a place of superiority over creation (Ps 8:4–8). The Psalmist emphasizes that "man left to himself is nothing," but it is God who grants man his position over the creation.³⁸ Coining it as a "reversal motif," Hubert Keener describes this movement as "the way in which YHWH makes his name excellent in the cosmos by maintaining the created order through the exaltation of weak and humble things over and against proud and self-strong things."³⁹

Third, Ps 8 utilizes enthronement language consistent with the enthronement language in the creation narrative. Instead of simply stating that man was created in the image of God, the Psalm explicitly states that God "crowned" (from the Hebrew verb עטר) him as a king (Ps 8:5). Specifically, God endows him with glory and honor, attributes which are characteristic of the rule of God and his appointed king (cf. Pss 21:6; 29:4; 45:4–5; 66:3; 96:7; Isa 24:23).⁴⁰ As God's enthroned king, Adam's primary function was to exercise dominion over all things, including every creature in God's created order (Ps 8:6–8). Specifically, the Psalmist declares that all things were put under the feet of God's king, a saying that indicates royal domination.⁴¹ God intended for his mastery over the

---

36. Keener, *Eighth Psalm*, 103; and Childs, "Psalm 8," 21–22. The LXX translates the Hebrew אלהים as ἄγγελος. Such a translation may have occurred out of an attempt at modesty. However, this Hebrew word is not normally used to refer to angels. In view of the connection to Gen 1, it seems best to translate is as "God" (Craigie, *Psalms 1–50*, 108; Ross, *Psalms*, 296).

37. Schüle, *Prolog*, 120.

38. Urassa, *Psalm 8*, 52.

39. Keener, *Eighth Psalm*, 59.

40. Levenson, *Creation*, 113; Kraus, *Psalms 1–59*, 183; and Schaefer, *Psalms*, 24.

41. Crouch, "Image of God," 15.

created order to be expressed through the rule of Adam. As in Gen 1, Ps 8 draws an important link between man's possession of the image of God and the commission to rule over other creatures.[42] The enthronement and its function in Ps 8 align with the creation narrative where God creates Adam in his image and appoints him to exercise dominion over the creation.

Adam in Second Temple Literature

Various texts in Second Temple Jewish literature reflect upon Adam's original place in the Genesis narrative.[43] Such a view reflects the original Genesis tradition of Adam's original position at creation. The "glory of Adam" is said to be above every living thing at creation (Sir 49:16),[44] and God creates him in his image (Wis 2:23; 2 En. 30:12). By creating Adam in his image, God endows him with his glory (4Q504 8.4).[45] As a result, God places Adam as his royal agent and grants him dominion over all creation, both the earthly creatures and the heavenly bodies (Jub. 2:14; Wis 10:2; 4 Ezra 6:45–46, 54; 2 En. 30:12; 31:3; 4Q504 8.6). As God's appointed ruler, Adam, along with all humanity after him, was meant to reflect God's rule by ruling the world "in holiness and righteousness" (Wis 9:2–3).[46] Adam

---

42. Murray, *Cosmic Covenant*, 98.

43. Scroggs, *Last Adam*, 25. The present section does not wish to argue that there was a singular, unified Adamic portrait present in Second Temple Judaism. John Levison has provided a thorough critique of those who would seek to construct a coherent "Adam myth" from Second Temple Judaism, arguing rather that each Second Temple Jewish text utilized the Adamic figure to suit its own context (Levison, *Portraits of Adam*). However, this section will briefly show that the portrait of Adam as God's first ideal king does appear in Second Temple Jewish literature.

44. The context indicates that Ben Sira seeks to present Adam as the first father of Israel. Bernardita Dianzon argues that Ben Sira desires to glorify Israel through the glorification of Adam. That is, in seeking to present the glory of Israel, Ben Sira presents Adam as the first human and Israelite who possessed glory that exceeded all creation. Further, Dianzon argues that "Adam theology, found in the Old Testament and intertestamental writings, fulfills the basic purpose of advancing a claim about Israel's place in God's purposes" (Dianzon, "Adam Language in Genesis," 11–13). Scroggs argues that this passage "probably" refers to the kingship of Adam (Scroggs, *Last Adam*, 22–23, 25; see also Levison, *Portraits of Adam*, 46–47).

45. Avemarie, "Image of God," 221–23. The writings at Qumran indicate elsewhere that Adam's glory did not necessarily pass to all of his descendants. Rather, God bestows "the glory of Adam" only upon the covenant community (CD III 19–20; 1QS IV 22–23; 1QH^a IV 27).

46. In the LXX, "ἐν ὁσιότητι καὶ δικαιοσύνῃ."

demonstrates his regal authority through the naming of the animals (Jub. 3:1–2) and through maintaining the garden (Jub. 3:15–16).

Philo presents a similar picture of Adam's original position at creation. Philo reasons that God created Adam (along with the rest of humanity) as superior to other earthly creatures by granting him the ability to reason[47] and by granting him the image of God.[48] As a result, God places Adam as king over all creatures and elements in creation.[49] Philo also exalts the first man as superior to all other humans who came after him.[50] He explicitly refers to Adam as a king and argues that his naming of the animals was proof of his regal authority.[51]

While in some cases Second Temple Judaism presents Adam as a glorious being, in other cases it presents a negative view of Adam that expounds upon the disastrous nature of his fall. Instead of reflecting God's holy and righteous rule, Adam's sin plunged humanity into a sinful state and brought death to all humanity (Jub. 3:17–31; 4 Ezra 3:6–11; 2 Bar. 17:3, 23:4). The effects of Adam's failure to exercise God's good rule reached beyond humanity itself. His failure had cosmological significance.[52] His failure brought corruption to all creation (4 Ezra 7:11–12). His sin brought a curse upon the land (Jub. 3:25) and negatively affected the animals (Jub. 3:28–29).[53]

Both the positive and negative picture of Adam presented in Second Temple Judaism highlight key aspects of his kingship. On the one hand, God granted Adam dominion over creation and commissioned Adam to maintain his good, created order. On the other hand, Adam's failure to rule as God intended plunged humanity into a sinful state, corrupted creation, and had catastrophic effects on the cosmos. This understanding of Adam's kingship and subsequent failure provides essential background for the Jewish hope in God's coming king. Davies aptly notes, "It was over against this background of a Fall which had involved the cosmos that

---

47. Philo, *Opif.* 65–68. Such a description demonstrates the Hellenistic influence on Philo's thought. For Philo, humanity is a composite creature made up of mortal body and immortal mind/soul (Dianzon, "Adam Language," 15–16).

48. Philo, *Opif.* 139.

49. Philo, *Opif.* 83–84, 142. Philo does exclude the heavenly beings from the dominion of Adam.

50. Philo, *Opif.* 136, 140.

51. Philo, *Opif.* 148–150.

52. Davies, *Paul*, 38–39.

53. Specifically, this passage in Jubilees states the animals lost their ability to speak.

that explicitly reflects on the Davidic covenant, grounds David's kingship in YHWH's anointing (Ps 132:10, 17).[61] This characterization means that whatever position, power, or authority that YHWH's king receives, it is grounded in YHWH's identity as Creator and Lord of all things.[62]

Second, at various points, these Psalms describe YHWH's enthronement of his king as a means to battle against cosmic forces of chaos.[63] That is to say, these Psalms often portray the opposition to God and his king by utilizing cosmic language.[64] As the Creator of the cosmos, YHWH has the unique ability to defeat and subdue all cosmic forces. Psalm 2:1–3 declares that the nations, kings of the earth, and rulers rise up against YHWH and his king. Such language is used elsewhere to describe cosmic chaos and rebellion.[65] As a response to their rebellion, YHWH counters by enthroning his chosen king (Ps 2:4–6). Psalm 18:4–5 describes the king being overcome by sinister cosmic powers.[66] YHWH wages war against these sinister forces and proves his power over them by delivering his anointed king (Ps 18:7–18). YHWH then empowers his king to battle against all his enemies and to have victory over them (Ps 18:32–43). Psalm 89:9–10 lauds YHWH as the one who defeats and subordinates hostile cosmic forces. YHWH declares that he has raised up and empowered a warrior for himself, whom he explicitly identifies as David (Ps 89:20–22). YHWH then grants his anointed king power over seas and rivers, which are portrayed within the Psalm as hostile cosmic

---

61. Specifically, the Psalm refers to David as YHWH's משיח. Generally, the Old Testament uses this term to refer to an eschatological human agent established by God who would deliver God's people and establish God's rule. Although this figure is most often depicted as a royal figure, ancient Judaism does use other figures (such as a priest or warrior) to depict the coming משיח. It should also be noted that royal messianism is not equivalent to Jewish reflections upon the ideal king. For example, Deut 17:14–20 gives a conception of Israel's ideal king but does not contain eschatological overtones. Some texts may not initially appear to be messianic in nature in their initial context, but once the messianic figure comes, they lend themselves to retrospective messianic interpretations (e.g., Pss 2, 110; Isa 9). For further discussion, see Jipp, *Christ Is King*, 29–31; Mowinckel, *He that Cometh*; Lucass, *Concept of the Messiah*.

62. Kraus, *Theology of the Psalms*, 122.

63. Scholars often refer to this concept as the *Chaoskampf* traditions, in which a deity engages in battle against forces of chaos. *Chaoskampf* traditions typically portray these battles in a cosmic setting. For more on this tradition, see Crouch, *War and Ethics*, 68–76.

64. Roberts, "Enthronement of Yhwh," 675–86.

65. Sasson, "Language of Rebellion," 147–54; Starbuck, *Court Oracles*, 161.

66. For more on the language employed by the Psalms to describe these cosmic powers, see Kraus, *Theology of the Psalms*, 134–36, and Creach, *Destiny of the Righteous*, 54–69.

forces (Ps 89:26).[67] The combination of YHWH's battle against hostile cosmic forces, the description of David as both warrior and YHWH's anointed, and YHWH's granting his king power over these same hostile cosmic forces suggests that the anointing of the king comes with the invitation for the king to join with YHWH in a cosmic battle.[68]

Third, these Psalms identify the royal Davidic figure as YHWH's son. In Ps 2:7, YHWH calls his enthroned king his son and proclaims that he himself has begotten the king.[69] Such language reflects the act of divine adoption in which YHWH calls out a king for himself, elevates him above the nations of the earth, and confers his own authority and power upon him.[70] Collins argues that the combination of begetting language with adoption language in this passage "suggests a closer kinship between king and god than is conveyed by 'adoption.'"[71] In Ps 89:27, the king appeals to YHWH by calling him father. YHWH promises to adopt the king as his firstborn son, and, as a result of this adoption, make him the most exalted of the earth's kings (Ps 89:28). The king's status as YHWH's son grants him authority not only over the nations of the earth but also, as mentioned in the preceding paragraph, over hostile forces in the cosmos (Ps 89:26). Though not explicitly calling the king YHWH's son, Ps 110 also utilizes language that conveys kinship. YHWH's initial invitation for the king to sit at his right hand bespeaks a close relationship between the two (Ps 110:1). YHWH declares that he has brought forth the king "from the womb of the dawn" and "like dew" (v. 3).[72] The LXX utilizes the Greek

---

67. On the use of water imagery to convey cosmic forces of chaos, see Day, *God's Conflict*.

68. Crouch, "Image of God," 18–20.

69. OT scholars have argued that the language of begetting in the Psalm depicts an enthronement ritual that may parallel Egyptian enthronement rituals. Adela Yarbro Collins and John J. Collins suggest that the Psalm was likely influenced (at least indirectly) by such Egyptian enthronement rituals (A. Y. Collins and J. J. Collins, *King and Messiah*, 10–15). Kraus correctly notes that while parallels between Ps 2 and other ancient Near Eastern traditions do exist, one should not "assume a single, unified concept in the ancient Near East" (Kraus, *Theology of the Psalms*, 113).

70. Kraus, *Theology of the Psalms*, 113.

71. A. Y. Collins and J. J. Collins, *King and Messiah*, 22. Starbuck suggests that the "begotten" language (from the Hebrew verb ילד) indicates that the king "participates in Yahweh's form" and possesses an ontological relationship with the divine (Starbuck, *Court Oracles*, 166). Such language does fall short of granting the king divine status. However, it does suggest that the Psalm claims a status for the king that is greater than human.

72. The first phrase is a translation of the Hebrew מרחם משחר, and the second is a translation of the Hebrew phrase טל ילדתיך לך borrowed from Kraus (Kraus, *Theology*

verb ἐκγεννάω to describe YHWH's establishment of his king (Ps 109:3). Put in simple terms, these metaphors assert that "just as Yahweh gives birth to the dew every morning, so, too, Yahweh has given birth to the king."[73] As in Pss 2 and 89, the imagery does not suggest that YHWH literally gives birth to the king. Rather, this imaginative language serves as a metaphor to convey the close kinship between YHWH and his king. The combination of these Psalms shows that there was a line of thought that viewed the ideal Davidic king as being adopted by YHWH. As YHWH's adopted son, he is granted the authority to exercise YHWH's royal rule.

Fourth, these Psalms assert that the scope of the king's rule extends over all nations and, at times, over the cosmos itself. These Psalms also assert that his rule is permanent. In Ps 2:8, YHWH's king declares that YHWH has granted him authority to rule over all nations of the earth. The king's reception of world dominion is grounded in YHWH's own lordship over the world.[74] In Ps 18:44–45 and 48, the king declares that YHWH has subjected the nations under the king's authority. The writer expresses YHWH's unending faithfulness to his מָשִׁיחַ, whom the Psalm explicitly identifies as coming from the Davidic line (Ps 18:51). Such faithfulness would keep the Davidic ruler on the throne forever. In Ps 21, YHWH grants unending days to his king (v. 5) and faithfully keeps his king from being overthrown (Ps 21:8). In Ps 45, the nations bow at the feet of YHWH's king (v. 6) and bring praise to his royal line forever (v. 18). In Ps 72, the king's authority extends "from sea to sea" and "to the ends of earth" (v. 8),[75] and all kings and nations bow before him (v. 11). As previously discussed, Ps 89 portrays the king's authority extending beyond the nations and over cosmic forces (v. 26). The Psalm affirms the permanence of YHWH's covenant with his king (vv. 27–28), and YHWH declares that the Davidic kingship would last forever (vv. 37–38). In Ps 110, YHWH subordinates the king's enemies under his feet (language that is similar to the subordination of creation under humanity's feet in

---

of the Psalms, 114). Psalm 110:3 is a notoriously difficult verse to translate and may only be understood with the use of text-critical emendation. Despite the various difficulties, most OT scholars agree that some sort of begetting/birthing imagery is in view. For more on translating/interpreting this verse, see Kraus, *Theology of the Psalms*, 114–15; Starbuck, *Court Oracles*, 148–53; and A. Y. Collins and J. J. Collins, *King and Messiah*, 16–19.

73. Starbuck, *Court Oracles*, 150.

74. Mowinckel, *Psalms*, 55.

75. Mowinckel draws a parallel to Babylonian traditions where "from sea to sea" means the whole of the known world (Mowinckel, *Psalms*, 55).

Ps 8) and grants the king authority to rule over his enemies (110:1–2). In Ps 132, YHWH expresses his intent to have David's line last forever (vv. 11–12). Psalm 144:2 declares that YHWH subdues the nations before his king. This characterization of God's king demonstrates the central hope that God would establish his rule over the nations through his anointed king.[76] The king's rule over the whole earth (and, at certain points, the cosmos itself) was meant to reflect the cosmic rule of YHWH.[77] As Kraus puts it, YHWH's ideal king "finds himself at the intersection of sacral enthronement and mythical cosmology."[78]

Fifth, while ruling over the nations, the characterization of the king's rule reflects the characterization of YHWH's rule. The king's function can be summarized under the titles of warrior, judge, and priest. As a warrior, the king defeats his enemies and the enemies of YHWH and brings them to justice (Pss 2:9–10; 18:33–43; 45:3–5; 89:23; 110:3). As a judge, the king's rule results in justice for the poor and oppressed (Pss 72:4, 12–13; 132:15b; cf. 22:26), and he makes just decisions (Pss 45:7–8; 72:1–2). His just rule brings peace, harmony, and prosperity for those under his reign (Pss 72:3, 6–7, 15–16; 132:15a; 144:12–14). As a Melchizedekian priest, the king seeks to bring the people under the kingship of YHWH (Ps 110:4). The combination of these functions demonstrates how God maintains cosmic harmony through his chosen king. "Justice and righteousness became the first and organizing responsibility of the king upon which all else depended."[79] In other words, one may, in some sense, find the hope of cosmic harmony within the Psalms in the eventual enthronement of God's ideal king.[80]

God's Ideal King in the Prophets

The conception of God's plan to install an ideal king through whom he would rule the cosmos continues into the writings of the prophets.[81]

76. Jipp, *Christ Is King*, 34.
77. Whitelam, "Israelite Kingship," 129–30.
78. Kraus, *Theology of the Psalms*, 121.
79. Mays, *Psalms*, 287.
80. Whitelam argues that the portrayal of YHWH's kingship throughout the Psalms places great stress on how he maintains cosmic order (Whitelam, "Israelite Kingship," 129). For references in the Psalms that allude to YHWH maintaining cosmic order, see Pss 47:3–9; 48:3–4; 74:12–14; 93:1–4; 98:2, 6; 99:1–2.
81. Lucass argues that while the themes of kingship are still present in the writings

Specifically, various texts in the prophets anticipate the installation of a Davidic king who will establish God's righteous rule over the earth. The royal Davidic figure appears to be the predominant figure behind the messianic hope within the prophets.[82] While many royal ideological texts in the prophets focus on the reestablishment of Israel, various texts demonstrate God's intent to enact his rule over the earth through his enthroned king.

Isaiah speaks of the hope that God will one day establish justice and righteousness throughout the earth. More than any other prophet, Isaiah views God accomplishing this task through a royal figure. This figure appears in three separate portraits: the king, the servant, and the anointed conqueror.[83] Isaiah 7:14 foretells the birth of a king called עמנו אל, a name that indicates that this ideal king would serve as a herald of God's presence.[84] Isaiah 9 envisions the enthronement of YHWH's king as the hope for the oppressed. The various appellations granted to YHWH's king indicate that the enthronement of the ideal king represents the enactment of YHWH's rule over the earth (Isa 9:5–6).[85] The king rises from the

---

of the prophets, they began to move away from the king as the central figure of salvation (Lucass, *Concept of the Messiah*, 94–121).

82. Daniel Block argues that this is not only true of the prophets, but that this is the predominant picture of the messiah throughout the OT. More specifically, Block pushes back against conceptions that seek to identify the messiah as prophet, priest, and king. He argues that prophetic and priestly elements are mostly absent from messianic passages. When they appear (especially in the case of the priest), they are simply describing the prophetic and priestly functions the king sometimes adopts (Block, "My Servant David," 17–56).

83. Motyer, *Prophecy of Isaiah*, 13. Motyer argues that the Isaianic literature is built around these three messianic portraits. There has been much debate regarding the messianic portrait in Isaiah. The present study does not intend to solve these issues, nor does it seek to advocate for a unified or conflicting messianic picture in Isaiah. Rather, it seeks to examine possible royal themes that underlie these messianic portraits.

84. Schibler, "Messianism" 99–100; see also Laato, *Star Is Rising*, 123–25; Barthel, *Prophetenwort*, 145, 174–75; and A. Y. Collins and J. J. Collins, *King and Messiah*, 36–37. Schibler suggests that this oracle initially has Hezekiah in view but also foreshadowed additional things to come. Matthew's quote of this prophecy (Matt 1:23) indicates that this prophecy was much discussed in the Jewish and Christian tradition in the centuries that followed.

85. In the immediate context of Isa 7, this oracle most likely refers to Hezekiah. However, this oracle is forward looking rather than retrospective. While it may be appropriate that the context of the oracle refers to Hezekiah, the character of the oracle opens the possibility of hope for future kingship beyond the reign of Hezekiah. Rabbinic literature wrestles with the connection between Hezekiah and the messiah. While there was some speculation that Hezekiah may have been the messiah, rabbinic literature came to regard Hezekiah as a model for the coming messiah (A. Y. Collins and J. J.

Davidic line and is promised a vast dominion. Peace and justice are the result of his reign (Isa 9:6–7).[86] Isaiah 11 also looks forward to a king who would rise from the Davidic line.[87] His ability to rule arises from his close relationship with YHWH. The king possesses YHWH's spirit and delights in obeying YHWH's commands (Isa 11:2–3). Because of his relationship to YHWH, the king rules with justice and righteousness (Isa 11:3–5; see also Isa 16:5; 32:1), and his reign brings peace and harmony throughout the world (Isa 11:6–9). As one enthroned by YHWH, the nations submit to his reign (Isa 11:10). The cumulative effect is that the hope of nature and nations is founded upon the establishment of YHWH's ideal king.

The servant songs of Isaiah provide more insight into the picture of God's ideal king. While there are numerous debates regarding the identity of the servant, it seems most likely that he is some sort of royal figure. Gordan Hugenberger provides a helpful summary of the evidence, which suggests a royal identity for this servant figure. First, the designation "servant" is commonly used to refer to royal figures. Second, the assertion of YHWH's placing his Spirit upon the servant (Isa 42:1) accords with royal identity. Third, the servant's work to bring justice upon the earth (Isa 42:1–4) reflects the work of a king. Fourth, the acknowledgment of the servant by earthly kings (Isa 49:7; 52:14–15) suggests a royal identity. Fifth, the botanical imagery in Isa 53:2 parallels the royal language of Isa 11:10.[88] Given this evidence, Richard Schultz rightly states that "a number of thematic, verbal, and contextual indicators suggest that the two are not only to be compared with each other but also are integrally related,

---

Collins, *King and Messiah*, 40–41; Laato, *Star Is Rising*, 125).

86. Such qualities also characterize YHWH's kingship in Isaiah (Isa 24:21—25:21). For more on justice and righteousness as characteristic of God's divine kingship, see Weinfeld, *Social Justice*, 181–83.

87. Unlike Isa 7 and 9, the oracle in Isa 11 does not have Hezekiah as its immediate referent. Rabbinic literature never connects Isa 11 with Hezekiah, and Hezekiah does not fit well within the oracle given that the king in Isa 11 does not begin to rule until after the destruction of Assyria (Laato, *Star Is Rising*, 125).

88. Hugenberger presents corporate Israel, a prophetic figure (namely, Deutero-Isaiah), or a priestly figure as other possible candidates for the identity of the servant. He eventually rejects the evidence for a royal interpretation and argues in favor of a Mosaic interpretation (Hugenberger, "Servant of the Lord," 105–40). Block provides a helpful critique of Hugenberger's Mosaic interpretation, the most significant point being that the rest of the OT does not portray Moses as an eschatological messianic figure. He argues that the Davidic king presents the most likely background for the servant (Block, "My Servant David," 43–48). For another helpful summary on different views regarding the identity of the servant figure, see Watts, *Isaiah 34–66*, 115–20.

if not identified. The king and the servant share similar descriptions and similar tasks in the book of Isaiah."[89]

In Isa 42, YHWH grants his spirit to his royal servant (Isa 42:1; cf. Isa 11:2)[90] and, through his authority as the Creator (Isa 42:5), commissions him. This commissioning proves YHWH's covenant faithfulness to his people and enlightens nations to YHWH's just rule (Isa 42:6). As one commissioned by YHWH, the royal servant executes justice and brings peace to the oppressed (Isa 42:1, 3–4, 7). In Isa 49:1–6, YHWH commissions his servant at birth to restore Israel.[91] YHWH also commissions his servant to bring salvation to the whole earth (Isa 49:6b).[92] The oracle in Isa 52–53 begins with YHWH's promise to exalt his chosen servant (Isa 52:13).[93] However, the oracle declares that the servant's exaltation would follow his humiliation. His appearance is so appalling that his exaltation shocks the kings of the earth (Isa 52:14–15).[94] He is not special in appearance, and the people initially reject him (Isa 53:2–3).[95] Like other royal ideological texts, YHWH intends to restore his relationship with the people through the servant. However, unlike other royal ideological texts, the servant's suffering and death accomplishes this restoration (Isa 53:4–11).[96] In a reversal of fortune, the servant's suffering and death leads to his victory, and he divides the spoils of his victory (Isa 53:11b–12).

---

89. Schultz, "King," 157–58. Lucass views the servant in Isaiah as a development of the king's role (Lucass, "Concept of Messiah," 95, 120–21).

90. Motyer takes note of this parallel portrait between the king of Isa 11 and the servant in the Servant Songs (Motyer, *Prophecy of Isaiah*, 13).

91. The servant is explicitly identified as Israel in v. 3. However, v. 5 indicates that the Lord would bring restoration to Israel through the servant, which indicates a distinction between corporate Israel and the servant.

92. Blenkinsopp, *Isaiah 40–55*, 299.

93. Though Isa 52–53 does not explicitly speak about enthronement, the language of exaltation may suggest that the enthronement of the servant is in view.

94. Block argues that משחת in Isa 52:14 could be derived from the Hebrew verb for anointing. In this case, the verse would be referring to a superhuman anointing (Block, "My Servant David," 50; see also Barthelemy, *Critique textuelle*, 384–87).

95. Such rejection may parallel the rejection experienced by the Davidic king in Psalm 89:38–51 (Laato, *Star Is Rising*, 145–48).

96. This motif has puzzled OT scholarship because there does not seem to be an obvious antecedent for portraying the royal messiah as a sacrifice. John Walton argues for a potential parallel with the Mesopotamian ritual of the substitute king (Walton, "Substitute King Ritual," 734–43). Block suggests the possibility that this oracle adapts the ritual for its own messianic purposes. "Whereas the substitute king ritual has a commoner taking on himself the curse that hangs over the king and dying in his place, the Servant Song has the king . . . taking upon himself the sins of the common people

Isaiah 59:14—63:6 presents an anointed conqueror/divine warrior who has characteristics of royalty. Like the king and servant in Isaiah, YHWH grants his spirit to this figure because he is YHWH's chosen one (Isa 59:21; 61:1).[97] YHWH commissions him to bring deliverance and vindication to the poor and oppressed, and his arrival means the restoration of the true kingdom of God (Isa 61:2-4; 63:1). This kingdom draws the nations to itself because it displays the glory of YHWH (Isa 60:1-5; 61:5-6, 9). He is clothed with salvation and righteousness (Isa 61:10), and the nations will witness his deliverance of YHWH's people (Isa 62:10-11). This figure completes his work when he subjugates the nations and executes YHWH's wrath upon them (Isa 63:1-6).

Other prophets anticipate the installation of God's ideal king. Jeremiah envisions a righteous king from David's line who will rule in a just manner (Jer 23:5; 33:15). Israel would receive security, prosperity, and justice as the result of his reign (Jer 23:6; 33:17). Ezekiel describes the royal figure as a Davidic shepherd who cares for the people as a shepherd cares for a flock (Ezek 34:23; 35:24). As one appointed by YHWH, this royal figure rules over the people under the authority of YHWH (Ezek 34:24). The Davidic figure's subordination to YHWH's authority is conveyed by the granting of the title נשיא (Ezek 34:23; 37:25; he is called a מלך in Ezek 37:24). This title is not meant to deny this figure's kingship but to highlight his subordination to YHWH's kingship and his role as YHWH's royal representative to the people.[98] YHWH refers to this king as עבדי, indicating a special relationship between YHWH and his king (Ezek 37:24).[99] YHWH unites the kingdom of Judah and the kingdom of Israel under the eternal reign of his chosen Davidic king, representing YHWH's faithfulness to the Davidic covenant (Ezek 37:22, 25; cf. 2

---

and being slain in their place" (Block, "My Servant David," 53–54). While these parallels are certainly intriguing, it is difficult to prove definitively any direct connections between the Mesopotamian rituals and the Suffering Servant. Rather, one could argue that this idea reflects other Jewish royal motifs in which God elevates his king from a position of obscurity to kingship.

97. In Isa 59:21, the emergence of this anointed conqueror is indicated within the MT by the switch from a third person plural pronoun to a second person singular pronoun (Motyer, *Prophecy of Isaiah*, 492–93). This figure is first referred to in the third person in Isa 59:21 but reappears speaking in first person in Isa 61.

98. Block, "Bringing Back David," 175–76. The use of this term to describe royalty is a distinctive feature of Ezekiel. See the discussion on the use of נשיא in Ezekiel from Block, "Bringing Back David," 183–88, and Joyce, "King and Messiah," 330–32.

99. Block, "Bringing Back David," 182.

Sam 7). The king's appointment "symbolizes the realities of the new age."[100] Micah 5 sees the emergence of a king from David's hometown (Bethlehem) who would rule over Israel and possibly suggests the preexistence of this king (Mic 5:1).[101] YHWH's authority and strength will empower the king's rule, and he establishes peace and security (Mic 5:3–4a). His greatness will extend throughout the earth (Mic 5:3b). Zechariah 9:9–10 foresees the king as having a worldwide dominion, and peace would characterize his reign. However, YHWH is the one who brings about the state of world domination and peace to the earth (Zech 9:1–8). The king merely mediates the worldwide rule and maintains the peace brought about by YHWH alone.[102] Thus, the king presented in Zechariah appears more passive in his role than the king presented in the other prophets.[103]

While the preceding prophets view God's ideal king as a Davidic figure, Daniel presents a slightly different picture of the ideal king. The ideal king in Daniel is clearly a figure of cosmic significance. In an apocalyptic vision, Daniel speaks of a figure who is "like the son of man" (Dan 7:13). Though debate on the exact identity of this figure persists,[104] the title "son of man" most likely serves to identify the figure as royalty.[105] The scene in Daniel takes place in the heavenly realm, indicating that the conferring of regal authority upon this figure has cosmic implications.[106] His en-

---

100. Block, "Bringing Back David," 183. Unlike other OT texts, the king does not play a part in restoration. Rather, YHWH alone restores the people and then places his king over them.

101. Lucass, *Concept of the Messiah*, 97.

102. See Duguid, "Messianic Themes," 267 and Laato, *Josiah and David*, 270.

103. Laato suggests that this passage presents an alternative royal ideology and serves as a critique against previous Davidic rulers for failing to live up to the Davidic ideal (Laato, *Josiah and David*, 300–301; see also Mason, "Messiah," 353–57). Collins views the passage as a sort of "throwback" to the time of the judges, though it does explicitly grant royal status to the figure (Collins, *Scepter and the Star*, 37).

104. For an overview of scholarship on the son of man figure in Dan 7, including different arguments regarding his identity, see Casey, *Son of Man*, 7–50; Beyerle, "Wolken," 1–52; and Goldingay, *Daniel*, 366–70.

105. Both Ps 8 and Dan 7 identify their respective royal figures as the son of man. Though it may not be possible to argue definitively that Dan 7 draws from Ps 8, one does notice a few parallels between the two. Paul Mosca identifies the following parallels: (1) the title "son of man," (2) the location of God's work in the heavens, (3) dominion over the animal kingdom in Ps 8 compared to the son of man's dominion over the beasts in Dan 7, and (4) Dan 7's positioning of the son of man "in the clouds of heaven," echoing the status of the son of man as "a little less divine" in Ps 8 (Mosca, "Ugarit and Daniel 7," 515–17).

106. Even though it is highly probable that the son of man is a royal figure, it is less clear on whether or not he is a Davidic figure. Collins argues against a Davidic

thronement occurs after God's struggle with and defeat of cosmic powers (Dan 7:2–12). This royal figure is more than a mere earthly king. He is a transcendent being. God removes the authority of the hostile cosmic powers (Dan 7:12) and bestows his sovereign power and authority upon him in the heavenly realm, which grants him authority to rule over all the kingdoms of the earth (Dan 7:14a).[107] Such enthronement also means that his kingdom is eternal and indestructible (Dan 7:14b). His enthronement indicates that God has granted the kingdom to the saints whom he represents (Dan 7:27).

Though each of the prophets present unique features in each of their depictions of God's ideal king, they display a few common themes. First, God is the one who enthrones his ideal king and empowers the king to execute his rule. Second, the king's enthronement indicates the enactment of God's rule over the earth (and, at times, the cosmos). The king is primarily the mediator of the rule of God, the supreme king, over the earth. Third, in most of the prophetic writings, the king arises from the Davidic line and is therefore the fulfillment of the Davidic covenant. Even in cases where the royal figure is not obviously Davidic (such as the suffering servant and the son of man), one can make reasonable arguments for a Davidic background. At the very least, these figures function in a similar way as the ideal Davidic king. Thus, the prophets often reflect the exalted picture of the Davidic rule presented in the Psalms. Fourth, as the mediator of God's rule, the king is a righteous figure who brings justice, salvation, and peace to the whole earth. Fifth, while some

---

interpretation, noting a lack of acknowledgment in the rest of Daniel to a Davidic figure. Instead, Collins argues that the angel Michael is most likely the son of man in Daniel (see Collins, *Daniel*, 308–10). Paul Mosca suggests that Ps 89 may serve as a crucial link between the Canaanite/Ugaritic tradition and the Danielic son of man. In this case, one could view Dan 7 as echoing Davidic kingship (Mosca, "Ugarit and Daniel 7," 496–517). Pieter de Vries also argues that Daniel's son of man is the Davidic king. He argues for linguistic and thematic links between Dan 7 and Pss 2, 89, and 110 (Vries, "Identity of Him," 17–20). Whether or not a Davidic king is in view in Dan 7, one should acknowledge that his function is remarkably similar to the function of the ideal Davidic king in the Psalms. Some have argued that the son of man is a corporate personality referring to Israel as a people (for example, Lacocque, *Book of Daniel*, 126, 146). However, it seems much more likely that it refers to an individual king who serves as the representative of Israel.

107. Collins argues that this idea marks a major eschatological shift that would play an important role within Judaism in the centuries that followed. Further, this paradigm would be crucial for affirming Jesus' messiahship, despite his "failure" to restore the kingdom of Israel on earth (Collins, *Scepter and the Star*, 45–46).

of the prophetic writings focus more on the king's restoration of Israel (for example, Ezekiel), the prophets also claim that God subordinates the nations under the rule of his king. The dominion of God's king is a worldwide dominion. In the case of Dan 7, God even subordinates the cosmic powers under his king.

God's Ideal King in Second Temple Jewish Literature

Jewish literature from the Second Temple period demonstrates hope in the arrival of God's ideal king. Collins argues that by the first century BC, the hope of the reestablishment of the Davidic king was "part of the common heritage of Judaism"[108] and "the common core of Jewish messianism."[109] Much of these writings builds upon the foundations of royal ideology set forth in the OT text.[110] Some Second Temple Jewish texts, like the Similitudes of Enoch and 4 Ezra, portray God's ideal king as a transcendent figure. Therefore, while Second Temple Jewish texts present a multifaceted picture of Jewish messianic expectation, God's ideal king is of continuing importance to the Jewish hope in the Second Temple period.[111]

When Second Temple Jewish texts look forward to a coming king, they often describe this king using Davidic language, especially in the pseudepigraphal writings. Psalms of Solomon 17–18 provides an explicit reference to the coming Davidic king and perhaps the most detailed description of his restoration and enthronement.[112] The psalms look forward to the restoration of a Davidic king who would reign over Israel (Pss. Sol. 17:21). He is anointed by the Lord (Pss. Sol. 17:32) and operates under the kingship of the Lord (Pss. Sol. 17:31). He receives strength and authority from the Lord (Pss. Sol. 17:33–34) and is a sign of the Lord's goodness (Pss. Sol. 18:5–6). The king's role is both as a political and

---

108. Collins, *Scepter and the Star*, 52.

109. Collins, *Scepter and the Star*, 78.

110. Condra, *Salvation for the Righteous*, 226–37. Condra argues that the royal messiah serves as the cohesive and prominent figure in early Judaism.

111. While the destruction of the Second Temple occurred in 70 CE, this section will focus on Jewish literature that dates as late as the end of the first century CE/beginning of the second century CE. Even though some of these writings are dated after Paul's death, they present ideas that would have conceivably existed during Paul's life.

112. On the social setting of Psalms of Solomon, see Collins, *Scepter and the Star*, 52–57, and Condra, *Salvation for the Righteous*, 240–21.

spiritual figure.[113] This king functions as a victorious warrior[114] who will destroy the unrighteous rulers and nations, purge Jerusalem of sinners, and subjugate the nations under his rule (Pss. Sol. 17:22–25, 30, 34).[115] The king also acts as a righteous judge who rebukes the wicked rulers and sinners (Pss. Sol. 17:36) and brings blessings upon Israel (Pss. Sol. 17:43). As the Lord's anointed king, he will establish righteousness and holiness so that all nations might see the glory of the Lord (Pss. Sol. 17:31–32). His reign will be holy because the Lord will grant him his spirit of wisdom, righteousness, and strength (Pss. Sol. 17:37, 18:7–8). Psalms of Solomon 17–18 reveals that the ideal king's reign is about more than the deliverance and establishment of Israel. Rather, "what is anticipated is the realization of God's purposes on earth through a cleansing of the people and the establishment of righteousness."[116] Though this passage concerns itself with the establishment of a righteous reign for Israel, it also views the ideal king's reign as extending over all nations.

The Similitudes of Enoch portrays God's coming king as a transcendent figure who will be granted a heavenly throne. The Similitudes employs a plurality of epithets in its portrayal of God's ideal king: the Righteous One (1 En. 38:2, 53:6), the Chosen One (1 En. 39:6; 40:5; 45:3; 49:2, 4; 51:3, 5; 52:6, 9; 53:6; 55:4; 61:5, 8, 10; 62:1), the Anointed One (1 En. 48:10; 52:4), and the Son of Man (1 En. 48:2; 62:5, 7, 9; 63:11).[117] Rather than viewing these as separate figures, the context of the Similitudes indicates that these epithets all refer to the same figure.[118] Rather than focusing on

---

113. Collins cautions against those who would seek to draw a sharp distinction between the political and spiritual nature of this king. Such a distinction could cause one to lean to one side over the other. However, Collins suggests that such a distinction/contrast is "anachronistic" and that "the spirituality of the psalms is rooted in political and national conceptions." (Collins, *Scepter and the Star*, 59).

114. Chester argues that this king is "not a warrior-Messiah," citing that the passage does not mention "force of arms" to describe the king's overthrow of the oppressors (Chester, *Messiah and Exaltation*, 343). However, such an assertion seems to ignore the overall tone of the passage.

115. Collins aptly notes that the initial role of the king in this passage is "undeniably violent" (Collins, *Scepter and the Star*, 58).

116. Condra, *Salvation for the Righteous*, 243.

117. For a brief summary of the contents of the Similitudes, see A. Y. Collins and J. J. Collins, *King and Messiah*, 87–88.

118. Charlesworth, "Jewish Messianology," 238–40, and Vanderkam, "Righteous One," 169–91. James Waddell rightly notes that it is not the individual elements of a tradition that define its ideology. Rather, it is the ways in which traditions combine these elements that define its ideology. This is especially true in the Similitudes of Enoch, where the plurality of epithets grants a full picture of who the text conceives God's ideal

the establishment of his kingdom on earth, the Similitudes places greater emphasis on this figure's enthronement in the heavenly realm and his role in executing judgment upon all beings in the cosmos.

The Similitudes points to the exalted status of God's ideal king over the whole cosmos in a few ways. First, the Similitudes views this royal figure as a transcendent being.[119] He is introduced as one "whose face was like the appearance of a man" (1 En. 46:1) and is often referred to as "the Son of Man."[120] He is also "like the one of the holy angels" (1 En. 46:1). This description indicates that this figure is more than a man "in the usual sense of the word."[121] While he is compared to the angels, his royal position indicates that he ranks higher than the angels.[122] Second, this royal figure is enthroned by the Lord (referred to in Similitudes as "the Lord of the Spirits," 1 En. 45:1; 46:6, 8; 47:1) and operates under his authority. The Lord seats him on the "throne of glory," a designation that seems to indicate the throne of God himself (1 En. 45:3; 51:3; 55:4; 61:8; 62:2–3, 5; 69:27, 29).[123] As one enthroned in the presence of the Lord, he possesses eternal glory and might, and the Lord grants him "the spirit of wisdom and the spirit of insight" (1 En. 49:2–3). His enthronement on the Lord's throne demonstrates his exalted status above all creatures in the cosmos and indicates that the Lord grants him power and authority so that he might execute the Lord's rule.[124] Third, the Similitudes alludes to the preexistent status of the enthroned king. The Lord chose him and kept him "hidden in his presence" before the creation of the world and

---

king will be (Waddell, *Messiah*, 17, 48).

119. Waddell, *Messiah*, 49–51. Andrew Chester argues that this figure is not a human figure that relates to the present realm but belongs to the heavenly realm (Chester, "Jewish Messianic Expectations," 31). However, Waddell rightly cites this figure's identification as the son of man as an identification of his human nature. See also Eskola, *Messiah and the Throne*, 91.

120. Collins asserts that it is "beyond doubt" that Similitudes alludes to the Danielic son of man in its description of this royal figure (Collins, *Scepter and the Star*, 197; see also Condra, *Salvation for the Righteous*, 256). However, he argues the Similitudes develops the identity of this figure beyond what one finds in Dan 7. He points specifically to passages that associate the son of man with the Davidic messiah (A. Y. Collins and J. J. Collins, *King and Messiah*, 86–90).

121. A. Y. Collins and J. J. Collins, *King and Messiah*, 89.

122. For more on the transcendent nature of God's king in the Similitudes, see Böttrich, "Menschensohnes," 76–79, and Kvanvig, "Son of Man," 179–215.

123. Waddell notes that "glory" designates the throne of "the Lord of the Spirits." The text does not indicate that there are two separate thrones. Therefore, the Lord and his chosen royal agent share the same throne (Waddell, *Messiah*, 91).

124. Rowland, *Open Heaven*, 105–6.

heavenly bodies (1 En. 48:3, 6; 62:6–7). While Similitudes falls short of describing this royal figure as an eternal being, the text clearly indicates that he existed before the created cosmos.[125] Fourth, the Similitudes describes this royal figure as a righteous being. In its first mention of this royal figure, the Similitudes calls him "the Righteous One" (1 En. 38:2; 53:6), and elsewhere, the text states that righteousness dwells with him (1 En. 46:3). Fifth, the worship given to the royal figure demonstrates his exalted status over the cosmos. The Similitudes declares that all people on the earth will worship this figure (1 En. 48:5), and the whole cosmos will rejoice at his enthronement (1 En. 52:3–5). All powerful kings of the earth recognize his throne and exalt him for his glorious reign (1 En. 62:3–6, 9).

As the one whom the Lord has exalted above and enthroned over all things in the cosmos, the royal figure in the Similitudes takes on the functions of the Lord's ideal king. Most significantly, this royal figure mediates the judgment of the Lord over the cosmos. As one ruling under the authority of the Lord, he rules with righteousness and truth (1 En. 39:6–7). His initial appearance signals the judgment of the wicked and spoils for the righteous (1 En. 38:2). This royal figure judges the work of sinners (1 En. 45:3) and the holy ones (1 En. 61:8), overturns kings and kingdoms who deny the Lord (1 En. 46:4–6), judges the angels (1 En. 55:4), and executes judgment upon sinners, oppressors, and hostile cosmic forces (1 En. 49:4; 62:2; 69:27b–29). His right judgment grants hope to the righteous ones who are oppressed by the wicked kings and evil cosmic forces (1 En. 48:4; 53:6). Ultimately, his judgment results in the destruction of the unrighteous and the eternal salvation of the righteous (1 En. 62:2–14).

Though certainly not as extensive as the Similitudes, 4 Ezra also gives a transcendent picture of God's ideal king. Unlike the Similitudes, this text explicitly states that this king will rise from the Davidic line (4 Ezra 12:32). His transcendent nature is revealed in that God has kept him hidden for many ages, suggesting that this figure is preexistent (4

---

125. Vanderkam seeks to dismiss the preexistence of this figure by arguing that these texts refer "to no more than premundane election and concealment of his identity" (Vanderkam, "Righteous One," 179–82). However, Collins astutely observes that it is difficult to understand why this figure's identity would need to be hidden if he did not yet exist. While noting the potential parallel to the Wisdom tradition in Prov 8, Collins also points to the LXX translation of Ps 110:3 as another significant parallel, which states that the king was begotten "before the Day Star" (A. Y. Collins and J. J. Collins, *King and Messiah*, 89–90).

Ezra 12:32; 13:26).[126] He is called "God's Son," indicating both his Davidic nature and his special relationship with the Most High (4 Ezra 13:32, 37). This king arises from the sea and takes a stand on Mount Zion so that he might bring judgment upon the ungodly and wicked kingdoms of this earth (4 Ezra 12:33; 13:38–39).

Second Baruch[127] speaks of a ruler whose reign brings peace to all of creation. His revelation (which, as in 4 Ezra, may indicate that he is a preexistent figure) coincides with a period of great abundance and prosperity upon the earth (2 Bar. 29:3–8). Thus, the author indicates that the arrival of God's anointed king initiates a period of bliss and reward.[128] He exercises judgment upon the powerful, wicked rulers of the earth (2 Bar. 40:1). He summons the nations to himself and slays those who have oppressed and ruled over God's people (2 Bar. 70:9; 72:2, 6). However, he spares the nations who have not oppressed God's people (2 Bar. 72:4). At the conclusion of his judgment, the anointed figure returns to his throne in the heavenly realms and brings peace, joy, and rest (2 Bar. 73:1).[129] Further, the author declares that the enthronement of this king will result in the reversal of the effects of the fall (2 Bar. 73:2–7).

In each of the above-mentioned texts,[130] God's coming ideal king reflects the attributes and functions often associated with the ideal

126. Collins, *Scepter and the Star*, 78.

127. This work was probably composed after 4 Ezra and after the destruction of the temple in 70 CE. It was probably originally composed in Hebrew or Aramaic and is a decidedly Jewish text (Collins, *Apocalyptic Imagination*, 178, and Stuckenbruck, "Messianic Ideas," 108).

128. Stuckenbruck, "Messianic Ideas," 109. Second Baruch 30:1–2 states that this royal figure's return "with glory" also coincides with the resurrection of the righteous. Scholars are divided on how to understand the "return" of this figure in 2 Bar. 30:1. Pierre Bogaert argues that the passage refers to an even more future event than 2 Bar. 29, in which case the passage has in view the resumption of his glory and his resurrection (Bogaert, *Apocalypse de Baruch*, 1:416). However, Collins argues that while this passage does refer to the resurrection of the righteous, it does not clearly state that the anointed figure raises from the dead (Collins, *Scepter and the Star*, 134). While the issue of this figure's resurrection in this passage remains murky at best, the overall point of the author is that the arrival of this anointed figure will result in prosperity and reward for the righteous.

129. Though 2 Bar. 73:1 does not specifically refer to the location of the throne, the king's revelation in 2 Bar. 29:3—30:1 suggests that his place of residence is in the heavens (Chester, *Messiah*, 348).

130. Again, it should be noted that the Similitudes does not refer to the Davidic king in the conventional sense. Perhaps the greatest distinction between the royal figure of the Similitudes and the Davidic king is that this royal figure does not establish a kingdom on earth like the Davidic king (Collins, *Scepter and the Star*, 205). However, one

Davidic king.¹³¹ His enthronement upon the Lord's throne is similar to the conception of the Davidic king's enthronement, particularly within the Psalms.¹³² His role as judge, which includes punishment of the wicked and salvation of the righteous, parallels the role of the ideal Davidic king. However, the Similitudes presents a remarkable development of this role in that the Lord's king is a heavenly judge to whom the Lord grants authority to bring judgment upon spiritual beings.¹³³ Both 4 Ezra and 2 Baruch portray this king as a transcendent figure and view his reign as having a profound effect upon creation itself.

Though the interest may be minimal, the writings at Qumran do demonstrate that a royal messiah¹³⁴ would play a role in the community's eschatological expectations.¹³⁵ In most cases, these writings conceive this

---

should note that this figure's enthronement in the heavens has significant implications for the kingdoms of the earth.

131. Collins, *Scepter and the Star*, 205. The Similitudes concludes with the curious identification of Enoch as the son of man figure (1 En. 71:13–17). This passage has puzzled many interpreters because the Similitudes gives very little indication that Enoch is the son of man until this point. Even more curious is that 1 En. 70:1 seems to draw a distinction between Enoch and the son of man. Vanderkam suggests that the son of man is the heavenly counterpart to Enoch (Vanderkam, "Righteous One," 182–83). Chester views this passage as suggesting Enoch is transformed into an "exalted angel" (Chester, *Messiah*, 65–66). However, Collins refutes both claims and suggests that this passage was added by a later Jewish redactor, perhaps to refute a Christian identification of Jesus with the son of man (Collins, *Scepter and the Star*, 200–202). For the present study, the exact identity of this royal figure is not important. What is important is the contributions that this text makes to the Jewish understanding of God's ideal king.

132. A. Y. Collins and J. J. Collins, *King and Messiah*, 90, and Hurtado, *One God*, 53.

133. A. Y. Collins and J. J. Collins, *King and Messiah*, 94.

134. Qumran scholars have long argued that Qumran literature presents a diarchic view of messianism in which a priestly messiah and royal messiah are presented as two distinct figures. These figures were expected to lead the community together in the last days. For the sake of the present study, this section will focus only on depictions of a royal messiah. For more on the two messiah schema, see Evans, "Diarchic Messianism," 558–67. For an argument against this two messiah schema, see Hurst, "Two Messiahs?," 157–80.

135. George Brooke argues that the royal messiah at Qumran comes to the fore in later Qumran writings. However, even when this royal figure does appear in Qumran writings, the stress is on his place under the sovereign kingship of God and how his rule informs the place for the community of God's elect (see Brooke, "Kingship and Messianism," 434–55). Craig Evans suggests that while the Qumran sect was certainly not a messianic sect, they also "did not entertain ideas of final victory over its enemies without the leadership of a royal Messiah" (Evans, "Qumran's Messiah," 138). Collins notes that the Davidic king had a "well-established place" in the eschatological expectations of the Qumran community (Collins, *Scepter and the Star*, 67).

royal figure in Davidic terms.[136] While reflecting upon the Davidic covenant, 4Q174 declares that the Davidic king will arise in the last days as an interpreter of the law (4Q174 1.10–12). The *pesher* on Genesis interprets Gen 49:10 as referring to the establishment of the eternal Davidic throne. This Davidic king will bring justice with him (4Q252 5.1–5). The *pesher* on Isaiah interprets Isa 11:1–5 as referring to the coming Davidic king whom God would place on a glorious throne (4Q161 3.18–20).[137] This king will conquer all his enemies, establish his rule over all people, and bring judgment upon all people (4Q161 3.21–22; see also 4Q285 frag. 4–5). This picture of the Davidic king is consistent with the picture of the Davidic king given in Psalms of Solomon 17–18, where the king defeats the unrighteous and brings judgment upon them.[138]

Widely known as "the son of God text," 4Q246 speaks of a coming royal figure whom it identifies as "son of God" and "son of Most High" (4Q246 2.1). Though the identity of this figure has been debated, it seems most likely that the passage refers to a Jewish messianic figure, particularly in terms of Davidic kingship.[139] The sonship language parallels OT language that speaks of the Davidic king in terms of divine sonship (2 Sam 7:14; Pss 2:7; 89:26–27).[140] Within the literature at Qumran, 4Q174 also gives precedent for sonship language concerning the Davidic king. Given his title as "son of God," this figure clearly has a special relationship

---

136. A variety of titles are used in reference to this royal figure. One should be careful about limiting studies on Qumran messianism to passages that only refer specifically to a "messiah/anointed." For more on the various titles used for this figure, see Evans, "Qumran's Messiah," 135–37, and the helpful chart in Condra, *Salvation for the Righteous*, 245.

137. Eskola notes that this passage reflects "the rather traditional belief that the Davidide shall rule over the nations at the end of days" (Eskola, *Messiah*, 85). He also argues that while the passage is eschatological in nature, it does not necessarily conceive of a heavenly enthronement. Rather, the emphasis seems to be on an earthly throne where the Davidic king would exercise rule over all nations of the earth.

138. Evans, "Qumran's Messiah," 146.

139. For a brief summary of the different views regarding the identity of the "son of God" in this passage, see Collins, *Scepter and the Star*, 171–85, or Ferda, "Naming the Messiah," 153–56. See also Puech, "Fils de Dieu," 271–86, for an argument on the Davidic messiah as the identity of the "son of God" in this text.

140. See Ferda's discussion on divine naming in the Hebrew Bible in Ferda, "Naming the Messiah," 168–71, as evidence for this figure's identity as God's Messiah. Collins also suggests that the "Son of Man" figure in Dan 7 could prove helpful in interpreting this text. While it may not be possible to argue that the text represents an interpretation of Dan 7, comparison between the two texts may prove beneficial to understanding 4Q246 (Collins, *Scepter and the Star*, 176–79).

with the ultimate divine King.[141] He overthrows the kingdoms of the earth and establishes an eternal kingdom (4Q246 2.3–5, 8). His reign brings peace on the earth, and all people pay homage to him (4Q246 2.6–7). Taking these Qumran texts together, the picture of God's ideal coming king in the Qumran literature remains fairly consistent with the picture of the ideal Davidic king in the OT.

In summary, Second Temple Jewish literature expresses hope in the restoration of God's ideal king. These writings primarily use Davidic kingship language (both explicit and implicit) to express this hope. God anoints this king and empowers him to exercise God's rule. The king is often portrayed as a victorious warrior who destroys the enemies of God's people and brings judgment upon the wicked. A few passages portray the coming king as a preexistent figure whose throne is in the heavens. Upon his enthronement, he acts as a judge who will punish the wicked and bring salvation and reward to the righteous. While Israel itself is often portrayed as the primary benefactor of the king's reign, many passages emphasize that the king's reign extends over all nations and (at times) over the creation itself. In one case (2 Bar. 73:2–7), the king's enthronement reverses the effects of the fall of Adam, God's original king. Thus, God's installment of his ideal king will result in peace and prosperity for all creation.

SUMMARY AND CONCLUSIONS

The OT and early Jewish literature present two primary figures that represent an ideal king through whom God seeks to enact his rule over the earth, creation, and/or the cosmos: Adam and the royal messiah arising from the Davidic line. After examining the presentation of both figures in Judaism, one may notice several parallels between the enthronement of Adam and the enthronement of the Davidic royal messiah. First, Judaism presents God elevating both figures from obscurity to kingship. God creates Adam from the dust and endows Adam with his image and his glory. As a result, Adam is viewed as originally being superior to everything else in creation. Likewise, Judaism presents an exalted picture of the royal messiah. God elevates David from shepherdship to kingship. The royal messiah is often

---

141. Collins rightly points out that regardless of the differences between a Jewish text like 4Q246 and the Christian understanding of Christ's divinity, the notion that the messiah was the son of God is firmly rooted in Judaism (Collins, *Scepter and the Star*, 190).

described in terms of divine sonship. At other points, he is described as a preexistent figure. Second, the enthronement of both figures is an act of God himself. Third, both figures possess a unique relationship with God. One sees Adam's unique relationship with God through his possession of God's image and the messianic king's relationship through his possession of sonship. Fourth, God grants a vast dominion to both figures. As God subdued the creation under Adam's rule, so also did God promise to subdue the nations, creation, and (at times) cosmic powers under the rule of the messianic king. Fifth, God empowers and commissions both figures to exercise his good rule. By endowing Adam with his image and glory, God desired that Adam would maintain his created order and commissioned Adam to reflect his righteous rule. As a result, God meant to mediate his blessings to his creation through Adam's rule. However, Adam's failure to fulfill his responsibility as God's royal viceroy plunged humanity, creation, and the cosmos into disorder and chaos. Similar to Adam's commission, God commissions the royal messiah to rule over the nations with justice and righteousness. The king is often portrayed as a victorious warrior who destroys the enemies of God's people and brings judgment upon the wicked. His reign brings order, peace, and prosperity to the people of God, the nations, and creation itself.

One may draw a couple of implications from these parallels. First, the enthronements of Adam and the Davidic royal messiah reveal God's intention to rule his creation through a royal viceroy. God's chosen king plays a vital role in maintaining the created order. Second, one could argue that the enthronement of the ideal Davidic king resumes the kingship Adam originally lost. Thus, while Adam's failure led to cosmic chaos, God reestablishes cosmic harmony by enthroning this ideal king. This royal ideology underlies much of the New Testament conception of Christ's kingship. Further, this ideology could have provided a foundation from which Paul could plausibly conceive of Christ as being the promised eschatological king who restores what Adam lost and through whom God would enact his reign over the whole cosmos. If this is the case, this ideology can provide further clarity on how Paul formed his cosmic Christology, especially in Colossians and Ephesians.

3

Cosmic Christ in the New Testament

IF ANCIENT JUDAISM LOOKED forward to the restoration of cosmic harmony through the enthronement of God's ideal king, the NT presents the fulfillment of this royal hope in the person of Christ. In previous attempts to frame the NT depiction of Christ's position in the cosmos, especially from Paul, scholars have had a strong tendency to look either to Hellenistic cosmologies or to Jewish conceptions of personified Wisdom. While one may be able to find some parallels between these ideologies and NT cosmic Christology, Jewish royal ideology provides a useful lens through which the NT authors could have conceived Jesus as fulfilling the role of God's ideal king through his cosmic enthronement. This chapter will examine the possible linguistic and conceptual correlations between Jewish royal ideology and the NT conceptions of Christ's position as it relates to the cosmos. While the goal is not to give a comprehensive cosmic Christology of the whole NT, an examination of relevant passages could give further insight into how Jewish royal ideology may have helped the NT authors frame their own cosmic Christology, which in turn could provide more conceptual background to the cosmic Christology of Colossians and Ephesians. This chapter will survey important regal themes within the Gospels, take a closer look at key passages in the undisputed letters of Paul that present Christ as God's enthroned Ruler over the cosmos, and examine some other relevant NT passages that utilize Adamic and Davidic motifs in portraying Christ as the cosmic King.

COSMIC CHRIST IN THE GOSPELS

When examining whether the NT depicts Christ as being cosmic Ruler, the recorded claims of Jesus in the Gospels are a good place to start. Whether Christ saw himself as the fulfillment of the promise of God's ideal king carries significant weight in how one views the rest of the NT. Did Paul and others build on Jesus' own claims when portraying his cosmic rule, or is Jesus' cosmic rule an invention of other NT writers? To answer this question, this study will examine the Gospels to discover whether Jesus thought of himself as and made the claim to be God's cosmic King.

Cosmic Christ in the Synoptic Gospels

While the Synoptic Gospels present a variegated picture of Jesus, each Gospel seems to demonstrate some level of interest in Jesus' royal identity. Matthew shows the greatest concern for Jesus' kingship, but Mark and Luke also include various themes and sayings of Jesus that hint at both his royal position and the scope of his kingship.[1] Therefore, this section will focus specifically on passages in the Gospels that allude to Jesus' royal cosmic authority. These allusions appear in Jesus' claims concerning his enthronement, his regal authority, and in the accounts of his birth and baptism.

The designation "Son of Man" (ὁ υἱὸς τοῦ ἀνθρώπου) appears in the Synoptic Gospels as Jesus' preferred form of self-designation.[2] Jesus often used this self-designation in reference to his own regal authority and to the parousia, an eschatological event which would be cosmic in nature.[3]

---

1. The question of Jesus' royal identity, specifically his messianic identity, has been a matter of significant debate in Gospel studies. One can reasonably argue that the Gospel writers present messianic portraits that differ both in their imagery and emphasis. However, the purpose of the present study is to examine whether the Gospel writers alluded to Jesus' kingship as being cosmic in scope—even if this motif is only a minor aspect of their portrait of Jesus—and if Jesus viewed himself as being cosmic King. For discussion on Jesus' royal/messianic identity in the Gospels, see Cullmann, *Christology*, 117–33; Fuller, *New Testament Christology*, 102–31; Charlesworth, "Jewish Messianology," 225–64; Schnackenburg, *Jesus in the Gospels*; and Gathercole, *Preexistent Son*.

2. Though this expression appears sixty-nine times in the Synoptic Gospels, this extensive use does not necessarily mean that these Gospels prefer a Son of Man Christology. The christological picture in the Gospels is more complex. The Synoptic Gospel writers simply demonstrate that this designation was what Jesus used to refer to himself (Cullmann, *Christology*, 182).

3. Wright notes three primary ways in which Jesus utilized the self-designation ὁ υἱὸς τοῦ ἀνθρώπου: (1) to refer to his humanity, (2) to refer to his royal and transcendent

In Mark 8:38, Matt 16:27–28, and Luke 9:26–27, Jesus warns about the impending judgment that will come upon those who deny him. As a clear reference to himself, Jesus declares that the Son of Man will come and will be endowed with the Father's glory. Luke heightens the christological assertion by claiming that Jesus possesses his own glory (ἐν τῇ δόξῃ αὐτοῦ) along with the Father's glory (Luke 9:26).[4] The angels will accompany him at his coming, further demonstrating his cosmic authority. In Matthew's account of this saying, Jesus explicitly states that he will come in his kingdom (Matt 16:28). As one endowed with the Father's glory, he will possess authority to bring judgment upon those who reject him and vindicate those who follow him (Mark 8:38; Matt 16:27; Luke 9:26).[5]

In Mark 13:24–25, Matt 24:29, and Luke 21:25–26, Jesus speaks of the cosmic disruption that will occur immediately preceding the coming of the Son of Man, affirming once again that his arrival is a cosmic event. Jesus then states that the Son of Man will come in the clouds (Mark 13:26; Luke 21:27), a clear allusion to the son of man passage in Dan 7:13–14. Matthew remains faithful to the LXX reading of Dan 7:13 by stating that Jesus will come ἐπὶ τῶν νεφελῶν τοῦ οὐρανοῦ (Matt 24:30).[6] Such a mode of transportation befits the nature of his coming and points to his heavenly authority.[7] Jesus claims that the Son of Man will come with all power and glory (Mark 13:26; Matt 24:30; Luke 21:27). Not only will he be endowed with God's glory, but he will possess the ability to establish and reign over a new kingdom.[8] He further demonstrates his cosmic

---

qualities influenced by Dan 7, and (3) as an Aramaic idiomatic circumlocution to refer to himself (Wright and Bird, *New Testament*, 220–25). For more on the use of ὁ υἱὸς τοῦ ἀνθρώπου in the Gospels, see Casey, *Son of Man*, 157–219; Kim, *Son of Man*, 38–98; Monzani, "Fils de l'hommes," 376–92.

4. Marshall, *Gospel of Luke*, 376–77.

5. Casey suggests that the saying in Mark 8:38 is a development of the sayings in Matt 10:33 and Luke 12:9 (Casey, *Son of Man*, 161–62). However, the context of Mark 8 fits more closely with the context of the accounts in Matt 16 and Luke 9. Therefore, examining the parallel passages between Mark 8:38, Matt 16:27–28, and Luke 9:26–27 seems more appropriate.

6. This reading suggests that Matthew "was aware that this was a reminiscence of Dan 7:13, and that, like Mark, he belonged to the Western Christian tradition of interpretation of this verse" (Casey, *Son of Man*, 177).

7. Darrell Bock points out that everywhere else in the OT, only God or the gods ride on the clouds (Exod 14:20; Num 10:34; Ps 104:3; Isa 19:1; see Bock, "Blasphemy," 76–77).

8. Concerning Mark's attribution of power to the Son of Man's coming, Morna Hooker refers back to Mark 9:1, which attributes power to the kingdom of God (Hooker, *Saint Mark*, 319).

authority by commanding the angels to gather his people (ἐκλεκτοί), a gathering that will extend from the end of the earth to the end of heaven (Mark 13:27; Matt 24:31).⁹ This cosmic authority alludes to the regal authority granted to the Son of Man figure in Dan 7:14 (ἐξουσία βασιλική, LXX), an authority which extended over all nations of the earth. In place of the gathering motif, Luke adds an exhortation from Jesus pointing to this coming as the promise of redemption for his people (Luke 21:28).¹⁰ In redeeming and vindicating his people, Jesus fulfills the role of a righteous royal judge.¹¹ As the one sent from heaven, he carries the authority to consummate the reign of God.¹²

In Mark 14:61–65, Matt 26:63–65, and Luke 22:67–71, the high priest questions Jesus about whether he would claim to be the Christ and the Son of God (Mark 14:61; Matt 26:63; Luke 22:67).¹³ This question not only pertains to Jesus' status as the Davidic Messiah but also to his relationship with the divine. The combination of these two elements suggests that the high priest questions whether Jesus views himself as a king who would have a cosmic reign. Jesus answers the question affirmatively and gives "a spectacular vindication of that claim" by giving an eschatological

---

9. Matthew more specifically states that the angels will be sent ἀπ' ἄκρων οὐρανῶν ἕως [τῶν] ἄκρων αὐτῶν. Luke does not include this gathering motif in his account.

10. Marshall, *Gospel of Luke*, 777.

11. Howard Lee ties this idea to the messianic expectation in Judaism in which the messiah mediates "the divine purpose and the aspirations of the community" (Lee, "Christology in Mark's Gospel," 192).

12. Concerning Mark's account, Dorothy Lee connects the authority that Jesus exercises over the angels to the authority that Jesus had previously demonstrated over the seas (Mark 4:35–41). In effect, Mark's Gospel portrays Jesus as one who has authority over all aspects of creation (Lee, "Christological Identity," 12–14).

13. In the Markan account, the high priest asks whether Jesus is the υἱὸς τοῦ εὐλογητοῦ. This change probably reflects the Jewish practice of avoiding direct use of God's name (see France, *Gospel of Mark*, 610). The Lukan account constructs these as two separate questions. The Sanhedrin (rather than just the high priest) questions Jesus whether he is the Χριστὸς, and after Jesus' response, he asks Jesus whether he is the υἱὸς τοῦ θεοῦ. Marshall argues that Mark's account simply conflates the two questions found in Luke. He suggests that because a Jew would not have equated the messiah with the son of God, the Lukan account seems to be the more likely way the high priest/Sanhedrin would have asked the question (Marshall, *Gospel of Luke*, 849). While it is certainly true that not every Jew would have equated the messiah with the son of God, one can still find the messianic king being granted divine status in some Jewish writings. As was seen in chapter 2, certain Jewish writings spoke of the ideal Davidic king in terms of divine sonship. In any case, the question in all three Synoptic Gospels remains the same. Did Jesus view himself as the Davidic Messiah who had unique relationship with the divine?

picture of his cosmic kingship.[14] In Mark 14:62, Jesus gives an affirmative response by uttering "I am" (ἐγώ εἰμι), which could represent an implicit claim at divinity by claiming the divine name.[15] His response contains a midrashic combination of Ps 110:1 and Dan 7:13.[16] First, Jesus claims that his accusers will see him sitting at the right hand of power (Mark 14:62; Matt 26:63; Luke 22:69), an allusion to the ideal Davidic king in Ps 110. This claim indicates three important things: (1) God would be the one to enthrone Jesus (indicated by the passive participle καθήμενον); (2) as one enthroned at God's right hand, Jesus shared a unique relationship with God in which he is granted divine power and authority;[17] and (3) his position at God's right hand indicates that his reign would be universal/cosmic in scope.[18] Second, Jesus claims that his accusers would see him return on/with[19] the clouds of heaven (Mark 14:62; Matt 26:63), an allusion to the son of man tradition in Dan 7.[20] This allusion again points to the cosmic significance of Jesus' return to establish God's kingdom. The fact that the council would see Jesus' enthronement (Mark 14:62; Matt 26:64) serves to vindicate Jesus' own regal authority.[21] The high priest/Sanhedrin recognize the significance of Jesus' claim by accusing him of blasphemy (Mark 14:63–64; Matt 26:65; Luke 22:71). This serious charge was about more than a simple claim to messianic identity. Rather, Jesus had positioned himself as one who shared the rule and honor that belonged only to God. Morna Hooker summarizes the seriousness of this

14. Juel, "Mark's Christology," 452.

15. Hurtado, *Mark*, 249; Geddert, "Implied YHWH Christology," 338; and Garland, *Mark's Gospel*, 168. Both Matthew and Luke soften Jesus' response to σὺ εἶπας (Matt 26:64; Luke 22:70). Though it is not a direct affirmation, this response is also not a denial of divine sonship.

16. Casey, *Son of Man*, 178, and Ellis, "Deity-Christology," 195.

17. Lee, "Christological Identity," 14.

18. Schnackenburg, *Jesus in the Gospels*, 56, and Strauss, *Davidic Messiah*, 142.

19. Mark uses the preposition μετὰ, but Matthew uses the preposition ἐπὶ. Again, Matthew's use of this preposition remains faithful to the LXX reading of Dan 7:13.

20. Luke omits this allusion in his account. This omission could represent an attempt by Luke to place emphasis on the present reign of Jesus, but it is not a denial of Jesus' future coming. Casey admits that any attempt to view this omission as a sign that Luke did not view Dan 7 as referring to Jesus' parousia goes beyond the evidence of the passage (Casey, *Son of Man*, 184).

21. Bock points to the context of Dan 7 in which the heavenly scene has a profound effect on the happenings on earth. That is, the enthronement of the son of man figure serves to vindicate God's people on earth. In the case of Jesus' claim, his enthronement serves a self-vindication (Bock, "Blasphemy," 75–76; see also Müller, "Menschensohn," 45).

claim well: "To claim for oneself a seat at the right hand of power, however, is to claim a share in the authority of God; to appropriate to oneself such authority and to bestow on oneself this unique status in the sight of God and man would almost certainly be regarded as blasphemy."[22]

Beyond these three sayings that appear in each Synoptic Gospel, a few other Son of Man passages in the Synoptics contribute to the picture of Jesus' cosmic kingship. In Matt 19:28 and Luke 22:28–30, Jesus discusses the role his disciples would have in the coming kingdom, but he grounds their role in his own kingly reign.[23] Jesus looks forward to the time when the cosmos would be renewed (Matt 19:28).[24] This time of cosmic renewal would occur when the Son of Man sits on the throne of glory (Matt 19:28), and the Father would appoint this throne/kingdom to Jesus (Luke 22:29). Luke places this saying in Jesus' discourse at the Last Supper. By placing this saying after the institution of the Lord's Supper (Luke 22:19–20) and the passion prediction (Luke 22:21–23), Luke's account indicates that Jesus would achieve this royal appointment through his death, resurrection, and exaltation.[25] Jesus tells his disciples that when he takes his rightful throne, he would assign them thrones in the kingdom from which they would preside as judges over Israel (Matt 19:28; Luke 22:30). The implication is that Jesus could assign the role of judge to his disciples because he as God's cosmic King serves as the ultimate judge.

Matthew 25:31–46 presents a picture of the final judgment in which Jesus as God's King plays a significant role. As in previous sayings, Jesus indicates that the coming of the Son of Man inaugurates the final

---

22. Hooker, *Son of Man*, 173. Bock adds that this charge of blasphemy may also have been seen as a challenge to the authority of the religious figures. Jesus' claim indicated that he would return to judge those who were judging him. The council could have seen this as a clear threat to their own religious authority that would have put the present societal structures at risk (Bock, "Blasphemy," 82–84). Ellis suggests that Jesus' definition of messiahship "in terms of a combination of Dan 7:13–14 and of Psalm 110:1" would have been considered blasphemous. That is, by combining these two texts, Jesus pointed beyond a messianic figure "to a manifestation of YHWH in God's throne room in 'a likeness as the appearance of a man'" (Ellis, "Deity-Christology," 195–97).

23. While these passages seem to reflect the same saying, they present the saying in remarkably different forms and appear in different contexts. For a discussion on the differences between the two passages, see Nolland, *Gospel of Matthew*, 798.

24. Luke does not include the phrase ἐν τῇ παλιγγενεσίᾳ in his account. Even though Luke does not explicitly mention a renewed cosmos, both Luke and Matthew's account have an eschatological bent.

25. Strauss, *Davidic Messiah*, 323–24. Matthew inserts this saying as a response to Peter's declaration that the disciples had left everything to follow Jesus (Matt 19:27).

judgment (Matt 25:31).[26] Jesus puts an emphasis on the glorious nature of his future reign, stating that he would come in glory and would sit on a throne. He displays his cosmic authority by coming with all the angels and by sending them to gather all nations to his glorious throne (Matt 25:32).[27] From his throne, Jesus carries out his role as the royal judge. To the righteous (described in the passage as τὰ πρόβατα), the enthroned King (βασιλεύς) grants life and an inheritance in the kingdom (Matt 25:34–40, 46b). To the wicked (described in this passage as τὰ ἐρίφια), he bestows eternal judgment (Matt 25:41–46a).[28]

Mark 12:35–37 and Matt 22:41–46 provide a saying in which Jesus speaks of his relationship to the Davidic throne. Jesus brings a question to the Pharisees about the complex relationship between the messiah and David. Jesus cites Ps 110:1 and questions why David would call his own son Lord.[29] Jesus also points out that David spoke in the Spirit (Mark 12:36; Matt 22:43). Thus, Ps 110:1 represents "God's evaluative point of view,"[30] meaning that the Χριστός is designated κύριος by God himself. While Jesus does not explicitly give an answer to the question he poses, both Gospel accounts imply that there is a valid answer to the question.[31] Jesus could be rejecting traditional messianic categories, specifically that the messiah had to be a descendant of David. This option seems unlikely because (1) Mark's Gospel does not suggest anywhere else that the Χριστός is not the son of David[32] and (2) Matthew's Gospel places a heavy emphasis on Jesus' Davidic ancestry.[33] Jesus could simply be pointing out that the station of the Χριστός is higher than David's position. While Jesus' question certainly has implications for the position of the Χριστός,

---

26. The idea of the coming of the Son of Man inaugurating the final judgment also appears in Dan 7:9–14 (Casey, *Son of Man*, 190–92; Evans, *Matthew*, 422).

27. The future passive συναχθήσονται indicates that Jesus appoints the angels with the responsibility of gathering the nations. This idea also fits with Jesus' saying in Matt 24:31 in which he indicates that the angels would be the ones to gather the elect from the ends of the cosmos.

28. Concerning the use of the imagery of sheep and goats, see Njeri, "Day of Judgment," 87–104 and Moscicke, "Final Judgement," 241–59.

29. Mark 12:37 states, αὐτὸς Δαυὶδ λέγει αὐτὸν κύριον, καὶ πόθεν αὐτοῦ ἐστιν υἱός. Matt 22:43 states, Πῶς οὖν Δαυὶδ ἐν πνεύματι καλεῖ αὐτὸν κύριον. . .

30. Kingsbury, *Christology of Mark's Gospel*, 48–50, 112.

31. Juel, "Origin of Mark's Christology," 455.

32. Juel, "Origin of Mark's Christology," 454.

33. Davies, "Jewish Sources," 500. Matthew uses the term "son of David" nine times in his Gospel, more than any other gospel writer.

his primary concern was with what David called his son, not his son's position. That is, why would David view his descendant as someone who surpasses him "in a transcendent manner"?[34] Daniel Johansson states the problem well: "What Jesus points to is that David calls him κύριος, precisely what David also calls the first κύριος."[35]

The implied answer relates to the origin and identity of God's ideal King. Oscar Cullmann suggests that Jesus seeks to point to his divine lineage over his Davidic lineage.[36] As a result, Jesus rightfully shares the divine throne with God and is granted authority to carry out the divine rule. Put clearly, Johansson argues, "There is an overlap between the figures through the word κύριος, but there is also a differentiation which is here reinforced by the presence of two figures designated κύριος. As elsewhere (e.g., 2:28; 11:9), the second messianic κύριος also shares divine prerogatives or attributes with the first κύριος—the divine throne."[37] The events that would soon follow Jesus' proclamation affirm his transcendent royal identity. After Jesus' death and resurrection, God would say to Jesus, "Sit at my right hand" (Mark 12:36; Matt 22:44; Ps 109:1 LXX). By posing the question of why David would call his own son "Lord," Jesus implicitly points to his enthronement as affirmation of his rightful identity as God's ideal King. He carries out the divine rule because he himself is divine. Therefore, it is appropriate for David to call his own descendant Lord.[38]

The birth narratives both in Matthew and Luke emphasize Jesus' identity as God's ideal King. Matthew begins his Gospel by identifying Jesus as the Son of David and by outlining Jesus' royal lineage (Matt 1:1–17).[39] The announcement that Mary carried a child from the Holy Spirit

34. Lee, "Christology in Mark's Gospel," 203.

35. Johansson, "*Kyrios* in Mark," 117.

36. Though Jesus does not explicitly identify himself as the Χριστός in this passage, the context of both Gospels makes it clear that Jesus is unambiguously referring to himself. Cullmann argues that Jesus does not necessarily reject his Davidic lineage but rejects the significance that Jews attached to this descent for salvation to be accomplished. In other words, the fact that Jesus came from God himself is more significant than his Davidic lineage (Cullmann, Christology, 131).

37. Johansson, "*Kyrios* in Mark," 117–18. Johansson considers this sharing of the divine throne in Mark 12:35–37 striking given that it follows a citation to the Shema in Mark 12:29. He suggests that Ps 110:1 further defines the Shema and "reinterprets monotheism" (Johansson, "*Kyrios* in Mark," 119).

38. Lövestam, "Davidssohnsfrage," 72–82 and Juel, "Origin of Mark's Christology," 455.

39. Davies suggests that the initial words of Matthew's Gospel (Βίβλος γενέσεως) parallel Gen 1:1. Thus, Matthew's Gospel starts by simultaneously looking back to the creation narrative while also looking forward to the arrival of God's Messiah. In effect,

(Matt 1:18, 20) suggests a divine inbreaking to the created world, a point he emphasizes in his reference to Isa 7:14 (Matt 1:23). The fact that he would be connected to Joseph, son of David, indicates his legal claim to the Davidic throne (Matt 1:20).[40] Matthew's presentation of Jesus' divine and Davidic lineage within his birth narrative strongly implies that Jesus was a King who would affect the cosmos itself.

Luke's birth narrative further emphasizes Jesus' status as God's ideal King from David. Luke 1:26–27 states that the angel Gabriel appears to a virgin who was betrothed to Joseph, who was a descendant of David (ἐξ οἴκου Δαυὶδ, Luke 1:27). Much like Matthew, Luke prepares the reader for both Jesus' divine origin and his royal-Davidic status.[41] Gabriel's announcement to Mary has four allusions to the ideal Davidic king presented in 2 Sam 7 and Ps 89. First, Gabriel announces the greatness of his kingship, which alludes to the ideal Davidic king's status above all other kings (Luke 1:32; 2 Sam 7:9; Ps 89:27). Second, Jesus would be called "Son of the Most High" (υἱὸς ὑψίστου), which alludes to the unique father-son relationship between God and the ideal Davidic king (Luke 1:32; 2 Sam 7:14; Ps 89:26). Third, God would give Jesus the throne of David, his father, which alludes to the promise that God would establish the throne of the Davidic king (Luke 1:32; 2 Sam 7:12–16; Ps 89:29). Fourth, Jesus' throne would be an eternal throne, and his kingdom will never end, which alludes to God's promise to establish the throne of the ideal Davidic king forever (Luke 1:33; 2 Sam 7:12–16; Ps 89:36).[42] The combination of these allusions suggests that Luke's birth narrative points to Jesus as the one who fulfills the promise of the ideal Davidic king. Further, Luke demonstrates that "Davidic-messiahship is co-referential with royal messiahship."[43] Gabriel's announcement concludes by pointing to Jesus' divine origin. Because of his conception by the Holy Spirit, Jesus would be called the Son of God (Luke 1:35). The implication is that Jesus'

Matthew views the arrival of the Messiah as a cosmic event which brings about a new creation (Davies, "Jewish Sources," 496–501).

40. Schnackenburg, *Jesus in the Gospels*, 103.

41. Strauss, *Davidic Messiah*, 87.

42. For more on these allusions, see Strauss, *Davidic Messiah*, 88–89, and Henrichs-Tarasenkova, *Luke's Christology*, 115–16. Casey argues that there is no obvious OT influence on this passage (Casey, *Son of Man*, 193). While Luke 1:32–33 does not give a direct citation to any OT passage, the various allusions do demonstrate that Luke probably had the OT motif of the ideal Davidic king in mind. Casey's assertion appears to be an overstatement.

43. Strauss, *Davidic Messiah*, 89.

status as God's ideal King is not only confirmed by his role but also by his origin.⁴⁴ That is, Jesus' royal identity is not derived simply from his relationship to David but by his unique relationship to God.⁴⁵ As God's promised King, Jesus brings redemption and salvation to his people and conquers their enemies (Luke 1:68–71).

Both Jesus' baptism and transfiguration also imply his status as God's ideal cosmic King. At Jesus' baptism, the heavens open, which demonstrates the cosmic significance of Jesus (Mark 1:10; Matt 3:16; Luke 3:21–22). Jesus also has the Spirit descend upon him, which was a quintessential sign of God's anointed king (Isa 11:2; 61:11).⁴⁶ God speaks from heaven and declares Jesus to be his beloved Son (Mark 1:11; Matt 3:17; Luke 3:22), a declaration also made about God's ideal king in Ps 2:7.⁴⁷ However, unlike Ps 2:7, God says nothing about begetting Jesus. This omission implies that Jesus did not simply become God's Son at his baptism, but rather God's declaration reflected the reality of his sonship.⁴⁸ A similar declaration occurs again at Jesus' transfiguration, where a voice from heaven once again declares Jesus to be his beloved Son (Mark 9:7; Matt 17:5; Luke 9:35).⁴⁹ By using messianic language to declare Jesus' identity as God's Son, the baptism and transfiguration do not present an enthronement like any other king. Rather, Jesus' divine and royal identity are tied together to validate Jesus' eventual enthronement as God's ideal King who exercises authority over the whole cosmos.

---

44. Strauss suggests that this is Luke's only significant modification to the OT Davidic tradition. Judaism grounds the Davidic king's sonship in his role, but Luke grounds it in his origin. This modification does not conflict with the Davidic tradition but exceeds it (Strauss, *Davidic Messiah*, 90–93).

45. Henrichs-Tarasenkova, *Luke's Christology*, 139.

46. Schnackenburg, *Jesus in the Gospels*, 48.

47. Both Cullmann and Schnackenburg argue that the saying is more likely derived from the suffering servant in Isa 42:1 (Cullmann, *Christology*, 276; Schnackenburg, *Jesus in the Gospels*, 48). Hays suggests that Gen 22 and the designation of Isaac as the "beloved son" stands behind this text (Hays, *Echoes of Scripture*, 140, 245). Christopher Maronde presents an extended argument for the voice from heaven utilizing the language of Ps 2 in the declaration of Jesus' divine sonship at his baptism. He argues that Ps 2:7 gives the closest verbal parallel to the declaration, and the fact that it is a direct address aligns more closely with the direct address given in Ps 2:7. Thus, he views the declaration as a combination of the address in Ps 2:7 and the descriptors of the servant in Isa 42:1 (Maronde, "Beloved Son," 331–35).

48. Maronde, "Beloved Son," 334.

49. Luke's account includes the title ὁ ἐκλελεγμένος, a title often associated with God's ideal king.

Christ's Cosmic Kingship in John's Gospel

John's presentation of Jesus' royal identity in his Gospel focuses on Jesus' status both as an otherworldly figure and as the Son of God.[50] The title "son of God," which has significant royal connotations in ancient Judaism, appears at least eight times in John's Gospel (John 1:49; 3:18; 5:25; 10:36; 11:4, 27; 19:7; 20:31).[51] Jane Heath suggests, "John emphasizes that Jesus is king, but he underscores also that this is not a title or role that is readily understood in the usual political or religious categories."[52] A couple of passages in John's Gospel will serve to illustrate this theme.[53]

John's initial prologue immediately portrays Jesus as a cosmic figure. John describes him as the embodiment of the divine Word who existed in the beginning with God (John 1:1–2). Such a declaration portrays Jesus to be a preexistent figure whose origin lies outside of the physical world. John bolsters this assumption by using language reminiscent of the creation account in Gen 1–2 LXX (ἐν ἀρχῇ; πάντα . . . ἐγένετο; ζωή; φῶς and σκότος).[54] The whole of the created universe comes into being through his creative activity (John 1:3–4). By describing Jesus as the preexistent Creator, John distinguishes between the timeless nature of Jesus and the temporal world.[55] His role as Creator of all things and the giver of life validates his right to rule over the whole created universe. John then explicitly identifies the incarnate Jesus as the divine Word who descended

---

50. One of the biggest distinctions between John's Gospel and the Synoptic Gospels is with reference to the kingdom of God. Whereas the Synoptics refer to the kingdom of God multiple times, John's Gospel only uses the phrase ἡ βασιλεία τοῦ θεοῦ twice (John 3:3, 5). John's Gospel puts more emphasis on the nature of Jesus' identity as God's King (Kvalbein, "Kingdom of God," 215).

51. One could also add John 1:34, which contains a text critical issue over whether the reading should be υἱός or ἐκλεκτός. For an overview of this debate, see Quek, "Study of John 1:34," 22–34.

52. Heath, "I Am a King," 242.

53. Though the otherworldly and divine nature of Jesus' kingship is a major part of the Christology of John's Gospel, this study cannot explore this theme in depth. For a fuller discussion of Jesus' kingship in John, see Kügler, *König*; Daly-Denton, *Fourth Gospel*; Kvalbein, "Kingdom of God," 215–32; Busse, "Metaphorik und Rhetorik," 279–318; Heath, "I Am a King," 232–53; and Van der Watt, "Spatial Dynamics," 1–7.

54. For a full discussion on the connections between John 1:1–18 and Gen 1–2, see Borgen, "Targumic Character," 288–95; Painter, "Rereading Genesis," 179–201, and Siliezar, *Creation Imagery*, 27–55. Some scholars have suggested the term λόγος refers to the recurring phrase in Genesis εἶπεν ὁ θεός (Borgen, "Observations," 289; Brown, "Creation's Renewal," 277).

55. Hamerton-Kelly, *Pre-Existence*, 203–4.

from heaven to the world (John 1:10–14).[56] John's prologue sets the foundation for his understanding of the nature of Jesus' kingship, as seen later in John 1 with Jesus' interaction with Nathaniel.

At his encounter with Jesus, Nathaniel declares Jesus to be both the Son of God and the King of Israel (John 1:49). The synonymous parallelism of these two titles demonstrates "that 'Son of God' should be heard as a royal honorific designation."[57] Given the prologue of John's Gospel, the title "Son of God" not only serves to designate his status as the Davidic king (hence the title βασιλεὺς τοῦ Ἰσραήλ), but it also says something about his metaphysical nature.[58] Jesus responds to Nathaniel's declaration by stating that he would see the opening of heaven and angels ascending and descending on the Son of Man (John 1:51).[59] The first part of Jesus' statement parallels the "opening of heaven" that occurred during God's royal pronouncement at Jesus' baptism. In the context of John 1, Jesus' declaration emphasizes that his rightful claim as God's King is not based solely in his Davidic ancestry. Rather, Jesus' kingship is grounded upon his divine, heavenly origin, and his kingdom extends beyond Israel to the whole created cosmos. When applied to Jesus, the title Son of God extends beyond a royal designation to a statement about Jesus' ontological relationship to God. Myers rightly notes, "For John, Jesus does not need to be made 'king.' . . . What needs to take place is a recognition of how Jesus is God's Son and King."[60] Jesus' declaration indicates that he is God's royal representative who connects heaven and earth, and he will bring both heaven and earth under his kingship.[61]

Pilate's questioning of Jesus in John 18 provides further insight on the nature and scope of his kingship. Much like Nathaniel's declaration of Jesus as the King of Israel (thereby receiving Jesus as his own King), Pilate interrogates Jesus on whether he is the King of the Jews (John 18:33), limiting the scope of Jesus' kingdom to geopolitical categories. Jesus responds to Pilate's question by stating that his kingdom is not of

56. In these verses, the κόσμος refers to the created world, perhaps specifically to the world of humanity.

57. Hays, *Echoes of Scripture*, 324.

58. Hays, *Echoes of Scripture*, 324.

59. Jesus alludes here to Jacob's vision of angels ascending and descending on a ladder between heaven and earth in Gen 28:12. For more on this allusion to Gen 28:12, see Dodd, *Fourth Gospel*, 245; Rowland, "John 1:51," 498–507; and Roberge, "Jean 1,51," 193–217.

60. Myers, "Son of God," 143.

61. Brown, *John I–XII*, 90, and Daly-Denton, *David*, 122.

this world (John 18:36), thereby challenging Pilate's own conceptions of kingship.⁶² Jesus rejects Pilate's terms of kingship and defines these royal categories in otherworldly ways.⁶³ Jesus does not reject the royal title, but, as in his dialogue with Nathaniel, indicates that his kingship originates in the heavenly sphere and exceeds the expectations that the people had of him. Jesus defines his role as King to be one who will testify truth (John 18:37). Heath makes an astute observation regarding the nature of this truth: "The encounter in the praetorium shows that truth is not merely a matter of right or wrong, but of actually hearing and rightly making sense of Jesus, as a person and as a figure who reveals God's kingship within the world."⁶⁴ Pilate's response ("What is truth?") demonstrates his failure to understand Jesus' kingship and kingdom as something that does not originate in a worldly system and cannot not be confined to geopolitical categories (John 18:38).

COSMIC CHRIST IN THE UNDISPUTED LETTERS OF PAUL

The Gospel writers demonstrate a clear concern for Christ's position as the ruler of the cosmos. Paul picks up this theme in his own letters and develops it in unique ways. Paul clearly views Jesus' position and work as having significant implications for the whole of the cosmos. This section will focus on key passages in the undisputed letters of Paul that reveal the terms in which he conceived of Christ as the enthroned ruler over the cosmos.⁶⁵

Cosmic Christ in Galatians

Though Paul does not give much explicit reference to Christ's kingship over the cosmos in Galatians, Paul's explanation of Christ as the one who

62. Heath, "I Am a King," 244, and Keith, "Jesus the Galilean," 46–47.

63. This rejection of Pilate's terms of kingship echoes a recurring theme throughout John's Gospel in which Jesus refuses to have his kingship defined by the expectations of the people (Kvalbein, "Kingdom of God," 230–31; Heath, "I Am a King," 242–46).

64. Heath, "I Am a King," 245.

65. By undisputed letters, this study refers to the seven Pauline epistles considered by the vast majority of scholars to be authentic: Rom, 1 Corinthians, 2 Corinthians, Galatians, Philippians, 1 Thessalonians, and Philemon. The goal of this section is not to examine each of these letters in detail. Rather, this section will focus on passages from this group of letters that give specific insight into how Paul spoke of Christ's cosmic kingship.

fulfills the Abrahamic covenant contains some implicit royal overtones. In Gal 3, Paul makes the argument that Christ's death under the law (the law that brings a curse upon humanity) fulfills the Abrahamic covenant to bring God's blessing to the gentiles. Paul recalls the Abrahamic covenant and maintains that this covenant is as unchangeable as any other human covenant (Gal 3:15). He notes that God's covenant with Abraham would not be fulfilled through many seeds (σπέρμασιν) but through Abraham's singular (σπέρματι) seed (ὡς ἐπὶ πολλῶν ἀλλ' ὡς ἐφ' ἑνός, Gal 3:16).[66] Paul then explicitly identifies this seed to be Christ. While scholars provide various solutions to Paul's curious explanatory note,[67] it seems likely that Paul reads the Abrahamic seed in a messianic sense. One can argue for the plausibility of this messianic interpretation for a few reasons.

First, the idea of the "seed" in Genesis carries potential royal overtones. Beginning in Gen 3:15, Genesis shows concern for the continuation of the "seed" through whom God would once again establish his king.[68] God emphasizes to Abraham that kings would arise from his seed (Gen 17:6-7, 16). This royal motif climaxes with the royal hope presented in Gen 49:10. Second, Paul's use of the singular σπέρμα could be a "catchword" that would draw to mind both the Abrahamic covenant and the Davidic covenant. The singular "your seed" appears in both the several

---

66. Whether the dative σπέρματί refers to a singular descendant or a group of descendants remains a matter of debate among NT scholars. Though the noun appears in the singular, one should note that this word is often used as a collective singular. Wright argues that Paul envisages a worldwide family (as opposed to many families) made up of both Jews and gentiles. He suggests the explanatory phrase ὅς ἐστιν Χριστός takes on a corporate meaning. The one family of which Paul speaks is the family created in Christ (Wright, *Climax of the Covenant*, 162–68). In a slight alternative to the argument of Wright, Ellis suggests that this verse reflects the Pauline conception of corporate solidarity. Ellis argues, "Israel was embodied in Messiah, and the Christian community formed the remnant of the true Israel" (Ellis, *Paul's Use*, 70–73). While the idea of corporate solidarity and the vision of one worldwide family seems to be in Paul's view, particularly in Gal 3:26–29, it seems rather difficult to view Christ as a corporate term in Gal 3:16. Rather, a plainer reading of Paul's argument reveals that the singular Christ fulfills this Abrahamic covenant, and the result is that God brings about one worldwide family through him (Collins, "Galatians 3:16," 75–86).

67. One can put the various proposals for the reason behind Paul's exegesis into three categories: (1) Paul was unjustified in his exegesis and argument; (2) Paul views the seed and the designated heir of the Abrahamic covenant as Christ Jesus, the Davidic Messiah; and (3) Paul's focus is on a singular family that exists in corporate solidarity with Christ (Collins, "Galatians 3:16," 76–79; McCaulley, *Son's Inheritance*, 146–54).

68. Alexander argues that Genesis is structured around the line of the seed that would eventually become a royal dynasty (Alexander, "Messianic Ideology," 23–27).

promises God makes to Abraham (Gen 13:15; 17:6, 8; 22:8; 24:7)[69] and in the covenant he makes with David (2 Sam 7:12–14; 1 Chr 17:10–14; Ps 89:3–4). Hays suggests that this treatment of the seed "bears evident potential for messianic interpretation . . . and it authorizes, by means of *gezerah shawah*, a messianic reading of other promissory texts in which the key word seed appears."[70]

Third, Paul bolsters this assertion by stating that the duration of the law's addition would last until the arrival of the seed (ἄχρις οὗ ἔλθῃ τὸ σπέρμα, Gal 3:19). This phrase alludes to the royal promise given in Gen 49:10,[71] a text that was interpreted as messianic within Judaism (4Q252 5.1–5).[72] Paul's insertion of τὸ σπέρμα indicates the link between the Abrahamic covenant, the royal pronouncement of Gen 49:10, and the promise of the ideal Davidic king (2 Sam 7:12–14; Ps 89:3–4).[73] Further, Christ's identity as the messianic King and fulfillment of the Abrahamic covenant gave him the rightful claim to the inheritance (Gal 3:18). The Psalms indicate that the whole earth is the rightful inheritance of God's king (Ps 2:7–8).[74] Christ's identity as the messianic King who fulfilled the Abrahamic covenant means that he has the rightful authority over all the nations and forces of this world (Gal 4:3–7).[75] All these things seem to indicate that Paul views the work and revelation of Christ as God's promised King to be the fulfillment of the Abrahamic covenant. For this reason, God forms a people made up of Jew and gentile who have put

69. There is some debate on whether Gal 3:16 draws primarily from Gen 17:8 or 22:18. Hays, Novenson, and McCaulley all look primarily to Gen 17:8 while Juel and Collins argue for Gen 22:18 (Hays, *Echoes of Scripture*, 85; Novenson, *Christ among the Messiahs*, 138–42; McCaulley, *Son's Inheritance*, 150–54; Juel, *Messianic Exegesis*, 85–87; and Collins "Galatians 3:16," 75–86). For the present study, it makes little difference from which text Paul is specifically drawing his argument. Rather, the main point is that Paul draws a messianic conclusion from the Abrahamic covenant.

70. Hays, *Echoes of Scripture*, 85. Novenson contends that Paul views Jesus' messiahship as axiomatic so that "nonmessianic scriptural testimonies apply to him through his messiahship" (Novenson, *Christ among the Messiahs*, 140–42).

71. For a robust argument on the presence of this allusion in Gal 3:19, see Hewitt, "Ancient Messiah Discourse," 398–411.

72. See ch. 2.

73. Juel, *Messiah Discourse*, 86, and Hewitt, "Ancient Messiah Discourse," 406–7.

74. McCaulley, *Son's Inheritance*, 157. See also ch. 2.

75. Paul speaks of the believers' liberation from τὰ στοιχεῖα τοῦ κόσμου. This phrase has been the subject of much debate among scholars. It seems likely that Paul is referring to some sort of cosmic power, though the nature of this power is difficult to determine. For further discussion, see Kooten, *Cosmic Christology*, 60–70, and McCaulley, *Son's Inheritance*, 178–82.

on Christ and are now one in Christ (Gal 3:26–28).[76] The result is that believers now share in the fate of Christ himself.

The formation of this new people represents the new cosmic order brought about by the reign of Christ. Paul asserts that the cross of Christ (and his subsequent resurrection) eliminates the old order in which people were distinguished on the basis of circumcision (Gal 6:12–14). Rather, Christ's work inaugurates the "new creation" in which circumcision counts for nothing (Gal 6:15). Paul's language also echoes Gen 1 and indicates that believers have been transferred from the old creation order (the dominion of Adam) to the new creation order (the domain of Christ).[77] This language also points forward to God's intent to consummate a new cosmic order ruled by Christ, his royal agent.

Cosmic Christ in 1 Thessalonians

In an encouragement to the Thessalonian church under persecution, Paul presents a description of the coming of Christ in 1 Thess 4:13–18. This description contains a few elements that reflect Jewish conceptions of the enthronement of God's ideal king. First, Paul claims that Christ will descend from heaven.[78] The implication is that Christ has been reigning in heaven and arrives to enact his cosmic authority over the earth. That is, Christ's heavenly enthronement grants him the ability to enact God's reign over the earth.

Second, Paul declares that believers will be gathered to meet (εἰς ἀπάντησιν) Christ in the air (1 Thess 4:17). The word ἀπάντησις occurs only in two other places in the New Testament (Matt 25:6; Acts 28:15), where it communicates going out to meet someone in a welcoming manner. A slight variant to this word (ὑπάντησις) appears in John 12:13, where it speaks of the people going out to meet Jesus and welcome him as their King. Hellenistic literature also often uses the term ἀπάντησις in reference

---

76. Paul's reference to putting on Christ could be a potential allusion to Adam. That is, the believers' putting on of Christ implies that they have put off the old man, Adam (Son, *Corporate Elements*, 57–58; Hays, *Faith of Jesus Christ*, 204).

77. Bruce, *Epistle to the Galatians*, 273.

78. Specifically, Paul mentions that the κύριος would descend from heaven. One can be fairly confident that Paul refers to Christ with this title because Paul (1) grounds the hope of the believer specifically in the death and resurrection of Christ (1 Thess 4:14), (2) refers to Christ as the "Lord Jesus" at various points in the letter (1 Thess 1:2; 2:15; 3:13; 4:1), and (3) previously mentions the coming of the "Lord Jesus" as the center of the church's hope (1 Thess 2:19).

to a formal reception of a coming king or royal dignitary.[79] When combined with the term παρουσία, which "became the official term for a visit of a person of high rank, especially of kings and emperors visiting a province,"[80] it seems probable that Paul uses such language to indicate that believers will receive Christ as their King when he returns. As God's ideal King, Christ then comes to reestablish God's good order over the earth.

Third, Paul closely connects the royal coming of Christ with the day of the Lord (1 Thess 5:1–2). Paul says the day of the Lord would be a day of judgment upon the wicked (1 Thess 5:3) and a day of vindication for those who belong to Christ (1 Thess 5:9). The implication is that one of Christ's primary functions as God's King is to administer God's good judgment over the whole earth. This concept aligns with Jewish royal conceptions that view God's ideal king as the one through whom God would administer his judgment upon the wicked and through whom he would vindicate the righteous (Ps 2:9–10; 89:23; Isa 49:1–6; 63:1–6; Pss. Sol. 17:22–43; 1 En. 38:2; 45:3; 61:8; 62:2–14).[81]

Cosmic Christ in the Corinthian Letters

Paul gives an extraordinary christological confession in 1 Cor 8:6 that is foundational for how he views Christ's position within the cosmos. In a Shema-style confession (Deut 6:4), Paul declares first that there is εἷς θεὸς ὁ πατὴρ ἐξ οὗ τὰ πάντα καὶ ἡμεῖς εἰς αὐτόν (1 Cor 8:6a). Paul remarkably asserts that a full understanding of the one God includes Christ: καὶ εἷς κύριος Ἰησοῦς Χριστὸς δι' οὗ τὰ πάντα καὶ ἡμεῖς δι' αὐτοῦ (1 Cor 8:6b).[82] One can see the parallelism Paul draws between God and Christ as follows:

εἷς θεὸς ὁ πατὴρ
   ἐξ οὗ τὰ πάντα καὶ ἡμεῖς εἰς αὐτόν
εἷς κύριος Ἰησοῦς Χριστὸς
   δι' οὗ τὰ πάντα καὶ ἡμεῖς δι' αὐτοῦ.[83]

---

79. Peterson, "Einholung des Kyrios," 682–702; Bruce, *1 and 2 Thessalonians*, 102, and Gundry, "Brief Note," 39–41.

80. BDAG, 780–81.

81. See ch. 2.

82. That Paul reconfigures the Shema with a christological component is widely accepted in NT scholarship (Dunn, *Christology in the Making*, 179–80; Hurtado, *One God, One Lord*, 97; Hagner, "Paul's Christology," 19–38; Wright, *Climax of the Covenant*, 128–29; Fee, *Pauline Christology*, 89–90; and Leese, *Christ*, 71–72).

83. Some scholars suggest that Paul adopts a pre-Pauline confessional formula (for

Three aspects of this confession are relevant to the current discussion: (1) Paul's use of the term εἷς with both θεὸς and κύριος Ἰησοῦς Χριστὸς, (2) the use of the prepositions ἐκ, εἰς, and διά, and (3) the semantic scope of πάντα.

Paul's double-use of εἷς brings clarity to the unity between God and Christ, and it stands in direct contrast to his double use of the plural πολλοὶ (1 Cor 8:5) to describe the idols and false gods. Paul's affixing of the titles θεός and κύριος to πατήρ and Ἰησοῦς Χριστὸς also seeks to draw Jesus into close relationship with God while maintaining a monotheistic reading.[84] The result is that Paul explicitly identifies Jesus with the one true God, meaning that his position and function within the cosmos arise from his divinity. The result is that Paul gives "a statement of the highest possible Christology."[85]

Paul's use of the prepositions ἐκ, εἰς, and διά provide the key for the distinction between the Father and Jesus.[86] Paul declares that all things are from (ἐκ) and for (εἰς) the Father, meaning that God is the source of creation and goal of creation's redemption. Paul then uses two διά prepositional phrases to show that Jesus is the agent of the first creation and of the new creation of believers.[87] Christ's role as God's agent/mediator then serves as the central theme of Paul's reworked Shema.[88] This theme reflects Jewish regal traditions in which God's ideal king serves as the mediator of God's rule over creation but with one key addition. Paul supersedes these regal traditions by presenting Jesus not only as God's

---

example, Horsley, "Background" 130–35). However, it seems more likely that Paul, given his extensive knowledge and commitment to Jewish monotheism, created this christological formulation himself. However, the source of this confession matters little because, in both cases, Paul's use of it indicates that it is representative of his own Christology.

84. Leese, *Christ*, 72.

85. Wright, *Climax of the Covenant*, 132.

86. There has been much discussion on the use of prepositions in the construction of ancient cosmologies. Dunn suggests that the use of these prepositions typically represented Stoic thought (Dunn, *Romans 9–16*, 701; see also Hamerton-Kelly, *Pre-Existence*, 130). Further studies have shown that the use of these prepositions does not necessitate a Stoic background. Rather, these prepositions are used in both Greek and Jewish philosophical cosmologies (Sterling, "Prepositional Metaphysics," 219–38; Leese, *Christ*, 75–76).

87. That agency is in Paul's mind is clearly indicated by the use of the preposition διά with the genitive pronouns.

88. Capes, *Divine Christ*, 166. See also the discussion on the theme of mediation in 1 Cor 8–10 from McDonough, *Christ as Creator*, 158–67.

King over creation but as an active participant in the creation act as God's creative agent.⁸⁹ Jesus' kingship surpasses all preceding kingships in that he preexists all other kingships and is the agent through whom all creation exists. As he was God's agent in the original creation, so is he God's agent to bring about a new creation in his people (ἡμεῖς δι' αὐτοῦ, 1 Cor 8:6). Paul's understanding of Christ's role in creation then clarifies his understanding of Christ's kingship.

The semantic scope of the term πάντα gives clarity to the extent of Christ's rule. Edward Adams demonstrates how the immediate context of 1 Cor 8 indicates that Paul has the whole universe, both physical and spiritual, in view. Paul states that the existence of the one God negates the possibility for the existence of any other gods in the world (1 Cor 8:4). Adams then rightly suggests that the cosmos correlates with the phrase "whether in heaven or on earth" (1 Cor 8:5) and is "contextually equivalent to the phrase τὰ πάντα in v. 6."⁹⁰ Given these contextual markers, it seems clear that Paul views Christ as a King whose reign is cosmological in scope.⁹¹ The oneness Christ shares with the Father, his role as God's mediator/agent in original and new creation, and the cosmological scope

---

89. Many scholars view Jewish Wisdom traditions as informing Paul's view of Christ as God's creative agent (Schweizer, *Neotestamentica*, 105–9; Gibbs, *Creation and Redemption*, 71; Horsley, "Background," 130–35; Dunn, *Theology of Paul*, 269–74). Dunn takes this view further by suggesting that in identifying Jesus with Jewish Wisdom, Paul identifies Jesus with God's creative power and action but not as a preexistent being (Dunn, *Christology in the Making*, 174–82). The problem with this view is that the preposition διά consistently fails to appear in Wisdom literature when describing Wisdom's relationship to creation. Further, the OT gives no clear text presenting personified Wisdom as God's agent in creation. Even the instances in Wisdom of Solomon which may present Wisdom as an agent in creation are debatable (Richardson, *Paul's Language*, 296–304; Hurtado, *Lord Jesus Christ*, 126; Fee, *Pauline Christology*, 102–5, 598, 609–18; Romanov, "Through One Lord," 391–415). Therefore, it is doubtful that Jewish sayings on personified Wisdom traditions can fully explain Paul's reworked Shema. Much more will be said on this in the next chapter's discussion on Paul's Christology in Colossians.

90. Adams, *Constructing the World*, 140.

91. This assertion is contra to the argument by Jerome Murphy-O'Connor that 1 Cor 8:6 is primarily soteriological. Murphy-O'Connor originally argued that 1 Cor 8:6 is exclusively soteriological while all cosmological interpretations are unfounded (Murphy-O'Connor, "I Cor 8:6," 253–67). Murphy-O'Connor has since modified his position to acknowledge some cosmological significance to τὰ πάντα but still argues that the content is primarily soteriological (Murphy-O'Connor, *Keys to First Corinthians*, 70–75). Bauckham notes that, in a sense, τὰ πάντα relates to salvation because new creation is in view. However, the new creation is cosmic in scope (Bauckham, *God of Israel*, 216).

of his reign indicate that for Paul, "the Messiah has always been God's means of mediating his presence to the world."[92]

In 1 Cor 15:20–28, following a discussion on the importance of the resurrection to the believers, Paul looks to Christ's resurrection and his future reign as the hope for the believers' resurrection. This passage is replete with regal imagery alluding back to Adam and to Jewish traditions concerning the ideal Davidic king. In response to those who might doubt the resurrection of the dead, Paul emphatically declares that Christ, through his own resurrection, has inaugurated the resurrection age (1 Cor 15:20). Paul then draws an explicit typological parallel[93] between Adam and Christ (1 Cor 15:21–22).[94] This parallel suggests that in Paul's mind, Adam and Christ are both individual and corporate entities.[95] Both Adam and Christ stand at the head of two ages, and their actions have had significant cosmic consequences.[96] The destructive force of death was able to enter into the world through Adam (1 Cor 15:21a). Paul's thought alludes to the Genesis tradition, which viewed the sin of Adam, God's regal ambassador, as the reason for the corruption of creation. Paul viewed Adam's sin as a cosmic problem that required a cosmic solution.[97] For Paul, the resurrection serves as the cosmic solution to the problem of

---

92. McDonough, *Christ as Creator*, 168.

93. Typology is a much debated but prevalent concept in the NT and serves as a key exegetical principle for how the NT authors interpreted OT texts. Beale defines typology as "the study of analogical correspondences among revealed truths about persons, events, institutions, and other things within the historical framework of God's special revelation, which, from a retrospective view, are of prophetic nature and escalated in their meaning" (Beale, *Use of the Old Testament*, 14). One should note three important characteristics about NT typology: (1) It is derived from God's working in history. (2) The OT type stands in correspondence and contrast with the NT antitype. (3) The NT antitype often stands as greater than its corresponding OT type. For more discussion on typology, see Ellis, *Paul's Use*, 126–35; Goppelt, *Typos*; Baker, "Typology," 313–30; Hoskins, *Jesus as the Fulfillment*, 21–23; and Beale, *Use of the Old Testament*, 13–27.

94. Martinus de Boer suggests that Paul is responding to a gnostic anthropological dualism held by some in Corinth. These Corinthian pneumatics held that the pneumatic man awaited liberation from the natural man. Thus, bodily death served as the liberation, and there was not bodily resurrection. Paul then appropriated this anthropological speculation around this two-man schema and "qualified it with his own typological contrast between Adam and Christ" (De Boer, *Defeat of Death*, 102–10). While this view is possible, it seems more necessary to understand Paul's Adam-Christ typology, first, as Paul's own reflection on the creation narrative and Adam's role in creation.

95. Son, *Corporate Elements*, 59–63.

96. Bruce, *1 and 2 Corinthians*, 145–46 and Thiselton, *First Epistle to the Corinthians*, 1221.

97. De Boer, *Defeat of Death*, 114.

death and that solution is brought about through Christ (1 Cor 15:21b), whom Paul identified in the preceding verse as inaugurator of the resurrection age (ἀπαρχὴ τῶν κεκοιμημένων, 1 Cor 15:20).

Paul clarifies his premise of v. 21 in v. 22 by substituting the locative preposition ἐν for the preposition διά. Paul's switch of prepositions clarifies how he views the relationship between Adam and Christ and between their respective dominions. Further, πάντες must be understood as those who are either in Adam or those who are in Christ.[98] Those who remain in Adam share in Adam's destiny, but those who are now in Christ share in Christ's destiny (see also 1 Cor 15:44-49).[99] While Adam's failure to steward God's righteous rule resulted in the entrance "of a death-dealing rule,"[100] Christ's resurrection reverses the effects of Adam's rule and guarantees life and resurrection to all those who belong to him. As a result, those who belong to Christ and his dominion now bear the image of the one from heaven (1 Cor 15:49).

Paul then unfolds the order[101] in which Christ will bring about this cosmic destiny utilizing regal language. Paul places Christ as the assurance of the coming kingdom (ἀπαρχὴ Χριστός),[102] and the full realization of Christ's life-giving reign will occur at the parousia (1 Cor 15:23). The term παρουσία was often used to denote the coming of an imperial figure.[103] Paul sets the stage for his "little apocalyptic drama"[104] by casting Christ in the role of the messianic King, a fact Paul's overwhelming use of

---

98. Son, *Corporate Elements*, 45.

99. Paul's use of Adam-Christ typology in these verses illustrates the two modes of human existence (the two σώματα). These verses are less concerned with the reign of Christ and are more concerned with answering key anthropological questions. For a full discussion on this passage, see Adams, *Constructing the World*, 145-46, and Son, *Corporate Elements*, 47-51.

100. Jipp, *Christ Is King*, 207.

101. The word τάγμα denotes an orderly division or rank (Barrett, *First Adam to Last*, 354). The word was also used in military contexts to describe the division of troops. One could argue that Paul uses this word to depict Christ as gathering and leading an army made up of his people into battle (Thiselton, *First Corinthians*, 1229; Jipp, *Christ Is King*, 205).

102. The term ἀπαρχὴ is derived from OT imagery in which it denotes to first portion of a crop or flock that is offered to God. The first portion serves as the assurance of the full harvest. "Used figuratively . . . 'firstfruits' symbolizes the first installment and that part including, as by synecdoche, the whole" (De Boer, *Defeat of Death*, 109).

103. BDAG, 629-30, and Thiselton, *First Corinthians*, 1230.

104. Lindemann coins this term in his discussion on 1 Cor 15:23-28 (Lindemann, "Korinthische Eschatologie," 383).

the messianic title Χριστός in 1 Cor 15 also confirms.[105] As God delegated authority to Adam, so he now delegates authority to Christ to rule over the coming kingdom. Paul then lays out the responsibilities that Christ has as God's King.

Paul begins with the end goal of Christ's reign: to turn his rule over to God the Father (1 Cor. 15:24a). However, this turning over of the kingdom can only happen when Christ defeats every cosmic power (πᾶσαν ἀρχὴν καὶ πᾶσαν ἐξουσίαν καὶ δύναμιν, 1 Cor 15:24b). Paul's language "reflects what originally denotes the superhuman agencies of apocalyptic, including demonic powers, but may in Paul indicate every structural power against which the individual is helpless and held in bondage as victim."[106] Given the cosmic context of Paul's discourse, it seems that he is primarily focused on cosmic, supernatural powers who oppose the purposes of God. These are the powers who were able to corrupt and enslave humanity and creation as a result of Adam's failure to steward God's righteous rule. The destructive effects of Adam's failure will be undone only when these powers are fully abolished.

Paul describes Christ's reign between now and the end using language from Ps 110 and Ps 8.[107] Paul first states that Christ must continue to reign until God places all his enemies under his feet (1 Cor 15:25; Ps 109:1 LXX).[108] This allusion indicates that Paul viewed Christ as fulfilling the promise of the ideal Davidic/messianic king in the present (indicated by the use of the present infinitive βασιλεύειν). Like the Davidic king, God subordinates his cosmic enemies under the feet of Jesus and grants him authority to rule over them. Paul slightly modifies the language of the Psalm by clarifying that all of Christ's enemies will be subordinated to him, the last of which will be death itself (1 Cor 15:26).

---

105. Fee, *Pauline Christology*, 108–9, and Novenson, *Christ among the Messiahs*, 143–44.

106. Thiselton, *First Corinthians*, 1232, and Fitzmeyer, *First Corinthians*, 572–73. Witherington suggests that Paul seeks to supplant an imperial eschatology that portrays the emperor as a divine figure (Witherington, *Conflict and Community*, 304–5). While Witherington's argument sheds light on the social context of Corinth, he unnecessarily limits the semantic scope of Paul's language. Given Paul's later statements about the defeat of death, it seems very likely that Paul certainly has demonic and supernatural powers in view, though this does not discount the possibility that he may be including geopolitical powers in his thought as well.

107. Hays notes that this passage offers the earliest documentation of a christological interpretation of these two Psalms (Hays, *Echoes of Scripture*, 84).

108. ἕως ἂν θῶ τοὺς ἐχθρούς σου ὑποπόδιον τῶν ποδῶν (Ps 109:1 LXX).

Paul further expands the scope of this cosmic subordination when he states that God placed all things under Christ's feet (1 Cor 15:27; Ps 8:7 LXX).[109] In alluding to Ps 8, which reflects upon Adam's original position in creation, Paul keeps his Adam-Christ typology in the background of his explanation of Christ's kingship.[110] The subordination of all things under Christ reflects the creation mandate in which God commissions Adam to subdue the earth (Gen 1:28). By citing these two Psalms together, it seems that "Paul associates the eschatological work of the Messiah from Psalm 110 with the protological work of Adam in Psalm 8."[111] Put simply, Christ's work as God's Messiah fulfills the regal responsibilities that Adam originally possessed at creation. Paul clarifies that God would not be subordinated under the reign of Christ because he is the one who subjected all things under Christ (1 Cor 15:27b). Christ, as the son, then subjects himself under God the Father so that God might be all in all. Such subordination does not refer to Christ's person but to his role as God's regal agent. Christ's role as God's King is to restore the order in creation lost by Adam so that the one God might be exalted throughout the whole cosmos.[112]

In 2 Corinthians, Paul correlates the identity of believers with the regal identity of Christ. Paul claims that God has established Timothy, Paul, and the Corinthian believers together in Christ and that they have received a mutual anointing (χρίσας ἡμᾶς) by the seal of the Spirit (2 Cor 1:21–22). The LXX often uses the verb χρίω to speak of the anointing of royalty (1 Sam 10:1; 16:13; 1 Kgs 1:39).[113] Paul's play on words indicates

109. πάντα ὑπέταξας ὑπὸ τῶν ποδῶν αὐτοῦ (Ps 8:7 LXX).

110. Son, *Corporate Elements*, 47. Many scholars acknowledge the clear Adam-Christ typology in 1 Cor 15:21–22 but then fail to mention its impact on 1 Cor 15:27 (Fee, *Pauline Christology*, 109–12, 114–16; Novenson, *Christ among the Messiahs*, 144–46; Jipp, *Christ Is King*, 206–9). This could be due to the view that Ps 8 simply reflects on humanity rather than just on the individual Adam. However, one could argue that Ps 8 reflects on humanity's position at creation through the lens of Adam. Given Paul's explicit mention of Adam in 1 Cor 15:22, it does not seem far fetched—it is perhaps even likely—that he still has Adam-Christ typology in mind in 1 Cor 15:27.

111. McDonough, *Christ as Creator*, 86. This could be an example of *gezirah sheva* (גזרי שוה), a rabbinic hermeneutical technique wherein one utilizes one verse to clarify the meaning of another verse (Keener, *Eighth Psalm*, 150–52; Urassa, *Psalm 8*, 166; Morissette, "Psaume VIII, 7b," 313–42). This technique was to be used only if two Torah statements used identical expressions (Strack and Stemberger, *Talmud and Midrash*, 21).

112. Wright, *Climax of the Covenant*, 30; Fee, *Pauline Christology*, 113; and Jipp, *Christ Is King*, 208.

113. Harris, *Second Corinthians*, 205–6.

two things. First, Paul's use of the title Χριστός is a conscious affirmation of Jesus as God's "Anointed par excellence."[114] Second, Paul views believers as having a share in the royal identity of Christ, which indicates that believers would also share in Christ's reign.[115] God's people find their identity, function, and future in Christ, God's anointed King.

Because believers are incorporated into Christ, they now reflect the glory that belongs to Christ. In contrast with the glory that belonged to Moses, believers now behold the glory of the Lord because his glory has been granted to them (2 Cor 3:18). Paul's reference to the glory of the Lord is likely a reference to the glory belonging to Christ, especially since Paul explicitly identifies Jesus Christ as Lord in 2 Cor 4:5.[116] The point is that Christ serves as the expression of God's glory, and believers, by means of the Spirit, now reflect and are being transformed into that same glory.[117] Paul further emphasizes this point by identifying Christ as the true bearer of the divine image (2 Cor 4:4). Such language indicates that Paul "has himself intended to move beyond the mirror imagery toward the biblical basis for this language: Genesis 1:26, 27."[118] Paul's language here could be another implicit reference to his Adam Christology.[119] Christ, as the one who shares the divine glory, reclaims the image lost by Adam and bears this image in a way Adam never could. As a result, God, through Christ, restores and transforms believers into the image for which they had originally been created.

---

114. Hengel, "Messiah of Israel," 6. See also Novenson, *Christ among the Messiahs*, 147.

115. Thrall, *2 Corinthians 1–7*, 155 and Jipp, *Christ Is King*, 140–41.

116. Fee, *Pauline Christology*, 179.

117. Specifically, Paul declares that believers are being transformed into the same image (τὴν αὐτὴν εἰκόνα). Whether Paul refers here to the image of God or Christ is up for debate. Paul uses the language in this verse primarily in the context of his mirror imagery. Thus, Paul's Adam Christology is not the impetus behind the εἰκών in v. 18 (Fee, *Pauline Christology*, 184). Wright argues that the "image" in this verse does not suggest that believers are transformed into the same image as Christ. Rather, Paul is asserting that believers are transformed into the same image as their fellow believers (Wright, *Climax of the Covenant*, 188). Even if Wright is correct, the point remains the same. In this case, believers are being transformed into the same image as one another, but that glorious image is one that they receive as a result of their incorporation with Christ their King.

118. Fee, *Pauline Christology*, 185.

119. Oropeza, "New Covenant Knowledge," 421.

Such knowledge of Christ causes Paul to no longer understand Christ according to the categories of the old order (2 Cor 5:16).[120] Rather, those who are in Christ are now a new creation because they now belong to the new order brought about by the exalted Christ (2 Cor 5:17). While Paul's focus is on the soteriological implications of Christ's work, his language implies that Christ's work has serious implications for the whole creation.[121] This concept aligns with the Jewish hope that God would reestablish his good rule over creation through the enthronement of his ideal king (Pss 72:3–11; 132:11–12; Ezek 37:22, 25; Zech 9:1–8; Pss. Sol. 17–18; 2 Bar. 73:2–7).[122]

Cosmic Christ in Romans

In his opening to his letter to the Romans, Paul declares Jesus to be a descendant of David and the appointed Son of God (Rom 1:3–4).[123] Such a declaration indicates two things: First, Paul viewed Jesus' descent from David as significant to Jesus' identity. Christ's Davidic descent was part of God's promise spoken in the OT (Rom 1:2). In declaring Jesus to be the seed of David, Paul alludes to 2 Sam 7:12–14 in which God promises David that he would establish the throne of David's seed and would enter into a father-son relationship with him.[124] Further, Paul uses language that reflects messiah language found in ancient Judaism (ἐκ σπέρματος Δαυὶδ . . . Χριστοῦ, Rom 1:3–4).[125] For Jesus to fulfill the requirements of God's ideal king, it was necessary for him to partake in fleshly human existence (κατὰ σάρκα). Christ's descent from David fulfills God's promise

---

120. Fee, *Pauline Christology*, 197 and Novenson, *Christ among the Messiahs*, 166–67. On the adverbial use of κατὰ σάρκα in v. 16, see Harris, *Second Corinthians*, 428.

121. Lioy, "New Creation Theology," 73.

122. See ch. 2.

123. Some have argued that Rom 1:3–4 is a pre-Pauline formula (Dunn, "Jesus—Flesh and Spirit," 40–68; Jewett, "Redaction and Use of an Early Christian Confession," 99–122). However, Novenson rightly points out that even if this is a pre-Pauline formula, it still very much represents Paul's own view (Novenson, *Christ among the Messiahs*, 172).

124. Hays, *Echoes of Scripture*, 85, and Whitsett, "Son of God," 661–81. Whitsett also connects this passage to Ps 2.

125. Novenson argues that Paul's expression in this passage reflects idioms used in 2 Sam 22 and Ps 18. While Paul may or may not have been aware of this parallel, Novenson rightly suggests that Paul inherits and utilizes linguistic resources that reflect the messianic figure in Judaism (Novenson, *Christ among the Messiahs*, 168).

to bring about his ideal king through David's line. Paul views Christ's Davidic lineage as an important aspect of this royal identity.¹²⁶

Second, Paul's initial declaration draws a parallelism between the royal Davidic designation and divine sonship. The result of such parallelism shows that Paul considered Christ's divine sonship, in part, to say something of his royal position within the cosmos itself. Paul declares Christ to be God's Son before he speaks of his human birth (Rom 1:3a), which could be a possible allusion to Christ's preexistence and thus his heavenly origin.¹²⁷ The indication is "that the Son 'came' from heaven to 'come' from the seed of David κατὰ σάρκα."¹²⁸ Christ's resurrection from the dead not only affirmed that he was the fulfillment of the royal Davidic covenant, but his resurrection serves as the means by which he is granted a divine royal designation (Rom 1:4).¹²⁹ Paul characterizes this enthronement as one that is done in power, indicating that Christ demonstrates the power of God though his rule (Rom 1:4). His present enthronement is according to the Spirit (κατὰ πνεῦμα ἁγιωσύνης). Standing in parallel with κατὰ σάρκα, this phrase indicates that Christ's reign "is now marked by the qualities and attributes of the Spirit" (Rom 1:4).¹³⁰ As one whose kingship is marked by flesh and spirit, Jesus' reign naturally extends over both realms of flesh and spirit. The extent of his reign leads Paul to declare that Jesus himself shares in divine lordship (Ἰησοῦ Χριστοῦ τοῦ κυρίου ἡμῶν, Rom 1:4). In view of Christ's kingship, Paul proclaims his commission to bring about obedience to God's King among all nations (Rom 1:5).¹³¹ In this way, Paul shows that the hope of the ideal Davidic king extends beyond the Jewish people to all nations.

---

126. Schlatter, *Romans*, 5; Fee, *Pauline Christology*, 240–42; and Jipp, *Christ Is King*, 168–72. This is contra to the argument made by Per Beskow, who suggests that the early church did not place great significance on Jesus' Davidic descent but traced his kingship to his divine sonship (Beskow, *Rex Gloriae*).

127. Jipp, *Christ Is King*, 174. One should note that Paul does not make an explicit reference to Christ's preexistence in this passage. However, given Paul's expression of Christ's preexistence later in the letter (Rom 8:3), one could argue that preexistence is presuppositional to Paul's declaration in this passage (Fee, *Pauline Christology*, 242–43).

128. Fee, *Pauline Christology*, 42.

129. The participle ὁρισθέντος means that Christ is installed or designated to a position of rule (Jipp, *Christ Is King*, 175).

130. Jipp, *Christ Is King*, 177. Fee argues that the Spirit in this context "has to do with the heavenly, eschatological sphere of life, into which Christ himself by resurrection has now entered" (Fee, *Pauline Christology*, 244).

131. Whitsett, "Son of God," 676.

Romans 5:12–21 places Christ's enthronement and reign in a cosmic framework and compares Christ's reign with Adam's reign.[132] Specifically, Paul examines how the actions of Adam and Christ affected their given dominions. Paul's repeated use of the genitive ἑνὸς ἀνθρώπου to refer to both Adam and Christ and the description of Adam as a τύπος τοῦ μέλλοντος (Rom 5:14) makes this comparison explicit. Adam and Christ represent two realms of human existence. The dominion of Adam is marked by his failure to rule with righteousness. Paul begins this passage by pointing out that it was through one man that sin entered the world, which subsequently allowed the entrance of death. Paul alludes to the Gen 1–3 tradition in which God establishes Adam as his royal ambassador. Adam was to be the "prototypical human" who would steward the righteous reign of God.[133] Rather than stewarding God's righteous rule, Adam sinned, and those who live under the dominion of Adam are now joined with Adam in his sin (ἐφ' ᾧ πάντες ἥμαρτον, Rom 5:12)[134] and follow the pattern of sin that now reigns over them (ἁμαρτωλοὶ κατεστάθησαν οἱ πολλοί, Rom 5:19).[135] As a result, Adam's act "was determinative for (many) men who belong to him."[136]

---

132. When discussing this passage, De Boer limits his definition of "cosmic" as a referent to the whole of the human world, not to the whole universe or earth (De Boer, *God's Apocalypse*, 61). While the immediate context of Rom 5:12–21 does seem to focus on the human world, this passage illustrates "the cosmic contention for the lordship of the world" (Käsemann, "Primitive Christian Apocalyptic," 136). Paul views the reign of Adam and Christ as having significant implications for the whole of the created universe, a theme which he explores further in Rom 8. Therefore, understanding Paul's expression of the kingdoms of Adam and Christ is vital to understanding his cosmic program in Rom 8.

133. Jipp, *Christ Is King*, 182.

134. One can take the phrase ἐφ' ᾧ as either a causal conjunction or a relative clause. Given the difficulty of finding the proper antecedent for ᾧ, it seems most likely that this phrase is a causal conjunction. If this phrase is indeed causal, it begs the question whether Paul refers to individual sin ("because all personally sinned") or corporate sin in Adam ("because all sinned in Adam"). Given the context in which Paul is speaking of two realms of human existence that are attached to Adam or Christ, the corporate sin in Adam view seems most likely (Son, *Corporate Elements*, 52–53). For a helpful discussion on the various views on the meaning of ἐφ' ᾧ, see Cranfield, *Romans I-VIII*, 274–79.

135. Paul's statement here does not necessarily absolve humanity of personal responsibility. The tension between corporate destiny and personal responsibility appears in Jewish literature on Adam's sin. For Paul, both concepts (the corporate personality of Adam and the personal responsibility of all those who follow Adam's pattern) belong together (De Boer, *God's Apocalypse*, 64–65; see also Moo's analysis of Rom 5:12 in Moo, "Type of the One," 153–54).

136. Son, *Corporate Elements*, 54.

Adam's failure to fulfill the role of God's ideal king unleashed the power of sin and death upon the cosmos. What is interesting about Paul's interpretation of Adam's story is the way in which he personifies sin and death and presents them as cosmological powers. Paul views the plight of humanity as part of a cosmic conflict between God and the evil cosmic powers.[137] Paul uses royal imagery to demonstrate Adam's complicity in the dominion of sin and death (ἐβασίλευσεν ὁ θάνατος, Rom 5:14; ὁ θάνατος ἐβασίλευσεν διὰ τοῦ ἑνός, Rom 5:17; ἐβασίλευσεν ἡ ἁμαρτία ἐν τῷ θανάτῳ, Rom 5:21). Rather than exercising God's good rule, Adam unleashed the oppressive rule of sin and death, a rule which enslaves all humanity.[138] This idea reflects the common Jewish belief that Adam's failure brought sin and death to all humanity (Jub. 3:17–31; 4 Ezra 3:6–11; 2 Bar. 17:3, 23:4). Adam's failure to fulfill his role as God's royal ambassador brought about a cosmic conflict that necessitated the enthronement of a new ideal king who would be able to subdue these powers and thus save humanity.

It is against this backdrop that Paul presents the life-giving work of Christ. Paul indicates the comparison between Christ and Adam using the introductory formula ὥσπερ/ὡς ... οὕτως καὶ (Rom 5:12, 15).[139] Paul sets Jesus as the antitype to Adam (τύπος τοῦ μέλλοντος, Rom 5:14), meaning that Paul views Jesus and his kingship in correspondence and in contrast with Adam and his kingship. Paul sees a correspondence between Adam and Christ in that they both have a dominion entrusted to them and act in a way that affects everyone under their dominion.[140] More specifically, both Adam and Jesus establish the reign of something through their work.[141] Paul then brings Christ into sharp contrast with Adam through an examination of the effects of Christ's rule. Whereas

---

137. De Boer, *God's Apocalypse*, 66–67. Beverly Roberts Gaventa coins these as the "anti-God powers" and suggests that sin and death are "cosmic partners" capable of exerting their power over the cosmos (Gaventa, "Cosmic Power of Sin," 229–40; Gaventa "Neither Height nor Depth," 268–69). Other helpful discussions on sin and death as cosmic powers include Adams, *Constructing the World*, 171–74, and Lee, *Cosmic Drama*, 157–61.

138. Kirk, *Unlocking Romans*, 105, and Gaventa, "Neither Height nor Depth," 270.

139. The adverbial ὥσπερ appears in v. 12 while the form ὡς appears in v. 15. One should also note that v. 12 contains the protasis (ὥσπερ) but no apodosis (οὕτως καὶ). The reason for this is most likely that Paul resumes the comparison he began in v. 12 in v. 18 (Son, *Corporate Elements*, 53–54).

140. Moo describes it as a "structural similarity between Adam's relationship to his 'descendants' and Christ to his" (Moo, "Type of the One," 155; see also Son, *Corporate Elements*, 54).

141. Kirk, *Unlocking Romans*, 103.

Adam's trespass resulted in death for many, Christ's obedience resulted in grace abounding to many (Rom 5:15). Whereas Adam's failure brought judgment and condemnation to all under his dominion, Christ's righteous act brought justification and life to those under his dominion (Rom 5:16, 18). Whereas Adam's actions enslaved humanity under the reign of sin and death, those who receive grace and righteousness through Christ will participate in his reign (Rom 5:17, 21). Whereas Adam's one act of disobedience made those under his dominion sinners, Christ's one act of obedience makes those under his dominion righteous (Rom 5:19).

Paul goes further than a comparison and contrast between Christ and Adam. He stresses that Christ's work and dominion far surpasses the work and dominion of Adam. Paul's use of (1) the introductory formula εἰ ... πολλῷ μᾶλλον (Rom 5:15, 17) and (2) his description of the abundance of grace surpassing the increase of sin (οὗ δὲ ... ὑπερεπερίσσευσεν, Rom 5:20) both emphasize that Christ's work overcomes and surpasses Adam's work.[142] In sum, Paul portrays Christ as God's ideal King, who, in his person and actions, surpasses God's first king, Adam; liberates humanity from the effects of Adam's reign; and enables his people to participate in his rule in the world to come.[143]

In Rom 8:18–39, Paul builds upon the themes established in Rom 5:12–21 and extends his discussion on the effects of Adam's and Christ's reigns beyond the world of humanity to the whole of creation. While Paul does not explicitly mention Adam in this passage, Paul's language draws the reader back to Adam and the creation story.[144] Paul begins Rom 8 by reminding his readers that in order to overcome the shortcomings of the law, God sent his Son in the flesh (Rom 8:3). Paul's statement "unpacks the significance of his messianic confession" in Rom 1:3 when he states that Christ appeared according to the flesh.[145] Given his statements in Rom 5:12–21, Christ's entrance into the Adamic dominion was necessary for him to rescue humanity from the enslaving effect of Adam's reign and to claim the Davidic throne. Paul then explains that believers no

---

142. Son, *Corporate Elements*, 54–55.

143. Kirk, *Unlocking Romans*, 102–3.

144. Adams provides a helpful list of criteria for identifying an "Adam motif" in Paul's letters. His criteria are as follows: (1) an explicit mention of Adam, (2) a reference to the Gen 1 story, especially references to man's creation in the image of God and as male and female and the commission for humanity to rule over the earth, (3) an echo/allusion to Ps 8, and (4) reference to Jewish speculations about Adam's original state and the effects of his sin (Adams, "Paul's Story," 25).

145. Jipp, *Christ Is King*, 184.

longer walk according to the flesh, an indication that one exists under the dominion of sin and death, but now walk according to the Spirit, an indication that one exists under the dominion of Christ (Rom 8:4–11). The result is that those who live under the dominion of Christ receive life and sonship and are the beneficiaries of future glory (Rom 8:12–18).

With these things in mind, Paul considers the effects of Adam and Christ on the whole of creation itself. Paul presents the κτίσις as a victim of the suffering and enslavement to the powers of the present age that eagerly awaits its renewal (Rom 8:19–22). A few things are worth noting in this passage. First, Paul's use of the term κτίσις rather than κόσμος marks a significant shift in Paul's discussion. Scholars primarily have argued for four views on the meaning κτίσις: (1) all creation, (2) nonhuman creation/nature, (3) the world of humanity, and (4) subhuman creation and unbelieving humanity.[146] Options three and four can be eliminated quickly because Paul uses the term κόσμος previously in Romans to refer to the world of humanity (both believing and unbelieving). A shift in terms makes little sense if Paul still intends to limit his scope to humanity. It seems unlikely that the term could refer to the unbelieving world since Paul elsewhere stresses human culpability for sin but here states that the κτίσις is an unwilling participant of subjection.[147] Additionally, Paul contrasts believers with the κτίσις in vv. 22–23. Considering this contrast, one can also eliminate option one, which views the use of κτίσις in this passage as embracing heaven, earth, and every human being.[148] Therefore, it seems most likely that Paul refers to the nonhuman creation. Paul's declaration then aligns with the Genesis narrative and Jewish writings in which Adam, as God's first king, is considered responsible for the corruption not only of humanity but of nature itself.

Second, Paul casts the κτίσις as a passive participant in the cosmic conflict. Paul utilizes the passive verb ὑπετάγη to speak of how the κτίσις entered its present state of enslavement (Rom 8:20a). Paul emphasizes this point when he states that this subjection happened through unwilling subordination (Rom 8:20b). While God seems to be the most likely referent for the participle ὑποτάξαντα, Paul's point is that Adam's failure

---

146. For a full discussion on these four views, see Hahne, *Corruption and Redemption*, 177–81. One unusual view argued by Fuchs is that the term refers to the angelic world (Fuchs, *Freiheit des Glaubens*, 109). However, this view has never gained any significant traction.

147. For a full repudiation of this view, see Adams, *Constructing the World*, 176–77.

148. Adams, *Constructing the World*, 176, and Hahne, *Corruption*, 179.

occasioned the event in which God subjected the creation to share in Adam's fallen state.¹⁴⁹ As God's royal ambassador to creation, Adam was accountable to God for how he ruled, and his actions affected the world for which he cared.¹⁵⁰ The demise of the κτίσις was tied to the demise of its first king, Adam. The result is that the κτίσις "has been rendered unable to fulfill the purpose for which it was intended: displaying His [God's] glory."¹⁵¹ Paul then states that the κτίσις will one day experience liberation, a fate which it shares with believers (Rom 8:21). Even though its demise is owed to the failure of its first king, the κτίσις finds its future hope in the work of God's ideal King, Christ Jesus.

Third, Paul states the liberation of the κτίσις will occur when the sons of God are revealed (Rom 8:19). Paul's statement suggests that the fate of the κτίσις is inextricably tied to the fate of believers. Believers and the κτίσις experience solidarity in both their present suffering and in the hope of future glory (Rom 8:22–23). Paul's claim throughout Rom 8 that believers are sons of God (Rom 8:14–17, 19, 23, 29–30) indicates that they participate in Christ's royal messianic sonship discussed in Rom 1:4.¹⁵² Paul further defines the terms of the believers' sonship when he claims that believers are to be conformed to the image of God's son (Rom 8:29). This declaration echoes Gen 1:26–27 where Adam is endowed with the image of God, and it further develops Paul's Adam-Christ typology. Whereas Adam failed to realize and reflect God's image, Christ in his own humanity perfectly bore the divine image. Christ takes up this royal mantle so that he might become the firstborn (πρωτότοκος) of all believers. Paul's use of this title echoes Ps 88:28 LXX where the ideal Davidic king is set as God's πρωτότοκος.¹⁵³ Such language, along with Paul's opening statements on Christ's Davidic kingship in Rom 1:3–4, hints at a potential connection Paul makes between Adam and David. If Adam's failure resulted in the corruption of God's creation order, then the "coming Davidic king ... would push forward God's creation project as a whole."¹⁵⁴

---

149. Dunn, *Romans 1–8*, 471; Adams, *Constructing the World*, 178–79; and Jackson, *New Creation*, 157–58.

150. Hahne, *Corruption*, 188.

151. Jackson, *New Creation*, 152.

152. Scott, *Adoption*, 244–45; Peppard, *Son of God*, 138–40; and Jipp, *Christ Is King*, 187–91.

153. Leese, *Christ*, 115.

154. McDonough, *Christ as Creator*, 88.

Christ's ascension to his royal position assures both his power to rescue believers from the dominion of Adam and his incorporation of believers into his reign. While humanity under Adam lost their ability to participate in God's rule, believers under the reign of Christ are now able to participate in the rule of God. By joining believers to Christ and conforming them to Christ's image, God restores to them the royal image that Adam possessed at creation[155] and, consequently, restores his "original vision for humanity as a corporate entity."[156] Believers' participation in Christ's rule restores the rule over creation originally possessed by Adam and thus restores the creation order. In this way, the fate of creation and the cosmos itself is bound up in the fate of believers.[157] For this reason, the κτίσις awaits the revelation of the people of God.

Paul celebrates the reign of Christ and believers' participation in his reign in Rom 8:31–39. Paul declares that believers need not fear condemnation because Christ has been raised and has taken his place at God's right hand (Rom 8:34). Such language echoes Psalm 109:1 LXX when God tells his ideal king to sit at his right hand and points to Paul's understanding of Jesus as the fulfillment of the Davidic messianic hope. Christ's kingship grants believers hope as they live in a world still affected by the reign of sin and death (Rom 8:34b–37). Further, Paul states that the cosmic powers themselves (οὔτε θάνατος οὔτε ζωὴ οὔτε ἄγγελοι οὔτε ἀρχαὶ ... οὔτε δυνάμεις) cannot separate believers from God's love in Christ the Lord (Rom 8:38–39). Paul is confident in this fact because of Christ's position as King/Lord over the cosmos. Paul's declaration suggests that Christ's kingdom encompasses both the physical and spiritual realms. Put simply, Paul "signals that all dimensions of creaturely life are effectively superintended by the dominion of Christ's saving love."[158] Further, believers have been joined to Christ, which means that they share in Christ's cosmic victory (Rom 8:37) and rule over these powers.

---

155. Stanley Grenz suggests the Rom 8:29 serves "as the final exegesis of Genesis 1:26–27" (Grenz, "Social God," 91).

156. Adams, "Paul's Story," 29.

157. Ziegler, "Love of God," 125.

158. Ziegler, "Love of God," 125.

Cosmic Christ in Philippians

The Christ hymn[159] in Phil 2:6–11 serves as a keystone discourse in Paul's christological belief. This hymn is of particular concern to the present study because it depicts Christ as an exalted royal figure. The opening phrase "being in the form of God" points to Paul's presupposition of the protological preexistence of Christ (Phil 2:6).[160] Paul utilizes the present participle ὑπάρχων rather than a finite verb to indicate Christ always being in the form of God. If Paul wanted to communicate that Christ was in this form only at the time he οὐχ ἁρπαγμὸν ἡγήσατο τὸ εἶναι ἴσα θεῷ,[161] he could have used the finite verb ἦν.[162] This participle also stands in temporal contrast with the aorist verb ἐκένωσεν and the participle γενόμενος (Phil 2:7), meaning that it was while Jesus was "being" in the form of God that he emptied himself by taking on another form. Moreover, such contrast makes most sense when it is presupposed that Christ existed as God prior to Christ taking on human likeness.[163] Paul's assertion that Christ existed in the form of God further confirms Christ's preexistent divine status. The word μορφή most likely points to Christ's possession of the

---

159. Whether or not Paul wrote this Christ hymn makes little difference. Whether Paul composed it himself or borrowed from another tradition, his inclusion of it in his writings indicates that its christological implications match his own Christology. For a full discussion on possible origin and genre of this hymn, see Brucker, *Christushymnen*, and Collins, "Origins of Christology," 361–72. Richard Weymouth has recently argued that this passage should be considered a prose narrative as opposed to a hymn, which is an intriguing proposition considering the Adam-Christ typology and the story of Christ's humiliation and exaltation that appear in the passage (Weymouth, "Christ-Story").

160. Hamerton-Kelly, *Pre-Existence*, 167–68. Dunn serves as the leading proponent against the view that this hymn says anything about Christ's preexistence or that it presents an incarnational Christology. Dunn argues that the hymn is an expression of Paul's Adam Christology. However, he argues that a preexistent-incarnational interpretation owes more to the gnostic redeemer myth than first century Adam Christology. Dunn may be correct in his denial of preexistence as the controlling concept of v. 6. However, this does not negate the possibility that Paul's presupposition of Christ's preexistence stands in the background of v. 6. On the contrary, the presupposition of Christ's preexistence makes more sense of Paul's Adam-Christ typology, a point which Wright astutely points out. In the words of Wright, "The presence of Adam Christology, then, says nothing of itself against pre-existence. It may actually require it" (Wright, *Climax of the Covenant*, 91–92). For more on Christ's preexistence as presuppositional for Paul's Christology, see Fee, *Pauline Christology*, 546–52.

161. Dunn makes this argument in denying that the hymn affirms Christ's preexistence (Dunn, *Christology in the Making*, 310–11).

162. Fee, *Pauline Christology*, 376n19.

163. Fee, *Pauline Christology*, 377.

essential characteristics and nature of the divine.[164] Such an understanding of the word further confirms Christ as the preexistent one.

The phrase ἐν μορφῇ θεοῦ also serves as an implicit reference to Gen 1:26, thus introducing Paul's Adam-Christ typology as an underlying theme of this passage.[165] Though Paul's use of μορφή differs from the LXX rendering of צלם as εἰκών, the words have very similar meanings.[166] Paul makes this implicit allusion more evident when he speaks of Christ's action as one who exists in the form of God. Paul begins by stating that Christ did not consider equality with God as something to be grasped (ἁρπαγμὸν). Wright's discussion on the meaning of this word depicts the implicit link Paul makes between Adam and Christ. He argues that the object to be grasped (equality with God) is already in Christ's possession. Adam's original sin was his attempt to grasp equality with God, something that did not rightfully belong to him, but Christ, who rightfully possessed divine equality, voluntarily renounced this status so that he might undo the effects of Adam's sin. In fact, it was Christ's equality with God (τὸ εἶναι ἴσα θεῷ, Phil 2:6) that uniquely qualified him to undo Adam's sin.[167] For this reason, Christ, the one in the form of God, took on the form of a servant (Phil 2:7a). Christ's obedience to death (Phil 2:8) parallels Paul's comparison between the disobedience of Adam and the obedience of Christ in Rom 5:19. The self-humiliation and obedience of Christ in this passage serve as a direct contrast to the arrogance and disobedience of Adam.[168]

Paul presents the exaltation of Christ in the second half of the hymn using regal language.[169] That God exalted Christ speaks to Christ's heav-

---

164. Hawthorne, *Philippians*, 81–84. See also the discussion from Bockmuehl, *Philippians*, 126–29. For an extensive study on the noun μορφή, see Fabricatore, *Form of God*.

165. This background to the hymn has been widely attested in NT scholarship (Ellis, *Paul's Use*, 129; Kim, *Paul's Gospel*, 265; Hooker, "Philippians 2:6–11," 96–100; Wright, *Climax of the Covenant*, 56–98; Dunn, *Theology of Paul*, 281–88).

166. Kim, *Paul's Gospel*, 200–204, and Son, *Corporate Elements*, 56. Fee questions the validity of semantic overlap between μορφή and εἰκών and suggests that Paul uses μορφή because it was the only term that describe Christ's mode of preexistence and incarnation. He does leave open the possibility of a conceptual allusion to Adam (Fee, *Pauline Christology*, 377–79, 522–23).

167. See Wright's full discussion on ἁρπαγμὸν in Wright, *Climax of the Covenant*, 62–90. See also Hoover, "HARPAGMOS Enigma," 95–119.

168. In Wright's words, "Adam, in arrogance, thought to become like God; Christ, in humility, became human" (Wright, *Climax of the Covenant*, 91).

169. That Paul continues to draw upon Adam Christology in this half, as asserted

enly throne positioned above all other thrones in heaven and on earth (Phil 2:9).[170] This immediate turn from Christ's death to his exaltation echoes the Jewish royal motif in which God elevates his king from a position of obscurity to kingship (Ps 8:4–5; Isa 53:4–12).[171] This exaltation is also reminiscent of the royal Psalms in which God grants the ideal Davidic king a heavenly throne (Ps 2:6; 45:7; 89:27; 110:1).

Paul further clarifies Christ's exaltation by stating that God granted Christ the name above every name (Phil 2:9b). It is plausible that Paul's reference here could be to the divine name in the OT, meaning that Paul has attributed a rank to Jesus that is reserved for God alone.[172] If this is the case, then Christ's share in the divine means that he has a share in the divine, cosmic rule. This parallels royal Jewish motifs in which God appoints his ideal king to share in his divine rule (Pss 2:8; 72:8, 11; 89:26; 110:1; Isa 42:5–6; Dan 7:14).[173] Within the context of the Philippian hymn, Paul's depiction of Christ's kingship develops the identity of God's ideal king one step further. By presenting Christ from the outset as the preexistent divine one, Christ's enthronement and reception of the divine name is a reception of "no more than that which was always, from before the beginning of time, his by right."[174] In other words, the one who fulfills the Jewish hope of God's ideal king is one who has himself rightfully shared the divine name from eternity past. That God gave Christ the name above every name could also be an implicit allusion to Paul's Adam Christology. At creation, God granted to Adam the task of naming all animals (Gen 2:19–20). As the one who gave all creatures of the earth

---

by Dunn and Hooker, is doubtful (Dunn, *Christology in the Making*, 117–19; Hooker, *Adam to Christ*, 96–100). While Paul presents Christ's kingship in a way that supersedes the original dominion of Adam, Paul's focus in this half of the hymn is on the royal exaltation of Jesus. Paul utilizes Adam Christology in the first half of the hymn to contrast Adam and Christ's original place in creation and their subsequent actions. His Adam analogy ends once he turns his focus toward Christ's exaltation.

170. Richard Bauckham, "Throne of God," 65.

171. See the discussion on this Jewish royal motif in ch. 2. Jipp also observes that the revelation of Jesus' divine rule through his refusal to exploit his equality with God subverts the pattern of Greco-Roman kings and emperors who rose to their rank through the exercise of their power (Jipp, *Christ Is King*, 132; see also Vollenweider, "'Raub' der Gottgleichheit," 432).

172. Wright, *Climax of the Covenant*, 93–94; Hengel, "My Right Hand," 119–25; Bauckham, "Throne of God," 65–66; and Fee, *Pauline Christology*, 396–97.

173. See the discussion on this Jewish royal motif in ch. 2. See also Collins, "Worship of Jesus," 240–51; Oakes "Re-mapping the Universe," 318–21; and Jipp, *Christ Is King*, 133–34.

174. Wright, *Climax of the Covenant*, 94.

their name, Adam possessed the authority to rule over all creatures of the earth. God conferred upon Christ the name that is above every name, meaning he now expresses rightful authority over everything in the cosmos. Christ then supersedes the first Adam in that the name/authority given to him is far greater than the name conferred upon Adam. As a result, the scope of Christ's authority extends not just over the physical creation but over the whole cosmos.

Paul depicts the extent of Christ's rule when he states that everything in every sphere of the cosmos (ἐπουρανίων καὶ ἐπιγείων καὶ καταχθονίων) will submit to and worship Christ. Paul's comprehensive language includes all sentient beings under the rule of Christ.[175] Thus, these terms convey the idea that even the spiritual beings will recognize Christ as the exalted Lord. Since Christ preexisted in the heavenly realm, appeared in the physical realm via the incarnation, and is once again enthroned in the heavenly realm, he also is qualified to bring both the spiritual and physical realms under his regal authority. As a result, everything and everyone in the cosmos will proclaim Jesus Christ is the κύριος, a title that reemphasizes Christ's royal position.[176] That the Father receives glory through Christ's exaltation and enthronement (Phil 2:11) parallels Jewish royal ideology in which YHWH's glorious rule is made known throughout the earth through the enthronement of his ideal king (Isa 60:1–5; 61:5–6, 9; see also Isa 45:22–25).[177] Paul, like Jewish royal ideology, views the enthronement of Christ, God's ideal King, to be the primary means by which God would once again establish his rule over the cosmos.

In Phil 3:20–21, Paul lays out the specific implications that Christ's cosmic kingship has for believers. In contrast to those that are enemies of Christ (Phil 3:18–19), Paul states that believers currently possess a heavenly citizenship (Phil 3:20a). Paul assures the Philippian church that the realization of their present citizenship will occur at the arrival of the Savior, whom Paul immediately identifies as the Lord Jesus Christ (Phil 3:20b), a direct parallel to the title ascribed to Jesus in Phil 2:11. This undoubtedly resonated with the Philippian believers, as σωτήρ was a title

---

175. Witherington, *Philippians*, 154.

176. On the royal connotations of κύριος, see Fantin, *Lord of the World*. On the royal connotations of Χριστὸς, see Novenson, *Christ among the Messiahs*.

177. See ch. 2. Many scholars have connected Paul's language in Phil 2:9–11 to God's establishment of his universal sovereignty in Isa 45:22–25 (Wright, *Climax of the Covenant*, 93; Son, *Corporate Elements*, 57; Reumann, *Philippians*, 374).

often attributed to the Roman Caesar.¹⁷⁸ Combined with the titles κύριος and Χριστός, σωτήρ carries significant royal overtones. Just as Israel found hope in the coming of God's ideal king, so now believers find their hope in the coming of the currently enthroned cosmic King. Upon his arrival, Christ will transform their humble bodies (τὸ σῶμα τῆς ταπεινώσεως ἡμῶν, Phil 3:21). The genitive ταπεινώσεως echoes the verb ταπεινόω used in Phil 2:8 to describe Christ's self-humiliation. As believers share in Christ's humiliation, so they will also share in his exaltation through their own transformation.¹⁷⁹ Christ effectuates this transformation according to the power that enabled him to subordinate all things under his reign. Paul once again echoes to the language of Ps 8:7 LXX where God grants humanity dominion over creation. Jipp rightly observes that Paul's allusion "depicts Christ as exercising by his own agency the royal dominion over creation and the glory and honor intended for Adam."¹⁸⁰ Christ's enthronement to cosmic kingship enables him to share his transforming resurrection power with his people. As a result, believers are assured of their heavenly citizenship and participation in Christ's cosmic rule.

OTHER KEY NT TEXTS ON COSMIC CHRIST

Beyond the Gospels and undisputed letters of Paul, three other passages that contribute to the conception of Christ as a cosmic King are worth a brief mention: Acts 2:25–36, Heb 1:1–5, and Heb 2:5–9.¹⁸¹ Peter's sermon in Acts 2 is of interest because of the way Peter explicitly identifies Jesus as the fulfillment of the ideal Davidic king. Peter begins his identification of Jesus as the Davidic king by quoting Ps 15:8–11 LXX (Acts 2:25–28). In the Psalm, David reflects on the presence of the Lord on his right (ἐκ

---

178. Bockmuehl, *Philippians*, 235, and Fee, *Pauline Christology*, 402.

179. Hooker, "Interchange in Christ," 21, and Fee, *Pauline Christology*, 403.

180. Jipp, *Christ Is King*, 147. On the allusion to Ps 8 in Phil 3:21, see Wright, *Faithfulness of God*, 1292–94, and Fee, *Pauline Christology*, 405.

181. The current study does not include any passages from Revelation. One should acknowledge that Christ's position as the cosmic Ruler/King is a prevalent theme in Revelation. However, given the extent and complexity of this theme in Revelation, an adequate survey of Revelation's cosmic Christology is beyond the scope of this study. The current study also does not include any passages from most of the general epistles. Though these epistles have passages that may contribute to the overall NT picture of Christ as a cosmic figure, questions of dating and how these writings would have related to Paul's formation of his own Christology make an adequate treatment of these passages not overly relevant for the current study.

δεξιῶν μου)¹⁸² as that which establishes and upholds him (Ps 15:8 LXX; Acts 2:25). David also declares that the Lord would not abandon his soul to Hades or decay (Ps 15:10 LXX; Acts 2:27). Peter suggests that this promise cannot apply to David himself because David is still dead (Acts 2:29). Rather, in an allusion to 2 Sam 7:12–13 and Ps 132:11,¹⁸³ Peter claims that David was speaking as a prophet about the resurrection of his own descendent the Christ (Acts 2:30–31). Peter then explicitly identifies Jesus' resurrection as the fulfillment of the Davidic hope (Acts 2:32), meaning that Jesus himself must be the Christ.

Peter then explains that Jesus' resurrection led to his exaltation to God's right hand (Acts 2:33).¹⁸⁴ Peter further emphasizes Jesus' enthronement at God's right hand with a direct citation of Ps 109:1 LXX (Acts 2:34). Three things stand out about Peter's characterization of Christ's enthronement. First, God is the active agent who enthrones Jesus. Both the use of the passive participle ὑψωθείς and the citation of Ps 109:1 LXX where YHWH speaks directly to the ideal Davidic king implicates God's agency in Christ's enthronement. This characterization aligns with Jewish royal traditions that view YHWH's ideal king as being enthroned by YHWH himself. Peter pairs Jesus' resurrection and enthronement together to vindicate Christ's work as the fulfillment of the messianic hope.¹⁸⁵ Second, Peter insinuates Christ's cosmic authority by depicting the location of his enthronement in the heavens at God's right hand.¹⁸⁶ Third, Christ's enthronement is accompanied by his reception

---

182. Given Peter's later citation of Ps 109 LXX, Peter could be interpreting Ps 15 LXX with Ps 109:1 LXX. In this case, it could be an instance of *gezerah shevah*. For more on the meaning of Ps 15 LXX in Acts 2, see Barrett, *Acts*, 1:144–48; Keener, *Acts*, 944–46; and Holladay, "What David Saw," 95–108.

183. Strauss, *Davidic Messiah*, 138–39, and Keener, *Acts*, 952–53.

184. Given Peter's following quotation of Ps 109:1 LXX, it seems best to interpret this dative as referring to place rather than means. However, such an interpretation does not necessarily exclude God's agency in Christ's enthronement. Only God can enthrone a king at his right hand. Therefore, Christ's position at God's right hand naturally indicates that God enthroned him there. For an argument for means, see Barrett, *Acts*, 1:149; for place, see Bock, *Acts*, 132–33.

185. Hay, *Glory*, 71–72; Strauss, *Davidic Messiah*, 141; and Keener, *Acts*, 956.

186. David Hay argues that Acts does not ascribe the title κύριος to Christ in a cosmological sense (Hay, *Glory*, 72). However, the location of Christ's throne εἰς τοὺς οὐρανούς has clear cosmic implications. The location of Christ's throne says something about the scope of his authority. Even if Acts focuses more on Christ's rule in the interim between resurrection and parousia, it does not mean that Luke did not conceive of Jesus as being the cosmic Lord. Rather, Christ's current position as the cosmic Lord provides hope for the eventual full revelation of his cosmic lordship (Strauss, *Davidic*

of the Spirit, which he then pours out on his people (Acts 2:33). Christ's reception of the Spirit echoes the Jewish royal motif in which God's ideal king is anointed with God's Spirit (Ps 89:19-20; Isa 11:1-3; 42:1; 59:21; 61:1).[187] But in a unique turn, Peter also depicts Christ as the one who pours out the Spirit on his people and that this outpouring is proof of his enthronement. The OT reserved the role for the pouring out of the Spirit to God alone (Isa 44:3; Ezek 39:19; Joel 2:28-29; cf. Acts 2:17-18). In pouring out God's Spirit, Christ, as God's royal agent, fulfills an explicitly divine role.[188] Peter's declaration then represents a higher development of Jewish royal ideology. Christ is not only endowed with God's Spirit, but, as the divine one himself, proves his divine kingship by pouring out God's Spirit himself. Fourth, Peter ends his sermon by depicting Christ as one who has been brought from obscurity to kingship. Jesus was the one whom the Jews crucified, yet God has now declared him to be both Lord and Christ (Acts 2:36). As the Christ, Jesus fulfills the Davidic-messianic hope, and as the Lord, the fulfillment of this hope is revealed to be the divine one himself.[189]

Hebrews presents two passages which make explicit connections between Jesus and Jewish regal ideology. Hebrews 1:1-13 makes several explicit connections between Jesus and the ideal Davidic king. The writer identifies Jesus as God's Son whom he has appointed to be the heir of all things (Heb 1:2). The writer connects Jesus to the son spoken of in Ps 2:7 and 2 Sam 7:14 (Heb 1:2, 5). Given this context, part of Jesus' inheritance is the throne for the promised Davidic king.[190] The writer clearly views Jesus as the one who fulfills the Davidic hope and explains the various ways Jesus fulfills the role of God's king.

First, Jesus has a rightful claim to kingship because he serves as God's agent (δι' οὗ) in creation. The writer's peculiar use of the plural

---

Messiah, 142-43).

187. There may also be traces of Sinai-Moses themes in this declaration (Turner, *Power from High*, 267; Bock, *Acts*, 131-32; Keener, *Acts*, 958-59).

188. Keener, *Acts*, 957. Turner argues that the church's understanding of Christ as the one who pours out God's Spirit was a key factor in attributing divinity to him (Turner, "Spirit of Christ," 168-90).

189. Bock, *Acts*, 136-37 and Keener, *Acts*, 963.

190. Given the reference to Ps 2 in v. 5, it is possible that the κληρονόμος is an allusion to the inheritance of God's appointed king spoken of in Ps 2:8 (Ellingworth, *Hebrews*, 94-95; McDonough, *Christ as Creator*, 192-93).

αἰῶνας suggests that he views Jesus' creative role extending from original creation to new creation (Heb 1:2).[191] Jesus' role in creation serves as necessary background for the understanding of his kingship. The cosmic throne Jesus receives is one that has always been rightfully his because of his work in creating the cosmos. Second, the writer views Jesus' earthly work as the affirmation of his enthronement and inauguration of his kingship (Heb 1:3). Third, God's enthronement of Christ at his right hand affirms Christ's rightful claim to cosmic kingship. The writer alludes to Ps 109:1 LXX in v. 3 and quotes it in v. 13 to emphasize God's initiative in appointing Jesus to cosmic kingship. Fourth, God appointed Christ to the cosmic throne as part of his plan to restore his good rule throughout the cosmos. As a result, Christ shares in God's cosmic rule. As God's appointed King, Christ mediates the glory and presence of God throughout the cosmos because he himself is divine (Heb 1:3a).[192] He does this by using his power to uphold the cosmos.[193] Additionally, the writer's allusion to 2 Sam 7:14 (Heb 1:5) and his use of many royal Psalms (Heb 1:5 [Ps 2]; 1:8–9 [Ps 45]; Heb 1:3, 13 [Ps 110]) indicates that God always planned to appoint a king over the cosmos and that his readers should have expected Christ's cosmic enthronement all along.[194] The writer also describes the rule of Christ by citing Ps 45:6–7 (Heb 1:8–9) and Ps 102:25–27 (Heb 1:10–12). Both Psalms originally describe the rule of God, but the writer attributes them to Christ's rule. Such attribution indicates that Heb 1 does not depict Jesus as simply ruling under God but with God. Christ's regal authority is one that uniquely belongs to him and extends over the whole cosmos, including the angels (Heb 1:4–6, 13).[195]

Hebrews 2:5–9 depicts Jesus' kingship over the cosmos using Adamic language, specifically by citing Ps 8:4–6. In returning to the theme of Jesus' superiority over the angels (Heb 2:5), the writer presents

---

191. McDonough, *Christ as Creator*, 200–204.

192. On the glory of God referring to his presence, see Buchanan, *Hebrews*, 6. The language, especially the word χαρακτήρ, is similar to the conception of Jesus as God's εἰκών (Ellingworth, *Hebrews*, 98–99).

193. This role is indicated by the phrase φέρων τε τὰ πάντα τῷ ῥήματι τῆς δυνάμεως αὐτοῦ. On the various possibilities for the meaning of the participle φέρων, see Ellingworth, *Hebrews*, 100–101.

194. Compton, *Psalm 110*, 22. For a full discussion on how the writer of Hebrews interprets the various OT passages cited in Heb 1, see Docherty, *Old Testament in Hebrews*, 144–81.

195. Compton, *Psalm 110*, 20.

Jesus as the true fulfillment of Ps 8.[196] One should note two reasons for the writer's use of Ps 8 in describing Christ's cosmic kingship. First, the writer reemphasizes the cosmic scope of Christ's authority (Heb 2:8). The writer makes the point positively by citing the language of Ps 8:6[197] and negatively in his comment on the text.[198] This authority is even greater than Adam's authority because it includes not only physical creation but the entirety of the cosmos. Second, the writer makes the point that Christ had to humiliate himself and suffer death to accomplish salvation for all (Heb 2:9). As a result, Christ has been crowned with glory and honor. The implication is that Christ regained the authority over creation that Adam lost. When drawn together with the picture of Christ's kingship in Heb 1 using royal Psalms, "the writer presents Jesus not only as having dominion over creation (as was God's intention for humankind according to Gen 1:26 and Ps 8) but also as the ruler of the cosmos."[199]

SUMMARY AND CONCLUSIONS

The NT consistently depicts Jesus as the one who fulfills the role of God's ideal king over the cosmos. The claims of Jesus in the Gospels (especially his "Son of Man" sayings) suggest that he understood himself to be the King through whom God would reestablish cosmic order. Jesus claims that he would be enthroned by God himself and would be endowed with divine glory. Further, Jesus claims that he rightfully shares in the divine throne and in God's rule over the cosmos. He describes his enthronement and eventual parousia as the events which signal the reestablishment of God's kingdom over the cosmos. At points, Jesus depicts himself as one who would have authority to command angels, which validates the cosmic scope of his authority. He also claims that he would carry out judgment upon the wicked and vindication for the righteous, thus fulfilling the role of royal judge. The birth narratives affirm both Jesus' divine origin and his legal claim to the Davidic throne. Jesus' baptism presents a royal pronouncement in which God declares Jesus to be his son. John's depiction of Jesus as the preexistent Creator validates Jesus' right to the divine throne

---

196. The writer indicates this with a change from the aorist participles ἠλάττωσας and ἐστεφάνωσας in Heb 2:7 to the perfect participles ἠλαττωμένον and ἐστεφανωμένον in Heb 2:9 (Ellingworth, *Hebrews*, 150).

197. πάντα ὑπέταξας ὑποκάτω τῶν ποδῶν αὐτοῦ (Heb 2:8a).

198. οὐδὲν ἀφῆκεν αὐτῷ ἀνυπότακτον (Heb 2:8b).

199. Grenz, "Jesus as *Imago Dei*," 619. See also Buchanan, *Hebrews*, 28.

and suggests that his coming kingdom would be one that exceeds typical sociopolitical categories. For Jesus, "the Son of God" is more than a regal title—it is an ontological description of his relationship to God. While Jesus lays rightful claim to the throne of God's ideal king, he achieves his enthronement over the cosmos through his death and resurrection.

Paul picks up these regal themes as he portrays Christ's cosmic kingship in his own letters. Paul's understanding of Christ's position in the cosmos both aligns and further develops ancient Jewish conceptions of God's ideal king. More explicitly than the Gospels, Paul sees Christ and his dominion as the antitype to Adam and his dominion. Whereas Adam's original dominion extended only over the physical creation, Christ's dominion extends over the whole cosmos. Whereas Adam's failure had catastrophic effects on the cosmos, Christ's enthronement brings the promise of the renewal of the cosmos. Whereas Adam's disobedience resulted in the loss of his position as God's ideal king, Christ's obedience resulted in his enthronement to a cosmic throne that was rightfully his from the beginning. Whereas Adam's failure subjected the creation/cosmos under the rule of hostile cosmic powers, Christ's enthronement liberates the creation/cosmos from the reign of these hostile cosmic powers and restores God's good rule over the cosmos. Whereas those who are under the dominion of Adam share in Adam's fate (death), those under the dominion of Christ share in Christ's fate (life).

Paul also viewed Jesus as the fulfillment of the messianic promise that God would reestablish his good order over the cosmos through the enthronement of his ideal king. Paul presents several crucial aspects of Christ's cosmic enthronement: First, Christ's lineage from the line of David gives him a rightful claim to the throne reserved for the ideal Davidic king. Second, Christ's cosmic throne is one that has always been rightfully his. Paul presents Jesus as God's agent in creation and as one who is and has always been equal with God. While Jewish royal ideology at times hints at the preexistence of God's ideal king, Paul presents Christ preexistence in more explicit terms and views his equality with God as essential to his right to rule the cosmos. Such a realization does not contradict Jewish conceptions of God's ideal king but serves to reveal in more explicit terms the identity of God's ideal king. Third, God is the one who has willfully chosen to exalt Christ to his right hand. Fourth, while Christ's cosmic throne has always been rightfully his, God enthrones him as a result of his self-humiliation, obedience to death, and his resurrection. These themes parallel a common Jewish regal motif in which God exalts his king from obscurity to kingship. Fifth, Christ's enthronement signals the subjection of everything in the cosmos and the defeat of every hostile cosmic power. God subordinates every cosmic power under the feet of Jesus. Through this subordination, not only will Jesus be exalted above everything in the cosmos, but God will once again make his glory known throughout the cosmos. In Paul's mind, God's original plan to subdue creation under his first king, Adam, and his promise to reestablish his dominion through the messianic king from David are fully realized in Christ's cosmic enthronement.

One may draw a few implications from this chapter: First, Jewish royal ideology provides a helpful framework through which one can understand NT conceptions of Christ's cosmic position. Second, and more specifically, Paul's understanding of Adam's original position in creation and of the ideal Davidic king provides plausible linguistic and conceptual frameworks that helped him form his conceptions of Christ's regal position over the cosmos. If this is the case, these frameworks may prove to be helpful in explaining the cosmic Christology of Colossians and Ephesians. Third, the idea of Christ as one who preexists, creates, and reigns over the cosmos is not unique to Colossians and Ephesians. While it may not necessarily be the major theological theme of every Pauline letter, Christ's cosmic kingship certainly aligns with the Christology of the undisputed Pauline letters. If this is the case, it may be more accurate to view the cosmic Christology of Colossians and Ephesians as providing further explanation of Paul's own cosmic Christology.

4

Cosmic Christ in Colossians

CHRIST'S POSITION AND ROLE in the cosmos becomes a major point of discussion in Paul's letter to the Colossians.[1] As with discussions on cosmic Christology in Paul's letters and in the NT, previous discussions regarding the cosmic Christology of Colossians tend to emphasize the role of either Hellenistic philosophy or Jewish conceptions of personified Wisdom. But given the influence of Jewish royal ideology on other cosmic christological texts in the NT, one should wonder whether Jewish royal ideology, particularly through the lens of the Adamic and Davidic king, may provide further insight into the background of the cosmic Christology in Colossians. This chapter will cover passages in Colossians that define Christ's role in the cosmos and explain his overall relationship with the cosmos. Specifically, this chapter will examine whether Paul utilizes any Adamic or Davidic themes as he articulates his own cosmic Christology. One should note that Paul does not explicitly mention Adam or David within the letter, but this does not mean that Paul could not have made implicit references to these figures. Paul's various allusions to Jewish regal texts and themes within the letter make it probable that his cosmic Christology was indeed heavily influenced by Jewish royal ideology. This assertion counters (1) Kooten's argument that Colossians presents an over-hellenized version of Pauline Christology[2] and (2) the

1. On Pauline authorship of Colossians, see ch. 1, 15n79.
2. The reasons for engaging extensively with Kooten's work were addressed in ch. 1.

argument for Jewish Wisdom as the primary influencer of the cosmic Christology in the letter.

COLOSSIANS 1:12-20

Kooten begins his study of Colossians by examining the concept of σῶμα in Col 2:8—3:4. He bases his entire study upon the idea that this passage serves as the center of the letter and that σῶμα is central to the passage.[3] This hermeneutical move significantly influences his interpretation of the letter. However, it seems Kooten reads the letter backwards because Col 1:15–20 provides the crucial christological foundation upon which Paul builds his argument of Col 2:8—3:4. The hymn describes Christ's relationship with the cosmos perhaps more explicitly than any other passage in Paul's writings. While most other scholars begin their examination of Colossian cosmic Christology with the hymn, there is a curious tendency to give insufficient discussion to Col 1:12–14.[4] These verses serve as a "prologue" to the Colossian hymn and provide key context for identifying potential conceptual backgrounds for the hymn.[5] The Colossian hymn builds on Paul's explanation of Christ's place in the cosmos in vv. 12–14.[6] Isolating the hymn from the context provided by these verses can lead to erroneous arguments regarding the background of the hymn.

---

3. Kooten, *Cosmic Christology*, 11–13.

4. For example, Tuckett argues that the opening of the hymn does not easily relate grammatically to vv. 12–14 (Tuckett, *Christology*, 75). Wright merely notes the Exodus motif in vv. 12–14 but fails to give significant discussion to the royal connotations of these verses and how they shape one's understanding of the hymn itself (Wright, *Climax of the Covenant*, 109). Beetham, who acknowledges the royal background of vv. 12–14, merely makes a passing reference to v. 14 before quickly attributing the hymn to personified Wisdom in Prov 8 (Beetham, *Echoes*, 131–32). In a recent exegetical discussion, Janusz Krecidlo concedes that the context of these verses "determines the main line of meaning for the interpretation of individual expressions contained in the hymn" (Krecidlo, "Reconciliation," 1137). He then proceeds to do almost no exegetical work on vv. 12–14.

5. This is not to suggest that Col 1:12–14 should be considered part of the hymn itself. Eduard Schweizer has argued that vv. 13–14 could have been part of the original poem that would have been recited or sung in early congregational settings (Schweizer, *Colossians*, 298–300). Wright points out the awkwardness of trying to fit these verses within the poetic structure of the Colossian hymn (Wright, *Climax of the Covenant*, 100).

6. Fee, "Old Testament Intertextuality," 202–3.

The Royal Prologue: Colossians 1:12–14

Colossians 1:12–14 serves as a "hinge" text that both concludes Paul's prayer of thanksgiving[7] and introduces the christological confession in vv. 15–20.[8] The story of cosmic Christ in Colossians does not begin in Col 1:15–20 but in Col 1:12–14. These verses represent a shift in focus from what God has done on behalf of believers to what Christ has accomplished. The "beloved Son" in v. 13 is the clear antecedent of the relative pronoun at the opening of the Colossian hymn. The Colossian hymn shifts the focus from who Christ is in relation to believers to who he is in relation to the cosmos.[9] Thus, recognizing the christological themes in vv. 12–14 should affect how one interprets the cosmic Christology of the Colossian hymn.

Paul suggests that to walk worthy of the Lord (Col 1:10)[10] means expressing gratefulness to God's granting the Colossians a part in the inheritance of his people (Col 1:12). Paul describes how God qualified the Colossians for such an inheritance. Paul declares that the Colossian believers have been delivered from the dominion of darkness and into the kingdom of Christ (Col 1:13). Paul's declaration implies the presence of two dominions within the cosmos. One is a domain ruled by darkness, by which Paul was most likely referring to cosmic, spiritual powers standing firmly against God and his people.[11] The second domain is ruled by Christ, the beloved Son of God. The implication is that these two

---

7. The participle εὐχαριστοῦντες (v. 12) functions adverbially along with the preceding participles (vv. 10–11) to describe the manner in which the Colossian believers were to walk (Moule, *Colossians and Philemon*, 55; Gibbs, *Creation and Redemption*, 101; Dunn, *Colossians and Philemon*, 75).

8. Käsemann argues that the author of Colossians joined vv. 12–14 with vv. 15–20 to form a redacted baptismal liturgy. In this case, the participle εὐχαριστοῦντες is a technical term used to introduce a liturgical confession (Käsemann, "Baptismal Liturgy," 149–68). While this argument is attractive, Käsemann's view falls short for three reasons. First, vv. 12–14 speak about the church while vv. 15–20 focus on the cosmos. Second, the use of the second-person plural in v. 12 with a switch to the first-person plural in v. 13 would be highly unusual in confessional material. Third, the technical use of the participle has been heavily disputed (Deichgräber, *Gotteshmnus*, 145; O'Brien, *Introductory Thanksgivings*, 73–74). For a full argument against Käsemann's view, see Sappington, *Revelation and Redemption*, 193–96.

9. Fee, "Old Testament Intertextuality," 202–4.

10. The infinitive περιπατῆσαι could indicate purpose or result. The difference is minimal, but given the exhortatory nature of Paul's prayer, it seems that the infinitive most likely indicates purpose.

11. Bruce, *Colossians*, 51, and Fee, "Old Testament Intertextuality," 206.

dominions stand against each other. Paul utilizes exodus imagery/language to illustrate the transfer of believers into the kingdom of Christ. Paul's language concerning the believers' inheritance (τὴν μερίδα τοῦ κλήρου) and their deliverance (ἐρρύσατο . . . ἀπολύτρωσιν) has significant linguistic ties to the OT exodus (Exod 6:6–8; 14:30; Deut 10:9; 15:15).[12] Just as God's people were delivered from the oppressive regime in Egypt and were brought into the land of promise, so now God has delivered the Colossian believers from the oppressive dominion of darkness into the kingdom of Christ. This language also alludes to the new exodus found in Isaiah (Isa 11:10–16; 42:6–7, 16; 43:16–21).[13] Isaiah 11 and 42 are of particular significance as both passages link this new exodus with the arrival of God's ideal king (Isa 11:1–9; 42:1–5). The implication is that the arrival of God's king inaugurates the new exodus in which God's people are once again delivered and redeemed.[14]

In a similar fashion, Paul conjoins the exodus imagery with an allusion to the ideal Davidic king. The relationship between the Father (τῷ πατρὶ) and his Son (τοῦ υἱοῦ . . . αὐτοῦ) parallels the father-son relationship God promised to have with David's royal descendant (2 Sam 7:14; Pss 2:7; 89:27). That the Son is beloved (τῆς ἀγάπης) parallels David's own declaration in which he praises God for his love for his household and him (2 Sam 7:18). Paul indicates that the beloved Son possesses a kingdom (βασιλείαν) given to him by the Father, which parallels God's promise to establish the kingdom of David's royal descendant (2 Sam 7:12–13; Pss 2:6; 89:20–22; 132:10, 17). This allusion indicates that Paul utilizes the title of "Son" as "covenant language and a royal title for the kings of the promised Davidic lineage."[15] Further, this allusion reveals Paul's own presupposition that Christ is the fulfillment of the promised Davidic king and that he is the agent through whom God brings about the redemption of his people (Col 1:14).[16]

---

12. For more on the Exodus motif in this passage, see Wright, *Colossians*, 61–63; Barth and Blanke, *Colossians*, 188, 90; Dunn, *Colossians and Philemon*, 74–77, 80; Fee, "Old Testament Intertextuality," 205–6; Beetham, *Echoes*, 81–95; and Beale, *Colossians and Philemon*, 62–68. Fee notes that Joshua repeatedly uses both μερίς (eleven times) and κλῆρος (thirty times) to refer to the apportioning of the land.

13. Beetham, *Echoes*, 86–87, and Beale, *Colossians and Philemon*, 63–65. See also ch. 2.

14. For more on the new Exodus motif in Col 1:12–14, see Shogren, "Presently Entering the Kingdom of Christ," 176–77.

15. Beetham, *Echoes*, 109.

16. Beetham, *Echoes*, 112, and Jipp, *Christ is King*, 102–3.

In summary, Paul prays that God would fill the Colossian believers with the knowledge of his will, along with the Spirit who gives wisdom and understanding (Col 1:9–10). Paul prays this confidently because believers already have access to all these things through their relationship to Christ the King. Paul then exhorts these believers to express their thankfulness to God because he has brought about a spiritual exodus in which the believers are no longer under the domain of darkness but have instead been placed in the kingdom of Christ. Christ then serves as the one who fulfills the Davidic covenant and the role of God's royal agent. These royal themes serve as a vital setup for the christological confession in Col 1:15–20 and must be considered in any interpretation of the hymn. Put simply, Paul declares how Christ's kingship brings redemption to believers in vv. 12–14 and then expands on the identity of Christ the King and the scope of his kingship in vv. 15–20.

The Royal Confession: Colossians 1:15–20

Colossians 1:15–20 appears to be an example of hymnic poetry. Many scholars seek a *Sitz im Leben* for this text.[17] However, considering the difficulty of reconstructing a *Sitz im Leben* without any textual evidence, it is perhaps better to treat this text as a Pauline composition that adapts and elaborates on Jewish (and possibly some Hellenistic) traditions.[18] The passage may also be properly labeled as an encomium, which was some sort of song/hymn of praise for an extraordinary figure.[19] While there have been numerous discussions regarding the structure of the hymn, most scholars agree that the hymn should be divided into two strophes.[20] The first strophe (Col 1:15–17) presents Christ as God's agent of creation, and the second strophe (Col 1:18–20) presents Christ as God's agent of redemption.[21]

17. Käsemann, "Baptismal Liturgy," 149–68; Aletti, *Colossiens 1,15–20*; Lohse, *Colossians*, 46–61; and Dunn, *Colossians*, 86–104.

18. Balchin, "Colossians 1:15–20," 65–93; Barth and Blanke, *Colossians*, 235; Helyer, "Cosmic Christology," 235–46; Dübbers, *Christologie*, 86–92; Smith, *Heavenly Perspective*, 158; Gordley, *Christological Hymns*, 118–19; and Krecidlo, "Reconciliation," 1136.

19. Krecidlo, "Reconciliation," 1135. For a full discussion on the use of encomiums in praise to rulers and kings within Hellenism and Judaism, see Jipp, *Christ Is King*, 81–100.

20. For a full discussion on the structure of the hymn, see Wright, "Poetry and Theology," 444–51; Smith, *Heavenly Perspective*, 153–59; Pizzuto, *Cosmic Leap*, 97–156; and Gordley, *Colossian Hymn*, 170–229.

21. Wright provides perhaps the most influential discussion regarding the structure

Cosmic Christ as King over Creation (Col 1:15–17)

Building on his earlier proclamation of Christ's royal identity (Col 1:13), Paul begins his christological confession by declaring Christ to be the image (εἰκών) of the invisible God and the firstborn (πρωτότοκος) of all creation (Col 1:15). Scholars have long debated whether Paul's use of εἰκών and πρωτότοκος alludes to Jewish conceptions of personified Wisdom or to the creation of Adam in Gen 1:26–27.[22] Many scholars will suggest that both motifs are present, but one is subservient to the other.[23] The majority opinion seems to lie with Hellenistic-Jewish ideas of personified Wisdom as the primary source of Paul's language. Dunn argues that the Hellenistic-Jewish Wisdom background "is a matter of broad consensus."[24] This current study, along with some recent scholarship,[25] aims to challenge this consensus. Therefore, before examining Paul's possible use of Adamic language in his description of cosmic Christ, it will be prudent to examine the arguments made for Jewish Wisdom as the primary explainer of Paul's language in this hymn.

The argument for Wisdom arises from a supposed link between the Colossian hymn, Prov 8:22–31, and the developments of this tradition in Jewish Wisdom writings.[26] One can summarize the argument for

---

of the hymn where he identifies the hymn as following a chiastic ABBA structure. In this case, each section begins with a christological title. Thus, one can divide the hymn as follows: (A) "who is the image ... the firstborn" (Col 1:15–16); (B) "He is before all things" (Col 1:17); (B) "He is the head" (Col 1:18a); (A) "who is the beginning" (Col 1:18b–20); see Wright, "Poetry and Theology," 444–51. For the purposes of the present study, this section will cover the hymn using the simple two strophe division.

22. Käsemann has argued for the gnostic redeemer myth as the primary source behind this hymn (Käsemann, "Baptismal Liturgy," 149–68). However, Käsemann's argument is no longer considered to be tenable as most scholars view Christian Gnosticism as a development that occurred after the writing of Colossians. For a full argument against Käsemann, see Yamauchi, "Alleged Evidences," 46–70.

23. For example, Grant Macaskill suggests that the Colossian hymn is not devoid of allusions to Gen 1 but that Wisdom should be viewed as the primary background (Macaskill, "Union(s)," 93–95).

24. Dunn, *Colossians and Philemon*, 86n8.

25. Scholars who have challenged this view include Ridderbos, *Paul*, 79–80; McDonough, *Christ as Creator*, 175–79; Dunne, "Regal Status" 3–18; Fee, *Pauline Christology*, 601; Jipp, *Christ Is King*, 101–6; Leese, *Christ*, 111–13; and Northcutt, "King of Kings," 205–24.

26. C. F. Burney is one of the earliest modern scholars to make this connection, and many arguments for Prov 8:22–31 as the primary background of the hymn have developed from his original article (Burney, "Christ as the ΑΡΧΗ," 160–77). Dunn provides the fullest and most well-known articulation of this argument (Dunn, *Christology in*

Wisdom under three primary points. First, scholars argue that both the Colossian hymn and Wisdom traditions use similar language in presenting a secondary figure who was present at the beginning of creation.[27] Speaking in the first person in Prov 8, Wisdom extols herself as being created[28] and established before the beginning (ἀρχή) of creation (Prov 8:22–26). Wisdom also claims that she was present with God as he created the world (Prov 8:27–29). Similar language concerning Wisdom's creation and existence before creation occurs elsewhere in early Jewish literature (Sir 1:4, 24:9; Wis 9:9). Second, scholars point to early Jewish texts which suggest Wisdom's involvement/agency in creation. Both Wisdom of Solomon and Philo seem to suggest that Wisdom had agency in creation (Wis 7:22; 8:4–6; 9:1–2; Philo, *Det.* 54).[29] Third, Wisdom advocates argue that the titles attributed to Christ in the Colossian hymn find their source in Jewish sayings about Wisdom. Proverbs 8 refers to Wisdom as "the beginning" (ἀρχή, Prov 8:22 LXX) and contains several mentions of her existence "before" (πρό) creation (Prov 8:23–27 LXX). Some scholars suggest that Paul's use of "firstborn" (πρωτότοκος, Col 1:15) echoes the "before" language of Prov 8.[30] Wisdom is called the "image [εἰκών] of his [God's] goodness" (Wis 7:26). Philo refers to Wisdom as both "the beginning" and "the image" (Philo, *Leg.* 1:43). Scholars also cite Philo's various uses of the title "firstborn" in relation to God's Word and reason, language that for Philo is interchangeable with Wisdom (Philo, *Conf.* 146; *Agr.* 51; *Somn.* 1.215; QG 4:97).[31]

Despite the wide acceptance for Wisdom as the primary background for the Colossian hymn, serious questions remain regarding the arguments listed above. On the first argument, it is certainly true that Judaism speaks of Wisdom being present with God at creation. However,

---

the Making, 163–96). Beetham argues that Paul does not allude to Prov 8:22–31 "in a strict sense, but rather to it in its first century CE interpretive development" (Beetham, *Echoes*, 113).

27. Gordley, *Colossian Hymn*, 67.

28. While the Hebrew verb קנה in Prov 8:22 can be translated as "possessed," the LXX uses the verb κτίζω, suggesting that Wisdom was created before the earth itself.

29. Some scholars will argue that Prov 8:30 contains a reference to Wisdom's agency in creation (for example, Witherington, *Jesus the Sage*, 612). However, such an interpretation serves as weak evidence given the ambiguity of the Hebrew term אָמוֹן and the equally ambiguous Greek participle ἁρμόζουσα used in the LXX.

30. Lohse, *Colossians*, 48; Dunn, *Colossians and Philemon*, 90; Beetham, *Echoes*, 133; and Krecidlo, "Reconciliation," 1139.

31. Lohse, *Colossians*, 48; Dunn, *Colossians and Philemon*, 90; Beetham, *Echoes*, 133; and Gordley, *Christological Hymns*, 125.

these texts clearly view Wisdom as a creation of God. Wisdom proclaims to have been created by God in Prov 8:22 LXX (Κύριος ἔκτισέν με ἀρχὴν) and in Sir 24:9 (ἀπ' ἀρχῆς ἔκτισεν με; see also Sir 1:4, 9). As will be seen below, the Christ hymn in no way indicates that Christ is the first created being. Serious questions also remain about whether the authors of these texts viewed Wisdom as a divine hypostasis or as a simple personification of a divine attribute.[32] The result is that "a sizeable distinction emerges between the comparison of Christ, a person, with Wisdom, a personification."[33] One should also note that no Jewish source presents a connection between personified Wisdom and the messiah.[34] That Christ is a person and not simply a personified attribute of God makes the identification between Christ and personified Wisdom more complicated than some scholars suggest.

The second argument might be the strongest and most important argument regarding Paul's potential use of Wisdom language. Christ's agency in creation seems to be the primary motivation for scholars turning to Wisdom motifs. Therefore, "the relationship of Wisdom to creation . . . is singularly the one point at which the whole enterprise found its origins and continues to find support in the literature."[35] Despite attempts to identify Wisdom as an agent in creation, the instances in which one could possibly interpret personified Wisdom as such remain ambiguous. While Prov 8:22–31 clearly speaks of personified Wisdom's presence at creation, the text does not clearly communicate that Wisdom was an active agent in the creation process. Sirach 24 only expresses concern for Wisdom's finding her place in creation (Sir 24:8) but does not suggest that she was an agent in creation. The strongest evidence for Wisdom's potential agency in creation may be found in Wisdom of Solomon (Wis. Sol. 7:22; 8:4–6; 9:9),

---

32. Fee, *Pauline Christology*, 607–9. Dunn himself hesitates to call these uses of Wisdom as a divine hypostasis and suggests that it should be consistently understood as personification within Judaism. However, he still suggests that these instances of personified Wisdom inform Paul's ideas regarding Christ's preexistence (Dunn, *Christology in the Making*, 170–76). The problem with such an assertion is that it is difficult to see how language concerning a personified attribute of God could possibly serve as the foundation of Paul's view of Christ's preexistence.

33. Dunne, "Regal Status," 5–6.

34. Ridderbos, *Paul*, 79. This is contra to Christian Stettler who tries to argue for a connection between Wisdom and the messiah in the Enoch tradition (Stettler, *Kolosserhymnus*, 337).

35. Fee, *Pauline Christology*, 609. See also Northcutt, "King of Kings," 208–9, who suggests that this is the driving motivation for finding Wisdom rather than any linguistic correlation.

but even these texts are highly ambiguous.³⁶ While the Colossian hymn states that all things were created "in [ἐν] ... through [δι'] ... and for [εἰς]" Christ (Col 1:16), Wisdom literature does not use this combination of prepositions to describe Wisdom's role in creation. More specifically, the preposition διά, which would most clearly communicate agency, never appears in Wisdom literature to describe Wisdom's relationship to creation, and no text indicates that God created the world "for" Wisdom.³⁷

The third argument proves to be the most susceptible to criticism and seriously calls into question whether Wisdom should be considered as the primary background of the Colossian hymn. While it is true that Wisdom is given the title of "image" (εἰκών), Jewish literature never calls her the "image of God" but only the "image of God's goodness." Such language presents "God's wisdom as 'reflected' in his goodness."³⁸ There is a significant difference between imaging a characteristic of God and bearing the actual image of God, a point some Wisdom proponents conveniently ignore.³⁹ Perhaps the more puzzling correlation made by Wisdom proponents is the supposed connection between "firstborn" (πρωτότοκος) and Jewish descriptions of Wisdom. Proverbs 8, the primary OT passage used to argue for the influence of Wisdom, never refers to Wisdom as the "firstborn" of creation.⁴⁰ Rather, Wisdom proponents strain to make a connection between the *before* language of Prov 8 and the use of πρωτότοκος in Col 1:15. Furthermore, the *before* language used in Prov 8 clearly refers to God's creating of Wisdom before all things, a meaning that is absent from the Colossian hymn. Jewish literature never uses the word πρωτότοκος in reference to divine Wisdom. Wisdom proponents call upon evidence in Philo,⁴¹ but Philo never uses the

---

36. Fee, *Pauline Christology*, 613–18.

37. Fee, *Pauline Christology*, 616; Bird, *Colossians and Philemon*, 148–49; and Sappington, *Revelation and Redemption*, 174.

38. Fee, *Pauline Christology*, 601.

39. For instance, Dunn mentions that Wisdom is called "the image of God's goodness" but does not explain why this title should correlate with Paul calling Christ the actual "image of God." He simply rules out the correlation to Adam because of v. 16 (Dunn, *Christology in the Making*, 188–89). After acknowledging that this title "does ultimately derive from Genesis 1:26–27," Beetham goes on to argue that the allusion should still be considered first as an allusion to divine Wisdom with Gen 1 as an echo in the background (Beetham, *Echoes*, 131–32). But if Paul wished to allude primarily to the Wisdom tradition, why did he explicitly use the language of Gen 1?

40. Fossum, *Image*, 24.

41. Dunn, *Colossians and Philemon*, 89–90; Beetham, *Echoes*, 133; and Krecidlo, "Reconciliation," 1139.

word πρωτότοκος in reference to Wisdom. Scholars suggest that Philo's description of the Logos as God's firstborn provides the link between πρωτότοκος and Wisdom since, as the argument goes, Wisdom and Logos are interchangeable terms/ideas for Philo. However, the actual word used by Philo is πρωτόγονος and is accompanied by the word "son" (Philo, *Agr.* 51; *Conf.* 146; *Somn.* 1.215; *QG* 4.97).[42] The fact that divine Wisdom is described using feminine terms makes this connection even more difficult to make. Therefore, the linguistic connection that supposedly exists between πρωτότοκος and Jewish Wisdom imagery is tenuous at best and altogether absent at worst.[43] All of the above objections do not necessarily discount any reminiscences of Wisdom imagery in Colossians, but it does suggest that viewing Wisdom as the primary source of Paul's language in the Colossian hymn remains highly problematic.

Upon closer examination, it appears that both the descriptions of Christ as the "image of God" and the "firstborn" have highly regal connotations. Paul begins his hymn of praise by referring to the royal beloved Son as "the image of the invisible God." The likely allusion for this title is Gen 1:26–27 for a few reasons. First, the antecedent of the relative pronoun ὅς in v. 15 and the pronouns that appear through the rest of the hymn are not "Wisdom" but the beloved Son in v. 13. This beloved Son is clearly presented as a royal figure since he is the one to whom God's kingdom belongs. Paul's use of exodus and royal Davidic language in vv. 12–14 suggests that he is reflecting upon Israel's story. Israel's story grounds the hope for restoration in the arrival of God's ideal king.[44] Wisdom proponents seemingly ignore this context,[45] but such strong regal

---

42. Fee, *Pauline Christology*, 320–21.

43. Ridderbos also notes that words such as image, firstborn, and beginning had a wide circulation and variety of uses within Jewish literature, which makes it unnecessary for Paul to be dependent upon Philo. He also cites fundamental material differences between Philo's speculations concerning the Logos and Paul's christological pronouncements in Colossians (Ridderbos, *Paul*, 80).

44. Dunne, "Regal Status," 10–11, and McDonough, *Christ as Creator*, 180–82.

45. For instance, Dunn simply argues that v. 16 disproves any potential allusion to Adam, but he does not consider how the context of vv. 12–14 might affect one's interpretation of the hymn (Dunn, *Christology*, 188). Both Beetham and Macaskill acknowledge "the beloved Son" as the antecedent but do not consider how this might affect their own interpretation of the hymn. Beetham goes so far as to acknowledge the potential royal connotations of πρωτότοκος but discounts it on account of v. 16 (Beetham, *Echoes*, 131–34; Macaskill, "Union(s)," 95).

imagery provides critical context for identifying the regal themes that appear in the Christ hymn.[46]

Second, the actual language of v. 15 (εἰκὼν τοῦ θεοῦ) more closely aligns with the language of Gen 1 (κατ' εἰκόνα θεοῦ, Gen 1:27 LXX) than any language in Wisdom literature.[47] In Gen 1:26-28, God's creation of Adam in "the image of God" suggests that God designated Adam as his original royal representative. God commissioned Adam to rule over and subdue the earth.[48] Paul also uses the combination of the terms εἰκών and πρωτότοκος in Rom 8:29, a passage which draws upon Adam and the creation story.[49] Thus, in presenting Christ as "the image of God," Paul not only places Christ in the position that Adam once possessed but demonstrates the ways in which Christ's rule and dominion far exceed the rule and dominion of Adam.

Third, Paul's allusion to Gen 1:26-27 in Col 1:15 correlates with his Adam Christology in his other letters. Paul previously states that believers have been transferred from the dominion of darkness to the dominion of Christ (Col 1:13). The contrast between these two dominions is reminiscent of his Adam-Christ statements in which Adam's reign ushered in the rule of sin and death while Christ's reign brought life (1 Cor 15:21-22; Rom 5:12-21).[50] This dominion of darkness directly resulted from Adam's failure as God's first king. As in previous examples of Paul's Adam Christology, Paul also presents Christ as superior to Adam. Many Wisdom proponents suggest that Paul's presentation of Christ as the Creator of the cosmos discounts or diminishes the possibility of an Adam Christology, but one of the main points of Paul's own Adam Christology is to present Christ as far superior to Adam. By presenting Christ as preexistent Creator, Paul demonstrates Christ's ability to undo the effects of Adam's reign and Christ's authority over the whole cosmos, which exceeds the authority given to Adam at creation. Christ's identity as the preexistent Creator makes him both the archetype after which Adam was created and the ideal antitype to Adam. The implication is that "Adam himself was a copy of Christ, the genuine image of God, and thus

---

46. Dunne, "Regal Status," 8, and Jipp, *Christ Is King*, 101.

47. Some scholars argue that the chiastic structure of the hymn itself is a midrashic exposition on Gen 1:1 (Manns, "Col. 1,15-20," 100-110; Smith, *Heavenly Perspective*, 156).

48. See the full discussion on Adam as God's first king in ch. 2.

49. See ch. 3.

50. See ch. 3.

his dominion was a copy of the absolute dominion exercised by God's anointed one."[51]

Paul emphasizes Christ's superiority over the whole cosmos with the addition of the genitive descriptor "invisible" (ἀοράτου). It is true that Christ is the visible manifestation of God himself, and one could argue that this descriptor simply assigns a revelatory function to the title "image of God."[52] Proponents of a Wisdom background suggest that as Wisdom is the agent through which God makes himself known, Christ as the "image of God" mediates the knowledge of God.[53] However, the adjective "invisible" does not just describe God as sensually unknowable but also serves to differentiate the transcendent God from the material creation and all other cosmic powers.[54] Given the regal connotations of the term εἰκών, to describe Christ as the "image of the invisible God" is to designate him as the royal ambassador of the one God who is supreme over all creation, meaning that he has the right to exercise regal authority over all things in the cosmos. As Adam served as God's visible, royal representative at creation, so Christ, in his humanity, took up and exceeds Adam's role as God's visible, royal representative over the whole cosmos. Christ's royal function then accounts for his revelatory function.[55]

The second title "firstborn" affirms the regal connotation of the first title "image of God." In broad terms, the title πρωτότοκος can indicate both temporal priority and priority in rank. While this title does assume Christ's existence before the creation,[56] the primary emphasis is on Christ's rank over the created cosmos based upon his unique relationship with the supreme God.[57] Again, ancient Jewish literature never refers to personified Wisdom as God's "firstborn" (πρωτότοκος).[58] The OT language

---

51. McDonough, *Christ as Creator*, 183.

52. Fossum, "Colossians 1:15–18a," 188, and Smith, *Heavenly Perspective*, 162.

53. Dunn, *Colossians*, 87–89, and Krecidlo, "Reconciliation," 1137. On the Platonic background for this idea, see Kooten, *Paul's Anthropology*, 93–95.

54. Dübbers, *Christologie*, 92, and Northcutt, "King of Kings," 219–20. This adjective appears in three other NT passages outside Colossians. In each case, it is a characteristic attributed to God (Rom 1:20; 1 Tim 1:17; Heb 11:27). First Timothy 1:17 and Heb 11:27 both use this term to distinguish God as supreme over all other competing powers.

55. Fowl, *Story of Christ*, 107.

56. Moule, *Colossians and Philemon*, 64.

57. Lohse, *Colossians*, 49, and Bruce, *Colossians*, 59.

58. Dunn asserts that the antecedent of πρωτότοκος is "most obviously Wisdom" (Dunn, *Colossians and Philemon*, 90). However, as has already been discussed, such a

describing the place of the ideal Davidic king as YHWH's son presents a more obvious linguistic parallel. Specifically, Paul's usage aligns closely with Ps 89:27 (Ps 88:28 LXX) in which God sets the ideal Davidic king as his "firstborn," exalts him over all kings of the earth, and grants him authority over cosmic forces.[59] This allusion also fits well with the regal description of Christ in Col 1:13. This regal background suggests that the genitive πάσης κτίσεως is subordinate to the "firstborn." Christ did not just exist before all creation, nor is he part of the created order. Rather, he is the transcendent ruler over all creation.

This title may also have some correlation with Adam. While the OT never refers to Adam as God's "firstborn," God does grant priority and dominion to Adam over his creation.[60] Paul pushes the priority and dominion of Christ beyond the dominion of Adam by ascribing to Christ authority over the whole cosmos. In bringing together the regal titles "image" and "firstborn," Paul forms an inextricable regal link between the creation and messianic tradition. In fulfilling the promise of the ideal Davidic king, Christ also regains the dominion over creation that Adam once lost. The way in which Paul incorporates Christ into Israel's story reveals that Christ was always the intended ruler of the cosmos who alone could restore cosmic harmony.[61]

In the remainder of the hymn, Paul elucidates the role of Christ as God's ideal King. Paul reveals that God's royal agent, Christ, is also his agent in creation (Col 1:16). Christ's role as God's agent in creation also grants him the right to rule over the cosmos.[62] Paul's language concerning Christ's role in creation consists of three prepositional phrases: "in [ἐν] him ... through [διά] him ... for [εἰς] him." That the cosmos was made through (διά) Christ, which echoes Paul's declaration in 1 Cor 8:6 (see also John 1:3 and Heb 1:2), indicates that Christ is God's agent in creation. That the cosmos was made for (εἰς) Christ indicates that Christ is the goal of creation, a role played by God the Father in 1 Cor 8:6. The meaning of the first prepositional phrase is a little more difficult to explicate. While

---

connection is very far from obvious.

59. See ch. 2. Others who recognize this allusion include Wright, *Climax of the Covenant*, 113; Barth and Blanke, *Colossians*, 248; McDonough, *Christ as Creator*, 184; Dunne, "Regal Status," 13; Sumney, "Writing 'in the Image,'" 199; Fee, *Pauline Christology*, 301; Northcutt, "King of Kings," 222; and Jipp, *Christ Is King*, 108.

60. McDonough, *Christ as Creator*, 184, and Smith, *Heavenly Perspective*, 163.

61. McDonough, *Christ as Creator*, 185.

62. This is clearly indicated by the use of the conjunction ὅτι in v. 16.

it is possible to understand this phrase as communicating agency,⁶³ it seems unlikely considering that the second prepositional phrase clearly communicates agency, and it would be odd for Paul to use two phrases communicating agency when describing Christ's role in creation. A more likely solution is that the first prepositional phrase serves as a comprehensive statement of Christ's role in creation while the second and third phrase extrapolate from the meaning of the first phrase.⁶⁴ In this case, the first phrase indicates the sphere in which all things were created.⁶⁵ The implication is that the whole created cosmos operates within the sphere of Christ's supreme rule because he is the agent through whom the cosmos came to be. With this assertion, Paul pushes Jewish royal ideology forward by asserting that Christ as God's ideal King rightfully claims authority over the whole cosmos because he himself is the Creator and goal of the cosmos.⁶⁶ That Christ is granted sovereign rule over the cosmos further supports the idea for creation and messianic ideology as the primary background of the hymn, especially considering that sovereign rule is not a major aspect of Wisdom motifs.⁶⁷

Paul specifies the scope of Christ's cosmic rule by declaring that Christ's creative power and cosmic authority extends to the physical and spiritual realms (τὰ πάντα ἐν τοῖς οὐρανοῖς καὶ ἐπὶ τῆς γῆς, τὰ ὁρατὰ καὶ τὰ ἀόρατα, Col 1:16). Further, Paul claims that every cosmic being/force in these realms exists under the creative dominion of Christ (εἴτε θρόνοι εἴτε κυριότητες εἴτε ἀρχαὶ εἴτε ἐξουσίαι, Col 1:16).⁶⁸ While Paul's proclamation certainly has implications for earthly political powers,⁶⁹ he is more likely referring to cosmic spiritual powers. Paul probably has in mind both the heavenly angelic powers and the evil demonic powers.⁷⁰ Paul uses these

63. Lohse, *Colossians*, 50–51.

64. Barth and Blanke, *Colossians*, 198, and McDonough, *Christ as Creator*, 185–86.

65. Schweizer, *Colossians*, 69; Bruce, *Colossians*, 197; Aletti, *Colossiens*, 99–100, and Fowl, *Story of Christ*, 109.

66. Jipp, *Christ Is King*, 109.

67. Steenberg, *Irenaeus on Creation*, 103, and Leese, *Christ*, 112.

68. Dunn proposes that the author is presenting a hierarchy of the heavenly powers (Dunn, *Colossians*, 92). However, this seems difficult to determine given that it is not Paul's primary objective in this passage to present a spiritual hierarchy. Elsewhere in Paul's letters, he does not list them in this order (Bruce, *Colossians*, 64; Barth and Blanke, *Colossians*, 202).

69. Barth and Blanke, *Colossians*, 201–2. Walter Wink argues that this refers to governmental powers (Wink, *Naming the Powers*, 66).

70. Wesley Carr argues that Paul has in mind the heavenly powers, not demonic

terms in other passages when describing the power of Christ over the cosmos (Rom 8:38; 1 Cor 15:24). This understanding also fits the characteristics of those whom Paul was refuting. Whoever these heretics were, it seems that they were boasting in their access to the spiritual realms and powers (Col 2:18).[71] Such boasting was empty because every spiritual power in the cosmos, whether good or evil, is subject to Christ's rule because they were all created by him.

As God's ideal King over the cosmos, Christ also maintains cosmic harmony. Paul proclaims that Christ "is before all things" (Col 1:17a). This phrase emphasizes both the preexistence and preeminence of Christ.[72] Wisdom advocates argue that this phrase provides a clear link between Christ and personified Wisdom.[73] However, when this language is applied to Wisdom, it speaks of Wisdom as being created before all things. Paul does not state that Christ was a created being but that he is before all things. The claim of Christ's preexistence aligns with Jewish

---

fallen beings (Carr, *Angels and Principalities*). However, Paul's statements later in Colossians concerning Christ's triumph over the rulers and authorities make this interpretation unlikely (Col 2:15). Clinton Arnold argues on the other end that this list refers specifically to evil spiritual beings who opposes the purposes of God (Arnold, *Colossian Syncretism*, 255). However, this statement seems unnecessarily restrictive considering Paul's primary point in the hymn is that Christ rules over everything and everyone in the cosmos. Kooten argues that the phrase does not refer to beings at all but simply to cosmic forces (Kooten, *Cosmic Christology*, 121). The personal nature of Paul's terminology makes this understanding very unlikely.

71. The exact nature of the Colossian heresy has been notoriously difficult to identify and has been a matter of much discussion. Scholars have made various contributions to this argument, and it is unnecessary to determine the exact details of the heresy for the present study. Despite the difficulty of determining what exactly the Colossian heresy was, a few key points have arisen from the contribution of various scholars: (1) The heresy was very Jewish in nature, indicated by references to circumcision (Col 2:11–13), eating and drinking laws, festivals, and the Sabbath (Col 2:16). (2) The heresy was probably influenced in some way by Hellenistic and pagan practices. (3) There was a heavy emphasis on the spiritual realm and access to the spiritual realm became a source for boasting. That is, those who claimed to access the heavenly realms claimed to be spiritually superior (Col 1:18). (4) There was a real fear of evil spiritual powers. (5) The heresy had some dualism that deprecated fleshly existence and called for ascetic practices in order to release one from his/her fleshly existence. For further discussion on the Colossian heresy, see the contributions of Lightfoot, "Colossian Heresy," 13–59; Bruce, "Colossians Problems," 195–208; Demaris, *Colossian Controversy*; Arnold, *Colossian Syncretism*; Martin, *Philosophy and Empty Deceit*; and Smith, *Heavenly Perspective*.

72. Aletti suggests that temporal priority is in view while Masson argues for superiority in status (Aletti, *Colossiens*, 103; Masson, *Colossiens*, 101). It could be that Paul was deliberately ambiguous so that both senses would be understood (Harris, *Colossians and Philemon*, 46–47).

73. Dunn, *Colossians and Philemon*, 93, and Beetham, *Echoes*, 134.

descriptions of the messiah as a preexistent figure (Ps 110:1; 1 En. 48:2–3, 6; 62:6–7), Gospel declarations that affirm Christ's preexistence (Matt 22:41–46; Mark 12:35–37; John 1:1; 17:5, 24), and Paul's other writings that presume Christ's preexistence (1 Cor 8:6; Rom 1:3; 8:3; Phil 2:6–7). The implication is that the King who creates and rightfully rules over the cosmos is the one who existed with God before the creation of the cosmos and is therefore supreme over the cosmos. Taken in this way, the prepositional phrase "before all things" (πρὸ πάντων) qualifies Christ as the one who has the right to exercise authority over all creation.[74]

As the preexistent, supreme King, Christ holds all things together in himself (Col 1:17b). Like v. 16, v. 17b refers to the sphere of Christ's cosmic rule. The verb συνίστημι, when appearing as an intransitive verb, refers to bringing something together and placing it in its proper order.[75] The use of the perfect tense of this verb indicates that Christ is the one who has maintained and upheld the order of the cosmos from its creation until now.[76] Christ's role in upholding the order of the cosmos reflects the regal commission given both to Adam and the ideal Davidic king. Upon endowing Adam with his image, God commissions Adam to rule over and subdue the earth, making Adam responsible for maintaining God's good order in creation (Gen 1:26, 28; Ps 8:6–8; Wis. 9:2–3).[77] That the enthronement of the ideal Davidic king would restore God's good order in the cosmos and would bring about cosmic stability is a major aspect of Jewish royal ideology (Pss 2; 18; 45; 72; 89; 110; Isa 11:6–10; Dan 7:2–14).[78] In holding all things together, Christ both restores the

---

74. Fowl, *Story of Christ*, 111.

75. Collins, "Colossians 1,17," 64–87. Some read this phrase in light of Stoic speculations of the Logos. In this sense, Christ would be the "cosmic glue" binding the universe together. Such speculations also suggest the Colossians presents the cosmos as Christ's own body (Kooten, *Cosmic Christology*, 10–19; Cox, *Same Word*, 171). Though there are some general resemblances between the language of Col 1:17 and Stoic Logos speculation, these resemblances are far from specific enough to be convincing. McDonough rightly insists that "a terse formula such as 'in him all things hold together' only makes sense when it is read within the larger philosophical or religious system within which it is embedded" (McDonough, *Christ as Creator*, 187; see also Jipp, *Christ Is King*, 111). Therefore, the regal context of the Colossian hymn should govern one's interpretation of this phrase.

76. Dunn suggests that it is God's wisdom characterized in Christ that holds the cosmos together (Dunn, *Colossians and Philemon*, 94). However, the text is very clear that it is Christ himself who holds the cosmos together.

77. See ch. 2.

78. See ch. 2.

cosmic order that Adam failed to maintain and fulfills the cosmic hope of the ideal Davidic king.

This royal background gives a more plausible alternative to Kooten's Stoic–Middle Platonic interpretation of the hymn. Kooten suggests that the notion that the cosmos was brought into being with Christ and holds together in Christ "is but one step . . . to the idea that the cosmos constitutes his body."[79] Kooten's argument is difficult to maintain for two reasons. First, his theory fails to recognize any of the obvious Jewish imagery within the hymn, particularly the regal imagery. Kooten never fully explains how the hymn's ascription of the titles "the image of God" and "the firstborn over all creation" coheres with his view.[80] Christ's identity as the "image of God" and "the firstborn over all creation" grounds Paul's understanding of the cosmos' creation and coherence "in him." The hymn does not present the cosmos as Christ's body but as his kingdom. Second, the hymn never explicitly refers to the cosmos as Christ's body, but it does explicitly identify the church as Christ's body.

Cosmic Christ as King over New Creation

As God's ideal cosmic King, Christ also has the responsibility to rule over the church. Paul declares Christ to be the head of the church, which is described as his body (ἡ κεφαλὴ τοῦ σώματος τῆς ἐκκλησίας, Col 1:18a).[81] The word κεφαλὴ can denote either source or authority. Those who argue for source suggest that Christ is the one who vitalizes the church through his presence and energizes the church through his power. Christ then utilizes the church as his instrument to continue to carry out his work on earth.[82] Paul also uses κεφαλὴ to denote source later in the letter (Col 2:19). While this aspect may be present, Paul's intent throughout

79. Kooten, *Cosmic Christology*, 23, 125.

80. Kooten merely mentions the terms when discussing the structure of the hymn. See Kooten, *Cosmic Christology*, 112–15.

81. Those who wish to argue that Colossians presents the cosmos as Christ's body argue that the genitive τῆς ἐκκλησίας was added as a later interpretive gloss. Fossum goes so far to say that it is "clearly identifiable as a gloss." Fossum, "Invisible God," 32; Lohse, *Colossians*, 42–43, 52–55, and Dunn, *Colossians and Philemon*, 94–95. However, such a gloss exists only in the imagination of these scholars as there is no textual evidence for such a reading. It seems those who argue for a gloss do so to make the text fit their own argument rather than from textual evidence itself. See Kehl, *Christushymnus*, 41–45.

82. Bruce, *Colossians*, 70, and Fee, *Pauline Christology*, 306.

the hymn is to demonstrate the absolute authority that Christ exercises over the cosmos.[83] Thus, when reading Paul's head-body metaphor in the overall context of the Colossian hymn, it seems that Paul's use of κεφαλή in v. 18 carries regal connotations. A parallel may be found in 2 Sam 22 when David celebrates God's anointing of him as king and praises him for making him "head of the nations" (2 Sam 22:44 LXX).[84] The regal nature of the metaphor seems even more apparent when one considers the parallel text in Eph 1:20–23, where the context of Christ's enthronement governs the meaning of the term κεφαλή. The regal authority with which Christ rules over the cosmos is realized in his rule over his corporate body, the church. As those who are subjected under the cosmic King, the church has realized its restoration to its cosmic authority and now operates according to the directives of the cosmic King.

Christ's role as the ruling head of the church indicates that he is the inaugurator of the new order. Paul continues by referring to Christ as the ἀρχή (Col 1:18b). Like the title "firstborn" in v. 15 and the phrase "before all things" in v. 17, this term can also refer either to temporal primacy, in which case it would be translated as "beginning," or primacy of status/rank, in which case it would be translated as "ruler." Wisdom advocates argue that the temporal sense is the primary meaning as the hymn continues to reflect Jewish traditions concerning Wisdom. As Christ the Creator stood at the beginning of the creation, so now also he stands at the beginning of a new creation.[85] Though it is probable that ἀρχή does convey a temporal aspect of meaning, it is likely that primacy of rank is also in view. Rhythmically, the term falls in the same position as the term εἰκών as it is also followed by the title "firstborn"[86] and serves as another allusion to Gen 1. As has already been discussed, the title εἰκών in both Gen 1:26–27 and in Col 1:15 carries significant regal connotations. By placing ἀρχή in

---

83. This does not discount the implications for those who wish to argue for source as the primary meaning. That Christ is the governing authority over the church also means that he vitalizes and empowers the church. Arnold defines the headship image according to the medical writers of the day who saw the head as both the ruling part of the body and the supply center. In this case, κεφαλή can simultaneously denote both authority and source. For this reason, it may be best to exclude neither source or authority from the meaning of κεφαλή (Arnold, "Jesus Christ," 346–66; Krecidlo, "Reconciliation," 1143).

84. For further discussion on the royal connotations of κεφαλή in the OT, see Jipp, *Christ Is King*, 114–15.

85. Dunn, *Colossians and Philemon*, 95–96; Gordley, *Colossian Hymn*, 222–23; Beetham, *Echoes*, 134; and Krecidlo, "Reconciliation," 1145.

86. Gordley, *Colossian Hymn*, 222.

a parallel position to εἰκών, the title probably also carries regal connotations. The title ἀρχή also appears in the LXX to describe a person in a position of authority and is often used as a royal appellation (Gen 49:10; Num 23:21; Deut 33:5). Isaiah 9:5–6 LXX uses the term to describe the authority of the coming messianic king.[87]

The regal connotation of ἀρχή becomes even more likely when one considers that Paul qualifies its meaning with the royal title πρωτότοκος.[88] Whereas Paul proclaims Christ to be the "firstborn over all creation" in the first strophe, he now calls him the "firstborn from the dead." Paul's use of "firstborn" in v. 18 seems ambiguous on the surface, but when one considers the royal context of the hymn, the meaning becomes much clearer. The royal Davidic background that underlies the use of "firstborn" in v. 15, along with the royal context of vv. 12–14, carries over to the use of "firstborn" in v. 18.[89] The meaning becomes clearer when one considers Paul's description of Christ as the Davidic King in Rom 1:3–4. Paul claims that Christ's resurrection serves as the means by which he is granted the divine, cosmic throne and fulfills the Davidic covenant. This association between Christ's resurrection and enthronement is also found in Rom 1:3–4, Eph 1:20–23 and Heb 1:3–13.[90] As the "firstborn of the dead," Christ not only stands as the cosmic King over the new creation order, but he also secures the destiny of those who belong to him (Col 1:21–23; 1 Cor 15:20–23; Rom 8:29). While Christ's resurrection certainly inaugurates the new creation/resurrection age, Paul emphasizes that Christ's resurrection secures his rightful place as the cosmic King who rules over the new creation age. Such an understanding of "firstborn" also allows one to suggest with high probability that Paul uses ἀρχή to communicate both Christ's role in inaugurating new creation and in ruling over the new creation.[91] To paraphrase, Paul states that "Christ is the beginning/ruler of new creation, the supreme king of the resurrection

---

87. Dunne, "Regal Status," 15 and Jipp, *Christ Is King*, 116–17.

88. The association of the terms ἄρχων and πρωτότοκος τῶν νεκρῶν is also found in Rev 1:5 where Christ is presented as the "ruler over the kings of the earth." This association could be suggestive of how ἀρχή should be translated in relation to πρωτότοκος in Col 1:18 (Dunne, "Regal Status," 16).

89. Gordley suggests that Christ is arguably being described as the "King of the dead" (Gordley, *Colossian Hymn*, 223).

90. On Rom 1:3–4 and Heb 1:3–13, see ch. 3. Ephesians 1:20–23 will be discussed in greater detail in the next chapter.

91. Jipp, *Christ Is King*, 117. Arnold also suggests that both the temporal and authoritative senses are present with the term ἀρχή (Arnold, *Colossian Syncretism*, 260–61).

age." Paul claims that all these things occur so that Christ might have the preeminent position over everything in the cosmos.

Though not directly, one can also see a correlation between Paul's declaration of Christ as the cosmic Lord of the resurrection age and his other statements regarding Adam Christology. As Adam was granted authority to steward God's good rule over creation, so now God has granted Christ the authority to rule over the new creation. By stating that Christ is the "firstborn from the dead," Paul presumes that the cosmos has been corrupted by death, which was brought about by Adam's failure as God's first king. Christ's kingship brings about the age of resurrection, reversing the effects of Adam's failure. The Colossian hymn does bring one point of further clarity regarding Paul's own Adam Christology. For Paul, Christ's enthronement over the whole cosmos as a result of his resurrection is a claim to the cosmic throne that has been rightfully his since before the creation of the cosmos. Therefore, while Adam was granted authority to rule over the physical creation, Christ has always been God's King over the cosmos. Only the rightful cosmic King could undo the effects of Adam's reign. Christ's resurrection simply proves that he has always been God's ideal cosmic King.

Paul continues the hymn by giving further justification for Christ's preeminence in the cosmos (indicated by the conjunction ὅτι in v. 19) and gives the grounds for Christ's work to reconcile the cosmos. Paul states that God determined to have his fullness dwell within Christ (ἐν αὐτῷ εὐδόκησεν πᾶν τὸ πλήρωμα κατοικῆσαι, Col 1:19).[92] The LXX uses the word πλήρωμα and its semantic equivalents in a cosmological sense to speak of God pervading the universe (Ps 71:19 LXX; Jer 23:24) and to

---

92. Whether the subject of the verb "determined" (εὐδόκησεν) is either "all the fullness" (πᾶν τὸ πλήρωμα) or "God" as the presupposed subject is a matter of debate. Since πᾶν τὸ πλήρωμα is stated in the verse, it may serve as the easiest possible solution. In this case, πᾶν τὸ πλήρωμα would be considered a personal designation of God. This construction would also parallel Paul's usage in Col 2:9 (ὅτι ἐν αὐτῷ κατοικεῖ πᾶν τὸ πλήρωμα τῆς θεότητος σωματικῶς), in which πλήρωμα takes κατοικεῖ as its verb (which appears as the infinitive κατοικῆσαι in v. 19) (Lohse, *Colossians*, 56–57; Moule, *Colossians and Philemon*, 70–71; Dunn, *Colossians and Philemon*, 101; and Stettler, *Kolosserhymnus*, 250). One may consider "God" to be the subject. If this were the case, πᾶν τὸ πλήρωμα would have to be considered as an accusative with the infinitive κατοικῆσαι. This option would also provide a smooth grammatical link with the masculine participle εἰρηνοποιήσας in Col 1:20. Barth and Blanke suggest that "a usage of εὐδοκέω is possible when God is presupposed as subject, and the Greek active infinitive with various subjects for εὐδοκέω and the infinitive is also an attested variant" (Barth and Blanke, *Colossians*, 211). In either case, the point is that God acts through his redemptive agent, Christ, by filling him with his fullness.

emphasize God's authority over creation (Ps. 23:1 LXX; 88:12).[93] In Ps 88 LXX, God grants his ideal king with his authority to rule over creation (Ps 88:26–30 LXX). In the Colossian hymn, God chooses to let his full divinity which pervades the cosmos dwell within his Son (see also Col 2:9). Paul does not suggest that God bestowed his fullness upon Christ after the creation of the cosmos, but this fullness of divinity belonged to Christ from before the creation of the cosmos.[94] Christ's eternal possession of full divinity qualifies him as God's royal agent to exercise divine rule over the cosmos.[95] Therefore, as Jipp notes, "a plausible interpretation of Col 1:19 would be one that stresses God's election of the Messiah as God's supreme vice-regent and God's decision to share all of the divine fullness with the anointed one."[96] This idea parallels Jewish royal ideology in which the ideal king's authority is grounded in God's enthronement of him (Ps 2:6; 110:1–3; 132:10, 17; Ezek 34:24; Dan 7:12–14).

Paul ends the hymn by outlining Christ's final task as God's cosmic King: the reconciliation of the cosmos. As with his agency in creation, Paul reveals Christ's agency in the work of reconciliation using the preposition διά (Col 1:20). Paul begins the hymn by setting Christ as the Creator and ruler of the cosmos, but the mention of Christ's cosmic reconciliatory work indicates a disruption between the cosmos and its Creator.[97] Paul presupposes the disruption of the cosmos through the failure of Adam's reign in Gen 1–3. As a result, all things in the cosmos need reconciliation "to him." The prepositional phrase εἰς αὐτόν could refer either to Christ or God. When Paul speaks of reconciliation in his other writings, he speaks of things being reconciled to God rather than to Christ (cf. Rom 5:10; 2 Cor 5:19; Eph 2:16). It would then make sense that Paul is once again speaking of the reconciliation of the cosmos to God. God is also the understood subject of the infinitive "to reconcile" (ἀποκαταλλάξαι), so one

---

93. Lohse, *Colossians*, 57–58, and Jipp, *Christ Is King*, 120–21.

94. Jeal, "Starting Before," 293.

95. The verb εὐδοκέω is often used in the LXX to describe God's election (2 Sam 22:20; Ps 67:17; 151:5). For more on the use of εὐδοκέω in the LXX, see Peppard, *Son of God*, 106–12. Some scholars detect a potential allusion to Ps 68:16 (Ps 67:17), where God is pleased (εὐδόκησεν) to dwell (κατοικεῖν) on Mount Zion. That Eph 4:8 clearly references Ps 68 strengthens the possibility of this allusion. Paul shifts the true dwelling of God from a place to the person of Christ. Christ has now become the locus of the divine presence in new creation. For more on this allusion, see Beetham, *Echoes*, 143–56, and Sumney, "Writing 'in the Image,'" 200–201.

96. Jipp, *Christ Is King*, 121–22.

97. See Barrett, *First Adam to Last*, 86, and Smith, *Heavenly Perspective*, 171.

could easily surmise that God reconciles the cosmos through Christ to himself. However, the context of the hymn suggests that the reference is to Christ. If Paul intended for the pronoun to refer to God, it seems strange for him to use a personal pronoun rather than a reflexive pronoun.[98] If the pronoun refers to Christ, it parallels the earlier use of the prepositional phrase εἰς αὐτόν in v. 16 where Paul clearly presents Christ as the goal of reconciliation.[99] That Christ is the referent of εἰς αὐτόν in v. 20 maintains the consistency of the hymn in which Paul views Christ as the agent and goal of both old and new creation.[100] In this case, one would interpret v. 20 as stating that all things in the cosmos are reconciled through Christ and for Christ. This idea does not diminish the importance of cosmic reconciliation to the Father. Rather, Paul conveys that God reconciles the cosmos to himself through Christ and for the glory of Christ the King.[101] The parallel between v. 20 and v. 16, which states that all things in the cosmos have been created through and for Christ, indicates that Christ's reconciliatory work is an act of new creation.

The means by which God accomplished this reconciliation is through Christ's blood shed on the cross (διὰ τοῦ αἵματος τοῦ σταυροῦ αὐτοῦ, Col 1:20). Christ's restoration of cosmic harmony through his death and resurrection is perhaps the most significant contribution that Paul and the other NT writers make to Jewish royal ideology. Rather than accomplishing cosmic harmony through military conquest (a common feature of Jewish royal ideology), Christ accomplished cosmic reconciliation through his sacrificial death and resurrection. The accomplishment of cosmic harmony through death and resurrection does subtly echo one key motif found in Jewish royal ideology: God elevates his ideal king from obscurity to kingship. Isaiah 52:13—53:12 exemplifies this motif where the royal servant's exaltation shocks the kings of the earth and is accomplished through his suffering and death.[102] Colossians 1:20 also parallels the hymn in Phil 2 where Christ's exaltation to the cosmic throne is accomplished through his humiliation (Phil 2:6–11).

---

98. Fee, *Pauline Christology*, 311.

99. Lohse, *Colossians*, 59.

100. Fee, *Pauline Christology*, 309–12, and Pao, *Colossians and Philemon*, 104.

101. Krecidlo suggests that the two interpretive options "to God" or "for Christ" should be treated as complementary. "This composition of the hymn can allow the reader to see its several complementary levels of interpretation as a proof of the author's poetic genius" (Krecidlo, "Reconciliaton," 1150).

102. See ch. 2.

That Christ achieved cosmic harmony through his own death stands as an unparalleled royal achievement.

Paul makes clear that Christ's reconciliatory work covers the whole created cosmos, "whether things on the earth or things in the heavens" (Col 1:20b). All beings and forces in the physical and spiritual realm come under the reconciliatory work of Christ. This declaration indicates that even the cosmic beings/forces that are hostile to Christ are part of his reconciliatory work. The infinitive "to reconcile" and participle "making peace" both appear in the aorist tense. Though the aorist participle and infinitive forms are relative in time and usually depend on the main verb, Paul does at times use aorist verbal forms in his other writings to indicate completed action (Rom 5:1; Col 3:9–10).[103] The use of the aorist tense in this passage occurs as Paul reflects upon how Christ can claim pre-eminence over the whole cosmos (Col 1:18). This context suggests that Paul is referring to a completed action, meaning that God completed the work of reconciliation through Christ's death and resurrection.[104] Kooten argues that this language points to a reconstitution of the cosmos in Christ and suggests that this conception diverges from Paul's cosmic Christology, which views the cosmic powers as being "subjugated and destroyed rather than reconstituted."[105] Kooten's argument hinges on the notion that the reconstitution of the cosmos is a reconstitution of the cosmic body, but the hymn makes no obvious reference to Christ having a cosmic body.[106] However, v. 20 does make an explicit reference to the incarnate body of Christ when he refers to his death on the cross.

---

103. In Rom 5:1, Paul states that believers have peace with God as a result of "having been justified by faith" (δικαιωθέντες). In Col 3:9–10, Paul utilizes two aorist participles (ἀπεκδυσάμενο and ἐνδυσάμενοι) with a present participle (ἀνακαινούμενον). Most likely, Paul intentionally uses these tenses the indicate that while the putting off of the old man and putting on of the new man is complete, the process of the church being renewed in Christ's image is ongoing.

104. Dunn argues that the aorist tense indicates that the expression of God's reconciliation has been completed, not the reconciliation itself (Dunn, *Colossians and Philemon*, 103). In this case, one might refer to these verbs as prophetic aorists. This serves as a good explanation of Paul's use of the aorist here but does not seem to capture the full idea. Rather, it is better to understand the work of reconciliation as complete with its realization occurring at the return of Christ.

105. Kooten, *Cosmic Christology*, 127–29.

106. Kooten argues that the fullness of God dwelling in Christ means that "the invisible God takes on the visible shape of the cosmic body" (Kooten, *Cosmic Christology*, 127). However, God's fullness dwelling in Christ likely emphasizes Christ's full possession of divinity and divine authority rather than a cosmic body.

Kooten's argument also rests on a faulty view of reconciliation. Cosmic reconciliation certainly includes salvation and peace for those who belong to Christ, but cosmic reconciliation implies subjugation of hostile cosmic powers under the reign of Christ.[107] In Jewish royal ideology, the enthronement of God's king signals the return of God's good rule over the nations and cosmos (Ps. 18:44–45; Isa 9:5–6; Mic 5:3–4; Zech 9:9–10).[108] The establishment of God's ideal king gives hope to God's people (Jer 23:5–6; Dan 7:27; Pss. Sol. 17:43; 1 En. 53:6) and signals defeat for God's enemies (Pss 2:4–10; 89:26; 144:12–14; Isa 63:1–6; Dan 7:12–14; Pss. Sol. 17:36; 1 En. 46:4–6; 69:27–29). In the same way, Christ's cosmic victory achieved through his death and resurrection provides hope for those who belong to Christ (Col 1:21–22) and signals defeat for those forces that are hostile to Christ (Col 2:15). The subjection of these powers brings about a restored cosmos that operates in perfect harmony under its cosmic King. As a result, Christ now stands as God's ideal cosmic King over both old and new creation. Rather than contradicting the cosmic Christology of other Pauline letters, the Colossian hymn's conception of God's reconciliation of the cosmos through Christ his King aligns with Paul's claims in his other letters that God would subordinate the whole cosmos under the reign of Christ (1 Cor 15:27–28; Phil 2:9–11).

COLOSSIANS 2:6–15

At the conclusion of the Colossian hymn, Paul applies the cosmic work of Christ to the lives of the Colossian believers. Paul explains how these believers became beneficiaries of Christ's reconciliatory work as they now stand "holy and blameless" before God (Col 1:21–22). As a result, Paul exhorts the believers to continue in the ministry of the gospel that continues to be proclaimed "in all creation under heaven" (Col 1:23). Paul's exhortation indicates that the Colossian believers joined the cosmic mission of making Christ known throughout creation. Paul then outlines his

---

107. Fee, *Pauline Christology*, 312–13. Moule comments that the idea of cosmic (or "universal") reconciliation is "the hardest to accommodate to the rest of St. Paul's thought" (Moule, *Colossians*, 62). However, when one considers that Christ's reconciliatory work has different applications (forgiveness for those who submit to Christ's cosmic lordship and subjection for those who are hostile to his lordship), the problem disappears.

108. Jipp notes that in Greco-Roman royal ideology, "Arguably the single most important trait of the good king was this production of peace and harmony through the defeat and pacification of the empire's enemies" (Jipp, *Christ Is King*, 122–27).

involvement in the ministry of the gospel as he strives to make the riches of the glorious Christ known to the gentiles (Col 1:24—2:5).

Paul continues to explain the implications of Christ's cosmic work in the lives of the Colossian believers. Paul begins by giving a general exhortation to continue to walk and grow in the ways of Christ. The exhortation marks a major rhetorical transition where Paul moves to the paraenetic section of the letter.[109] Thus, Col 2:6–7 serves as the general introduction to the paraenesis that follows. Paul grounds the reason for his exhortation in the fact that the Colossian believers received "Christ Jesus the Lord" (Col 2:6). Christ's lordship is the central confession of the gospel that the Colossian church received from Epaphras (Col 1:7). The Colossian hymn then gives expression to the lordship of Christ in both the creation of the cosmos and the reconciliation of the cosmos. The Colossian believers' acceptance of this confession implies that they received Christ as the fulfillment of the promised messianic king and that they surrendered themselves to the cosmic rule of Christ, which became "their primary frame of reference in this new life."[110]

Because the Colossian believers received Christ Jesus the Lord, Paul exhorts them to "walk in him" (ἐν αὐτῷ περιπατεῖτε, Col 2:6). The command to walk (περιπατεῖτε) conveys the manner in which the Colossian believers should live their lives.[111] Commentators typically take the prepositional phrase "in him" (ἐν αὐτῷ) to refer to the union that believers have with Christ and/or to their new identity defined by Christ.[112] While this understanding does capture the basic meaning of the phrase, Paul's exhortation to walk "in him" also recalls the cosmic rule of Christ laid out in the Colossian hymn, where he both establishes and maintains the order of the cosmos (Col 1:16–17). Interpreted against this background, one could plausibly translate "in him" as "in the sphere

---

109. Walter Wilson suggests these verses both conclude the first section of the letter and transition to the second section of the letter (Wilson, *Hope of Glory*, 241). For a helpful discussion on the rhetorical structure of the letter, see Copenhaver, *Historical Background*, 81–143.

110. Fee, *Pauline Christology*, 327. See also Dunn, *Colossians and Philemon*, 139–41.

111. Barth and Blanke, *Colossians*, 302–3; Heil, *Colossians*, 102; and Gupta, *Colossians*, 89.

112. Harris suggests that this phrase could either be locative (in him) or instrumental (by him) (Harris, *Colossians and Philemon*, 89). See also Dunn, *Colossians and Philemon*, 140; Sumney, *Colossians*, 128; Heil, *Colossians*, 102–3; and Beale, *Colossians and Philemon*, 172.

of his lordship."[113] Because the Colossian believers recognized that Christ is the rightful ruler of the cosmos, to walk in him means that they should conduct themselves according to the reality that they exist under the cosmic lordship of Christ. The Colossian believers conduct themselves this way as those who "have been rooted" and are "being built up in Christ (ἐρριζωμένοι καὶ ἐποικοδομούμενοι ἐν αὐτῷ, Col 2:7). The passive form of these participles indicates an external agent who roots and builds up these believers. Given Paul's assertion that the cosmos that exists under the sphere of Christ's lordship was created "through him," it seems likely that Christ's power to create and redeem the cosmos is the same power that roots and builds up the believers.[114]

Because they now exist under the cosmic rule of Christ, Paul cautions the Colossian believers not to be captured by false philosophy and deceitful teaching.[115] Paul characterizes the philosophy according to human traditions (κατὰ τὴν παράδοσιν τῶν ἀνθρώπων) and according to the στοιχεῖα τοῦ κόσμου (Col 2:8). The precise meaning of the latter characterization remains a subject of much debate. One can summarize the interpretations of this phrase into three basic positions: (1) basic religious principles, (2) elements of the universe, and (3) individual spiritual powers. According to the first view, στοιχεῖα τοῦ κόσμου refers either to the basic principles of the Jewish law or general principles that relate to both Jewish and gentile religious laws.[116] While Paul does reference different practices of Jewish law later in the chapter (Col 2:11, 16, 21–23), these practices seem to fit better under Paul's reference to the traditions of men. For this reason, interpreting στοιχεῖα τοῦ κόσμου as referring to religious

---

113. Fee, *Pauline Christology*, 326–27. See also Smith, *Heavenly Perspective*, 75.

114. Barth and Blanke point out that the use of the preposition ἐν (as opposed to the preposition ἐπί) with the verb ἐποικοδομέω is highly unusual and is therefore likely to be taken as an instrumental phrase (Barth and Blanke, *Colossians*, 304n22). It may also be possible to consider the participles as a reference to the teaching the Colossian believers had received (Dunn, *Colossians and Philemon*, 141). Even if this is the case, it seems best still to consider Christ as the primary agent who roots and builds up the Colossian believers as a result of their reception of the gospel of Christ.

115. The "philosophy and empty deceit" is probably a reference to the Colossian heresy that Paul seeks to address. Again, for the purpose of this study, it is not essential to identify the exact nature of the Colossian heresy. One should simply recognize that Paul characterizes the philosophy as arising from both human traditions and cosmic powers.

116. For proponents of this view, see Moule, *Colossians and Philemon*, 92; Carr, *Angel and Principalities*, 75; Sappington, *Revelation and Redemption*, 164–70; Bevere, *Inheritance*, 98–100; and Sumney, *Colossians*, 131.

principles and practices seems redundant. According to the second view, στοιχεῖα τοῦ κόσμου refers to the primary components in Greek thought that make up the universe: earth, water, air, and fire.[117] A variation of this view is that στοιχεῖα τοῦ κόσμου refers to astral powers that control the fate of the cosmos.[118] The problem with this view is that Paul directly contrasts the στοιχεῖα τοῦ κόσμου with Christ (οὐ κατὰ Χριστόν), a fact that becomes clear with the insertion of the negative particle οὐ before the prepositional phrase and the use of the conjunction καί to connect the two phrases. The result is a contrast between two personal sources that are together set up as a parallel to an impersonal source.[119]

The third position that views στοιχεῖα τοῦ κόσμου as a referent to spiritual beings seems to be the most likely interpretation. Paul's use of στοιχεῖα τοῦ κόσμου likely parallels his several references to the spiritual beings throughout Colossians.[120] There is also plenty of evidence that στοιχεῖα was used in both Greek and Jewish traditions to reference angelic and spiritual powers.[121] Angelic and demonic beings were also often viewed as the powers that lie behind the basic religious principles and the elemental forces that make up the cosmos.[122] In the immediate context, the contrast with Christ suggests that Paul uses στοιχεῖα as a reference to animate, personal beings. Paul's association of these beings with the deceitful philosophy could suggest that the reference is specifically to demonic beings.[123] If στοιχεῖα τοῦ κόσμου truly is a reference to personal spiritual powers, then it reiterates the cosmic authority of Christ. Rather than following the philosophies that arise from human traditions and the spiritual powers of the cosmos, Paul exhorts the Colossian believers to submit themselves to Christ, who is Lord and King over every power in both the physical and spiritual realm.

---

117. For proponents of this view, see Schweizer, "Slaves," 455–68, and Demaris, *Colossian Controversy*, 52–55.

118. Dunn describes this view as an extension of the view regarding the four elements since stars were made up of fire, one of the four primary elements (Dunn, *Colossians and Philemon*, 149).

119. Arnold, *Colossian Syncretism*, 188–89.

120. Arnold, *Colossians Syncretism*, 85, and Masson, *Colossiens*, 122.

121. On the religious-historical background of στοιχεῖα, see Arnold, *Colossian Syncretism*, 162–83.

122. On this point, see Dunn, *Colossians and Philemon*, 150–51, and Smith, *Heavenly Perspective*, 84–87.

123. Arnold, *Colossian Syncretism*, 189–90.

Paul asserts that the reason the Colossian believers should not submit themselves to any philosophy that does not align with Christ is because of the fullness of divinity that resides in his body (Col 2:9). Paul's language recalls his assertion of Christ's divinity in the Colossian hymn (Col 1:19). The phrase "fullness of the Godhead" (πλήρωματῆς τῆς θεότητος) refers to the glorious divine presence that pervades the entire cosmos and takes up residence in Christ himself. Paul's inclusion of the genitive θεότητος emphasizes that Christ was not merely a reflection of the divine but that he is God himself.[124] Paul further clarifies that Christ's full divinity resided in his incarnate body. Scholars interpret the adverb "bodily" (σωματικῶς) to convey either Christ's cosmic body, Christ's ecclesial body, or Christ's incarnate body. Kooten argues that the cosmological context of the letter suggests that "bodily" refers to Christ's cosmic body, which is made up of the rulers, powers (Col 1:16), the elements of the cosmos (Col 2:18), and other cosmic forces. He suggests that since "bodily" is not qualified by either the church (ἐκκλησία) or the "flesh" (σάρξ), it likely refers to Christ's cosmic body.[125] Kooten's argument is problematic primarily because there is no concrete linguistic connection in Colossians that would suggest that the creation and/or the cosmic forces make up a corporeal cosmic body of Christ. Kooten's argument relies on strained connections to Stoic physics, but such connections are unnecessary when Paul clearly qualifies the two senses of Christ's body as referring to either Christ's individual incarnate body (Col 1:19) or his corporate ecclesial body (Col 1:21; 2:11).

While Paul does refer to Christ's corporate ecclesial body at other points in the letter, the context of Col 2:9 does not easily convey this meaning. Therefore, σωματικῶς is most likely a reference to Christ's incarnate body.[126] This interpretation makes most sense as Paul sets the individual Christ against the human philosophies and spiritual powers. In explaining Col 1:19, Paul affirms that the fullness of divinity is expressed in Christ's incarnation. Paul's use of the present verb "dwell" (κατοικεῖ) emphasizes that Christ presently expresses this fullness in his resurrected

---

124. Sumney asserts that Paul's use of θεοτῆτος instead of θειοτής indicates a use of the most exalted language in Paul's description of Christ because θεοτῆτος could only apply to beings recognized as gods (Sumney, *Colossians*, 132–33).

125. Kooten, *Cosmic Christology*, 23–27. This view was first advanced by Ernst Lohmeyer (Lohmeyer, *Briefe*, 106–7), but it gained very little traction before Kooten.

126. The majority of scholars affirm this view (for example, Barth and Blanke, *Colossians*, 314; Sumney, *Colossians*, 133; Smith, *Heavenly Perspective*, 93; Beale, *Colossians and Philemon*, 177–78).

body.[127] As the one who is presently the fullness of God, Christ also possesses the divine honor and glory that characterizes God's ideal King. Whereas God's ideal king in Judaism needed God to bestow his honor and glory upon the king, Christ possesses divine honor and glory in his own body because his very nature is divine, and he is fully qualified to serve as God's royal representative who exercises God's rule over the cosmos.[128] Through his incarnation, Christ both fulfills the Jewish royal expectation that God's ideal king would appear "bodily" and exceeds these expectations by being God himself.

The implication for believers is that they are now filled by the one in whom the fullness of deity dwells (Col 2:10a). In broad terms, Paul's exhortation to the Colossian believers is that they have all that they need by means of their union with Christ, but the fact that they have been filled "in him" (ἐν αὐτῷ) also means that they exist in the sphere of Christ's reign and are the present beneficiaries of his cosmic lordship.[129] Paul references this connection when he reminds them that they have been joined to the one who is "the head over every ruler and authority" (Col 2:10b). Paul does not suggest that Christ has incorporated the rulers and authorities into his cosmic body.[130] Rather, Paul's expression recalls the Colossian hymn where he affirms Christ's cosmic authority by means of his agency in creation (Col 1:16). As Paul used the term κεφαλή to denote Christ's authority over the church, he uses it in Col 2:10 to denote Christ's authority over cosmic powers.[131] In making this assertion, Paul explains the blessing that comes when God transfers believers from the inferior dominion of darkness into the kingdom of Christ (Col 1:13). Paul's point is that because the Colossian believers are subject to the one who has subjected every cosmic power under his reign, they do not need to fear or submit to any other cosmic power.

Paul expounds upon the means and meaning of the believers' union with Christ in Col 2:11–15. Paul first states that in Christ the Colossian

127. This assertion is not to suggest that Christ only received divine fullness upon his resurrection. Rather, the adverb σωματικῶς refers to the whole of Christ's incarnational existence, including his present resurrected body (Barth and Blanke, *Colossians*, 314–15).

128. Wright, "Rulers and Authorities," 455.

129. Jipp, *Christ Is King*, 145.

130. Kooten argues for this interpretation (Kooten, *Cosmic Christology*, 23–24, 129).

131. This sense of κεφαλή counters any notion that Paul asserts that the rulers and authorities are somehow part of Christ's cosmic body (Barth and Blanke, *Colossians*, 316–17; Sumney, *Colossians*, 134–35).

believers experienced a spiritual circumcision by putting off their fleshly bodies (Col 2:11).[132] The "body of flesh" (σώματος τῆς σαρκός) could present an indirect reference to Adam in that the believers inherited their mortal, corrupt bodies from Adam.[133] For believers to enter Christ's kingdom, God needed to remove the corrupt body they inherited from Adam and his failed dominion.[134] Christ's death and resurrection brought about this spiritual renewal in which believers are now granted the characteristics of Christ their King (Col 1:22; 3:9–10).

Paul also states that the Colossian believers have been united with Christ in his death, burial, and resurrection (Col 2:12–13). God accomplished this union by canceling the "certificate of indebtedness" (χειρόγραφον) against those who now belong to Christ (2:14). The χειρόγραφον refers to some sort of legal ledger that records the various violations of God's law. Paul could possibly be referencing the Jewish idea of the heavenly book of the living (Exod 32:32–33; Ps 69:28; Dan 12:1; 1 En. 89:61–64), a book which records each person's good and bad deeds for the final judgment.[135] If this heavenly book is the referent, then Paul has placed the redemptive work of Christ on behalf of believers in a cosmic setting. Paul presents the sin of humanity as a cosmic offense, and the Colossian believers stood culpable in God's heavenly court because they had violated God's law. In an ironic twist, Christ, the rightful King

---

132. Kooten suggests that this assertion is also an implicit reference to Christ's putting off his own human body. He suggests that by putting off the body of flesh, believers reenact Christ's own putting off his flesh in his death (Kooten, *Cosmic Christology*, 129n34). However, Colossians does not suggest Christ's victory comes through putting off a human body so that he might take up a cosmic body. Rather, Christ's victory comes through the resurrection of his human body (Col 1:18).

133. Beetham, *Echoes*, 175–77. Paul makes a more direct reference to this motif in Col 3:9–10.

134. Some scholars note that Paul derives his circumcision metaphor from the OT's figurative uses of circumcision (Deut 10:16; 30:6; Jer 4:4; Ezek 44:7, 9) (Beetham, *Echoes*, 157–79; Sumney, "Writing 'in the Image,'" 202–5; Beale, *Colossians and Philemon*, 184–85). Beetham argues that the verse primarily echoes Deut 30:6. However, the multiple uses of the circumcision metaphor in the OT suggests that Paul is making a broader reference to the overall tradition.

135. For more on this understanding of χειρόγραφον, see Blanchette, "Cheirographon," 306–12; Nickelsburg, *Resurrection*, 11–42; Sappington, *Revelation and Redemption*, 214–20; Dunn, *Colossians and Philemon*, 165–66; and Smith, *Heavenly Perspective*, 97–102. Kyu Kim has recently argued that χειρόγραφον does not refer to a certificate of debt but to a declaration or oath that the Colossian believers made as part of a religious ritual (Kim, "Meaning of ΧΕΙΡΟΓΡΑΦΟΝ," 223–39). Kim's definition relies primarily on evidence from ancient Greek papyri, but he gives little consideration to the potential Jewish background.

of the cosmos, receives the punishment of the cosmic offense committed by those whom he has the right to rule. As a result, God cancels the χειρόγραφον through the death of Christ (2:14b).

Paul makes this cosmic setting even more explicit when he celebrates Christ's cosmic triumph in Col 2:15. The exact meaning of the participle ἀπεκδυσάμενος depends on whether Christ or God is the understood subject and on whether one interprets the middle voice as having a typical middle sense or as a middle with an active force. Further, if the basic meaning of the word refers to stripping someone of something, What is being stripped? If one argues for Christ as the subject, then the participle takes on the typical middle sense with Christ stripping himself of something. One may then argue that Christ has either stripped himself of his own flesh[136] or of the "rulers and authorities" (τὰς ἀρχὰς καὶ τὰς ἐξουσίας).[137] The former translation is difficult because the verse makes no direct mention of Christ's flesh, meaning that "flesh" would have to be the assumed direct object of the participle. It seems much more likely that the "rulers and authorities" serve as the direct object of the participle. That Christ "stripped himself of the rulers and authorities" is also a difficult interpretation because it would require an unexpected change of subject from God in vv. 13–14 to Christ in v. 15. This change in subject is not clearly communicated in the context. Additionally, that Christ was somehow clothed with the rulers and authorities and needed to strip them off suggests that Christ may have been subject to the rulers and authorities while on earth and needed to cast them off. Such a concept is foreign to Paul. Given these issues, God serves as the most likely subject of the participle ἀπεκδυσάμενος.[138]

If God is the subject, then the middle voice most likely carries an active force. In this case, "the rulers and authorities" remain the direct object of the participle, meaning that it was God who "stripped" the rulers and authorities. The middle voice is not completely lost because God performed this action out of his own interest.[139] The likelihood of this interpretation increases when one considers the parallels between Col 1:12–14 and Col 2:13–15. In Col 1:12–14, Paul draws a close connection between God's

---

136. Robinson, *Body*, 41, and Yates, "Colossians 2:15," 583–90.

137. Lightfoot, *Colossians*, 150; Dunn, *Colossians and Philemon*, 167–68; and Kooten, *Cosmic Christology*, 129.

138. Lohse, *Colossians*, 111–12; Barth and Blanke, *Colossians*, 333; Sumney, *Colossians*, 146; Pao, *Colossians and Philemon*, 172; and Beale, *Colossians and Philemon*, 201.

139. Smith, *Heavenly Perspective*, 108.

deliverance of believers from the powers of darkness (Col 1:13) and God's forgiveness of their sins through Christ (Col 1:14). A similar connection occurs in Col 2:13-15, where God's forgiveness of believers (Col 2:13-14) leads to his defeat of the cosmic powers (Col 2:15). The implication is that God's forgiveness of believers through Christ effectively releases believers from the authority of the cosmic powers so that they might come under the rule of Christ.[140] This parallel also means that "the rulers and authorities" most likely refer to hostile cosmic forces who rule "the dominion of darkness" (Col 1:13). If this is the case, then the participle ἀπεκδυσάμενος refers to God's stripping these powers of their authority and/or disarming them of their power.[141]

This understanding of the participle ἀπεκδυσάμενος helps determine the meaning of the participle θριαμβεύσας. Paul ends the verse with a picture of a royal triumphal procession. Paul declares that God has made a public display of the defeated cosmic powers by "triumphing" (θριαμβεύσας) over them. Paul's language probably draws upon the image of a Roman general celebrating victory over his enemies. The emperor or the victorious Roman general, often dressed in royal garb, would parade his defeated enemies through the streets and would receive honor and glory for his victory.[142] Paul ends by stating that this triumph occurred "in him" (ἐν αὐτῷ), a phrase which points to the critical role Christ plays in bringing about God's cosmic triumph. Whether one views the phrase as referring to Christ or to the cross, Christ's death on the cross serves as the means by which God brings about the defeat of hostile cosmic forces.[143]

---

140. Sappington, *Revelation and Redemption*, 211-13, and Beale, *Colossians and Philemon*, 200-201.

141. Lohse, *Colossians*, 112; Sumney, *Colossians*, 146; and Beale, *Colossians and Philemon*, 202. Carr and Yates argue that the "rulers and authorities" refer to the heavenly hosts that Christ would lead in a triumphal celebration (Carr, *Angels and Principalities*, 61-66; Yates, "Colossians 2:15," 581-83). For this view to be plausible, Christ would need to be the subject of the participle ἀπεκδυσάμενος and "the rulers and authorities" would need to function as the direct object of the main verb ἐδειγμάτισεν. Such a grammatical structure is difficult to reconcile.

142. Scholars widely attest to the use of the Roman victory image in Col 2:15 (for example, Yates, "Colossians 2:15," 579-80; Dunn, *Colossians and Philemon*, 168-69; Sumney, *Colossians*, 147; Gupta, *Colossians*, 98; Pao, *Colossians and Philemon*, 173; Jipp, *Christ Is King*, 126-27; Beale, *Colossians and Philemon*, 202.

143. The phrase ἐν αὐτῷ can be translated either as a locative (in him/the cross) or as an instrumental (through him/the cross) (Harris, *Colossians and Philemon*, 100). The instrumental translation makes the most sense of the context. If one chooses to translate it as a locative, then Paul's idea is that God brought about the defeat of the hostile cosmic forces within the sphere of Christ's work on the cross.

both Paul's and the NT's christological claims.[151] Christ's enthronement came as a result of his defeat of the cosmic powers via his death and resurrection (Col 1:18–20; 2:14–15). Paul's allusion to Ps 110 read in the context of his christological claim in the Colossian hymn also indicates the appropriateness of expanding its regal claims to include dominion over the whole cosmos.[152] Christ's placement at God's right hand means that he now participates in the divine rule over all things, including the heavenly realms. This reality mitigates any reasons the Colossians would have to boast in their supposed heavenly ascents. They were not to live out of a concern for heavenly beings but from a desire to know and submit to Christ their King.[153]

Paul's command to "seek" and "set your minds on things above" means that the Colossian believers were meant to orient their lives according to the inaugurated cosmic rule of Christ (Col 3:1–2). Such a life stands in contrast to those who would set their minds on "the things on the earth" (Col 3:2). Paul's exhortation does not draw a contrast between the metaphysical and the material, meaning that the Colossian believers needed to escape the material realm and ascend to the spiritual realm. Both the spiritual and physical realm belong under the reign of Christ. Rather, Paul's exhortation emphasizes the distinction between the old age where Adam fell on earth and the new age where Christ is enthroned in the heavenly realm (Col 3:9–10). The behavior of believers should reflect the ethics of Christ's kingdom instead of the ethics of Adam's fallen kingdom.[154]

Christ's enthronement not only had implications for the Colossian believers' present conduct but also provided security for their future destiny. The Colossian believers were to operate in submission to Christ with the hope that his cosmic reign would one day be fully realized. Paul reminds them that they have died to their former way of life, and their lives

---

110. In either case, the point remains that this verse, whether directly or indirectly, draws upon the royal ideology of Ps 110.

151. The NT writers cite Ps 110 more than any other psalm. Hay identifies thirty-three possible citations to Ps 110 in the NT (Hay, *Glory*, 15). For an extended discussion on the use of Ps 110:1 in Col 3:1, see Beetham, *Echoes*, 219–30.

152. Sumney, "Writing 'in the Image,'" 209–10. Sumney suggests that Paul simply expects his readers to accept this assertion because he does not immediately offer substantiation for the claim. While substantiation for the claim may not appear in Col 3, Col 1:12–20 offers the necessary grounds upon which Paul can make this christological claim.

153. Smith, *Heavenly Perspective*, 179.

154. Lincoln, *Paradise*, 126, and Smith, *Heavenly Perspective*, 180.

"have been hidden with Christ in God" (Col 3:3). Paul uses the perfect verb "hidden" (κέκρυπται) to convey something presently concealed that awaits future revelation.[155] Paul uses this verb earlier in the letter to describe the character of the gospel "mystery" that has been revealed to the saints (Col 1:26) and to God's wisdom and knowledge that has been hidden with Christ (Col 2:3). For believers, their "hiddenness" with Christ means that believers currently live according to the hidden reality of Christ's cosmic kingship. The use of the perfect tense indicates that their present lives on earth reveal the effects of their hidden life with Christ. Paul's language concerning the hiddenness of believers suggests that though Christ presently reigns over the cosmos, his reign has yet to be fully revealed.[156] Paul declares that this hidden reality will one day be made known. Such revelation can only occur when Christ is revealed (Col 3:4).

This revelation language bears some similarity to his statements regarding the destiny of believers in Rom 8, where the fate of creation is closely tied to the fate of believers (Rom 8:19, 22–23). Using the language of sonship, Paul identifies believers as participants in Christ's royal messianic sonship, meaning that they also participate in Christ's messianic rule (Rom 8:14–17, 19, 23, 29–30). Such identification with Christ explains creation's eager awaiting of the revelation of believers (Rom 8:19). Their revelation means that Christ's cosmic rule has been fully revealed.[157] Similarly in Col 3, Paul again identifies the believers' fate with Christ's fate. As Christ now fully defines their life, so Christ's destiny fully defines their destiny (Col 3:4). The Colossian believers could find their confidence in God's intent to reconcile the whole cosmos under the rule of Christ

---

155. Some scholars have argued that "hiddenness" refers to the protection believers have as they await their final revelation with Christ (Moo, *Colossians and Philemon*, 250–51; Pao, *Colossians and Philemon*, 213–14). However, this sense does not align with Paul's use of the verb earlier in the letter. Paul's subsequent mention of the believers' future revelation with Christ makes it much more likely that Paul uses this verb primarily to refer to something concealed awaiting revelation (Wright, *Colossians*, 132; Dunn, *Colossians and Philemon*, 206–7; Gupta, *Colossians*, 130; Beale, *Colossians and Philemon*, 268).

156. This distinction is important as it reveals that the eschatology of Colossians does not contradict the eschatology of Paul's other letters. Kooten argues that Colossians presents cosmic reconciliation as a completed act in that the cosmos has now been reconstituted in the shape of Christ's body (Kooten, *Cosmic Christology*, 129, 146, 209). Besides the problems associated with considering the cosmos to be Christ's body, Kooten's thesis ignores the "hidden" aspects of Christ's cosmic kingdom. Though Christ is presently enthroned as God's King over the cosmos, Paul's "hiddenness" language indicates that Christ's kingdom has not yet been fully realized.

157. For more on this motif in Rom 8, see ch. 3.

(Col 1:19–20). As in Rom 8, believers' final revelation at the appearing of Christ means the full realization of Christ's cosmic rule.

The appearance of believers with Christ "in glory" is an implicit reference to Paul's Adam Christology. The "glory" referred to by Paul is the glory that Adam originally lost because of his failure as God's first king. Christ has now taken up this "glory" so that God might restore this glory to humanity.[158] The implication for believers is that the glorious image originally possessed by Adam will be fully restored to those who belong to Christ, the true bearer of the divine image. This language echoes other Pauline texts in which Paul refers to God's intent to transform believers after the glory of Christ (1 Cor 15:44–49; Phil 3:20–21).[159] In Colossians, Paul explains that this restoration of glory happens as a result of believers' past death and resurrection with Christ (Col 2:20; 3:1), their present "hiddenness" with Christ (Col 3:3), and their future revelation with Christ (Col 3:4).

Paul makes another implicit reference to Adam with his use of the "old man/new man" metaphor in Col 3:9–11. While the impetus behind Paul's metaphor is ethical, his metaphor is grounded on his own Adam Christology, specifically the contrast he draws between the rule of Adam and the rule of Christ (1 Cor 15:21–22; Rom 5:12–21).[160] After giving some ethical implications of the Colossian believers' identification with Christ and his cosmic rule, Paul states that the reason for their ethical transformation is because they had "put off the old man with his deeds" (Col 3:9).[161] The old man refers to Adam and the effects of his failed reign. The Colossian believers were to live according to the reality that Christ had delivered them from the dominion of Adam. Therefore, they should no longer conform their lives to the ethics and practices of those who are under Adam's dominion.[162]

---

158. Dunn, *Colossians and Philemon*, 209, and Smith, *Heavenly Perspective*, 183.

159. Dunn, *Colossians and Philemon*, 209, and Beale, *Colossians and Philemon*, 270.

160. Cullmann, *Christology*, 174; Son, *Corporate Elements*, 57–58; Grenz, "Social God," 92; and Leese, *Christ*, 120.

161. The participles ἀπεκδυσάμενοι (Col 3:9) and ἐνδυσάμενοι are causal and suggest that the putting off and putting on occurred at the Colossian believers' salvation (Wolter, *Kolosser*, 178; Pao, *Colossians and Philemon*, 225; Beale, *Colossians and Philemon*, 279). Lohse and Yates argue that these participles are imperatival (Lohse, *Colossians*, 141; Yates, "Christian Way," 247), but this rendering is unlikely since these participles modify the series of imperatives given in vv. 5–9a.

162. Gupta, *Colossians*, 138.

Instead, Paul reminds them that they had "put on the new man."[163] The new man refers to Christ and the transformation that the believers experienced resulting from their transfer into his kingdom (Col 1:13–14). Paul characterizes this new man as being renewed "according to the image of the one who created him" (Col 3:10b). Paul's reference to the "image" (εἰκόνα) is a clear allusion to the original image granted to Adam in Gen 1:26–27. The "one who created" (τοῦ κτίσαντος) could refer either to God, who created Adam in his image, or Christ, who is God's agent in creation (Col 1:16). Though many scholars understandably argue that God is the primary referent,[164] a few contextual markers make it possible for Christ to be the referent.[165] In the immediate context, the Christocentric nature of the believers' new reality is made explicit in the following verse when Paul declares Christ to be "all and in all" (Col 3:11). Second, the broader context emphasizes that the Colossian believers have died and risen with Christ and await their glorification with him. This means that believers are being renewed in Christ's image. Third, the context of the letter points to Christ as the agent of creation (Col 1:15–16). Just as Christ was God's creative agent at the original creation, so also is he God's creative agent in the era of new creation. The new image into which believers are being transformed is not simply the original image given to Adam at creation but the image which Christ bears (Col 1:15). Those who now reside in the kingdom of Christ are being transformed together according to the image of their King, who now becomes the sole source of their identity (Col 3:11). Colossians 3:9–11 emphasizes that one of Christ's vital roles as God's King is to form a humanity who will perpetuate the rule of God and his own rule as God's King throughout the cosmos.

---

163. For an extensive discussion on the social, cultural, and contextual background of Paul's clothing metaphor in Col 3 (Canavan, *Clothing the Body of Christ*). Pao and Beale suggest that the use of the clothing metaphor could also be a reference to Adam. Whereas God provided Adam clothing as means to restore their relationship (Gen 3:7, 21), God's clothing of believers signifies the restored relationship between God and humanity (Pao, *Colossians and Philemon*, 225–26; Beale, *Colossians and Philemon*, 277–78).

164. Lohse, *Colossians*, 143; Dunn, *Colossians and Philemon*, 222; Beetham, *Echoes*, 242n63; Pao, *Colossians and Philemon*, 227; and Sumney, "Writing 'in the Image' of Scripture," 211.

165. The following contextual markers are discussed in Fee, *Pauline Christology*, 303–4. See also Wright, *Colossians*, 138–39, and Barth and Blanke, *Colossians*, 413–14.

SUMMARY AND CONCLUSION

Jewish royal ideology gave Paul a plausible framework by which he could conceive of and articulate the belief that Christ is the supreme King who rules over the whole cosmos. This chapter has attempted to show how Paul used both Adamic and Davidic language and themes to demonstrate Christ's identity and role as God's ideal King over the cosmos. While it would not be wise to discount any influence from Hellenistic or Wisdom traditions, Paul's use of regal themes in Colossians demonstrates the explanatory power of Jewish royal ideology on the cosmic Christology of the letter. Jewish royal language gives a viable alternative to those who primarily use Wisdom traditions to interpret the cosmic Christology of Colossians and to Kooten's Middle Platonic-Stoic interpretation. While Kooten argues that Colossians' cosmic Christology is an over-hellenized version of Paul's cosmic Christology, Jewish royal ideology reveals that Colossians' cosmic Christology aligns closely with Paul's cosmic Christology in his other letters. These royal themes also give deeper insight into Paul's ethical exhortations to the Colossian believers.

Paul presents Christ's position and role in the cosmos as the antitype of Adam's reign. Paul places Christ in Adam's original position as God's royal ambassador over creation and demonstrates how Christ's rule exceeds Adam's rule. Christ's role as God's agent in creation makes him the preexistent rightful King of the cosmos. Adam was granted the royal title "image of God" at creation, but Christ has always possessed the "image of God" as the eternal Son of God. Therefore, Christ has always been the rightful King of the cosmos, and he is the goal of the cosmos. Christ's work as Creator proves his power to undo the catastrophic effects of Adam's fall. Adam's failure plunged creation into chaos, but Christ's reign upholds and maintains cosmic order. Adam brought the cosmos under the "dominion of darkness," but Christ subdued the hostile cosmic powers under his reign. Adam was commissioned to subdue the earth, but Christ subdues every part of the cosmos under his reign. In this way, Christ fulfills God's original plan to exercise his good rule over creation through his ideal king.

Paul sees Christ regaining the dominion that Adam lost through his fulfillment of the messianic promise. Paul grants the title of "beloved Son" and "firstborn" to Christ. Both titles identify Christ as a royal figure and reflect the father-son relationship that God promised to have with the ideal Davidic king. As the one who has the divine fullness within himself, Christ possesses the honor and glory which belong to God's ideal king.

Christ's work in subjecting the cosmic powers reflects the Jewish royal motif in which God invites his ideal king to join with him in his battle against the hostile cosmic powers. Rather than achieving this cosmic victory through military conquest, Paul views Christ achieving this victory through his own death and resurrection. Rather than contradicting Jewish royal ideology, Christ's death and resurrection clarify the way in which God would enthrone his ideal king over the cosmos. As Jewish royal ideology views the enthronement of God's king signaling the defeat of the wicked and the vindication of the righteous, Christ's enthronement signals defeat for God's enemies and secures the destiny of his people. Paul presents Christ's cosmic victory as fully accomplished and states that he presently reigns over the cosmos. However, the cosmos awaits the full revelation of Christ's kingship.

Paul presents the church as the present realization of Christ's cosmic kingship. The church is the product of Christ's regal work in forming a new humanity that perpetuates the rule of God and Christ. Through Christ, God has delivered believers from the failed dominion of Adam and placed them under the dominion of Christ. Thus, the enthroned King of the cosmos is the one who rules over the church. Believers' subjection to Christ means that they do not need to fear or submit to any other cosmic power. As those under Christ's dominion, Paul exhorts the Colossian believers no longer to live according to the ethics of Adam's failed dominion but to live as those who are being transformed into the image of Christ their King until the full revelation of Christ's cosmic reign. In this way, Christ restores to believers the original purpose given to Adam, and believers now join with Christ in perpetuating God's good rule throughout the cosmos.

5

Cosmic Christ in Ephesians

PAUL VIEWS CHRIST'S COSMIC position and function as foundational to forming the church's identity in Ephesians.[1] Given the similarities between Colossians and Ephesians, one should explore whether the Adamic and Davidic royal themes that ground the cosmic Christology of Colossians appear again in Ephesians. Given that scholars have long recognized the influence of the OT on Ephesians,[2] it seems even more likely that Jewish royal ideology might lie behind Paul's cosmic christological assertions in Ephesians. Ephesians may also give further insight into Paul's view of Christ's cosmic kingship. The chapter will cover key passages in Ephesians that describe Christ's cosmic role and function using Jewish royal ideological language and themes. As with Colossians, Paul does not explicitly mention Adam or David in this letter, but one can reasonably argue that he alludes to Adamic and Davidic motifs. This chapter will also bring Ephesians into dialogue with Colossians to discover whether Ephesians critiques (as Kooten argues) or complements the cosmic Christology of Colossians. This chapter will also suggest that Jewish royal ideology serves as a plausible alternative to Kooten's Greco-Roman cosmological framework.

---

1. On Pauline authorship of Ephesians, see ch. 1, 15n79.
2. For examples, see Lincoln, "Use of the OT," 16–57, and Moritz, *Profound Mystery*.

THE RELATIONSHIP BETWEEN COLOSSIANS AND EPHESIANS

No one questions that a relationship between Colossians and Ephesians exists. The similarities in vocabulary, concepts, style, and structure make this relationship evident. The difficulty many scholars have found is in how to account for this relationship. Ernest Best outlines three basic possibilities: either (1) Ephesians depends on Colossians, (2) Colossians depends on Ephesians, or (3) neither letter depends on the other.[3] How one accounts for this relationship can significantly affect his/her views regarding the similarities and dissimilarities between Ephesians and Colossians. This is especially true of Kooten's own conclusions regarding the relationship between the cosmic Christology of Colossians and the cosmic Christology of Ephesians.

Kooten begins with the assumption that Colossians and Ephesians were written by two different authors with neither of them being Paul. He also assumes the view that the author of Ephesians was dependent on Colossians.[4] Further, Kooten argues that the Ephesians' author copied and adapted the literary structure of Colossians in such a sophisticated manner that it is without analogy.[5] Rather than using the structure of Colossians as a way to make his writing look Pauline,[6] the author of Ephesians adapted this structure so that he might present a critical commentary on Colossians.[7] Kooten suggests that the author of Ephesians reworked and reinterpreted various passages in Colossians and inserted new passages into the structure of his letter so that he might correct the cosmic Christology of Colossians. From this conclusion, Kooten then posits that the "interrelationships between the cosmologies of Ephesians, Colossians, and Paul are best explained within the framework of contemporary Greco-Roman cosmology."[8]

Kooten's picture of the relationship between Colossians and Ephesians is problematic for a few reasons. First, determining which letter

---

3. Best, "Who Used Whom?," 75.

4. This view was first championed by Holtzmann, *Kritik*, 35–129. For other arguments for this view, see Mitton, *Ephesians*, 55–58; Merkel, "Epheserbrief," *ANRW* 25.4:3212–20; and Lincoln, *Ephesians*, l–lviii.

5. Kooten, *Cosmic Christology*, 227–29.

6. This is the argument of Merklein, *Kirchliche*, 41, and Lincoln, *Ephesians*, lxviii.

7. Kooten, *Cosmic Christology*, 236.

8. Kooten, *Cosmic Christology*, 148–49.

depends upon the other is much more difficult than Kooten would like to admit. While the majority of scholars do favor the view that Ephesians depends on Colossians, other scholars have made plausible arguments that Colossians is dependent on Ephesians.[9] Best examines several parallel passages in Colossians and Ephesians and demonstrates the difficulty in determining the priority of either letter in each case.[10] The point is that if two different authors were involved in writing these letters, determining which author borrowed from the other is a highly problematic process. Second, Kooten's thesis would require that the author of Ephesians had a copy of Colossians in front of him as he wrote Ephesians, but there is no proof for this scenario.[11] Third, Kooten's timeline for when these letters were written and sent is questionable. He proposes that Colossians was written in AD 80 and Ephesians between AD 80 and 140. However, such a late date for Ephesians seems unlikely given its probable attestation by multiple early church fathers in the late first century and early second century AD.[12] Fourth, Kooten suggests that Ephesians uses certain terms from Colossians but with different connotations. For example, Kooten argues that while Colossians defines Christ's σῶμα in a cosmic sense, Ephesians defines Christ's σῶμα in an ecclesial sense.[13] Kooten's assertion fails because he does not recognize the clear ecclesial use of σῶμα in Col 1:17.[14]

When examining the relationship between Colossians and Ephesians, the simplest solution seems to be the most likely solution: Paul wrote both Colossians and Ephesians. The difficulty in determining the priority of either Colossians or Ephesians points to one author writing

---

9. Coutts, "Ephesians and Colossians," 201–7; Roon, *Authenticity of Ephesians*, 413–37. Roon argues that Colossians may have borrowed some from Ephesians but suggests that both letters depend on an Urtext.

10. Best, "Who Used Whom?," 79–93. See also Muddiman, *Ephesians*, 8–11.

11. Hoehner, *Ephesians*, 37.

12. For an extended discussion of the early church fathers' use of Ephesians, see Hoehner, *Ephesians*, 2–6. Clement of Rome possibly alludes to Eph 1:17–18; 4:4–6, 18; and 5:21. Ignatius of Antioch possibly alludes to Eph 5:1–2 and 6:11–17. Polycarp alludes to Eph 4:26. Kooten suggests that it is unlikely that Clement or Ignatius had knowledge of Ephesians but fails to give any justification for this assertion (Kooten, *Cosmic Christology*, 2). Further, he does not interact with any scholars who would challenge such an assertion.

13. Lincoln makes a similar argument, though he does not go so far to say that the Ephesians author desires to correct the Christology of Colossians (Lincoln, *Ephesians*, liii–liv).

14. See ch. 4.

both texts rather than one author depending on another author.[15] This view also accounts for any similarities and dissimilarities between the letters. The similarities are simply the result of both letters coming from the same author, and the dissimilarities are the result of each letter addressing different situations. As Hoehner aptly puts, "It is easier to believe that Paul wrote these two epistles, and that when he penned Ephesians, he would have similar vocabulary and content on similar topics and would vary in vocabulary when addressing different issues."[16] If Paul wrote both letters, it is likely that he wrote both letters either at the same time or very close together.[17] Paul's mention of Tychicus as the letter carrier of both Colossians (Col 4:7) and Ephesians (Eph 6:21–22) would also suggest that Paul wrote these letters around the same time. Therefore, the most likely scenario is that Paul originally wrote Colossians to encourage the Colossian church and to address the Colossian heresy. Since Tychicus, the letter carrier of Colossians, was from Ephesus and would return there after visiting Colossae, Paul decided to write a broader letter of exhortation to the church in the region of Ephesus.[18]

That Paul wrote both Colossians and Ephesians around the same time presents two implications that affect the following discussion on

15. Best suggests that "the similarities and dissimilarities of the two letters can be explained most easily on the assumption of distinct authors who were members of the same Pauline school and had discussed together the Pauline theology they had inherited." See Best, "Who Used Whom?," 96. This solution is much more difficult to prove. The easier solution would be to accept the internal evidence of both letters, which both claim to be written by Paul.

16. Hoehner, *Ephesians*, 38. Stanley Porter and Kent Clarke illustrate this point well in examining the use of the verb ἀποκαταλλάσσω in both letters. They argue that it would be unlikely for a pseudonymous author to use a newly coined term if he truly desired to imitate Paul. Further, if the Ephesians author wished to copy Colossians, it is unlikely that he would use this term since it carries a slightly different sense in Eph 2:16 (Porter and Clarke, "Canonical-Critical Perspective," 77–83).

17. Best, "Who Used Whom?," 95. Concerning date, it is most likely that Paul wrote Ephesians from his Roman imprisonment sometime between AD 61 and 63 (Barth, *Ephesians 1–3*, 50–52).

18. The inclusion of ἐν Ἐφέσῳ in Eph 1:1 remains a matter of great debate among textual critics. Some scholars argue for the omission of the phrase. According to this argument, this letter was meant to be a general letter, but it eventually became associated with Ephesus (Schmid, *Epheserbrief*, 125–29; Best, "Ephesians 1.1," 276–78). Kooten argues that Ephesians was written to the Laodiceans. Lincoln argues that it was written to Hierapolis and Laodicea (Lincoln, *Ephesians*, 3–4; Kooten, *Cosmic Christology*, 195–201). While these other arguments have merit, it seems best to retain the phrase ἐν Ἐφέσῳ and treat Ephesus as the original destination of the letter. Hoehner demonstrates that there is substantial internal and external evidence that warrants the retention of this phrase (Hoehner, *Ephesians*, 78–79, 144–48; see also Thielman, *Ephesians*, 11–16).

the cosmic Christology of Ephesians. First, if Paul utilized Jewish royal themes to articulate his cosmic Christology in Colossians, it seems likely that he may have used these themes again to articulate his cosmic Christology in Ephesians. Second, rather than contradicting the Christology of Colossians, Paul complemented and expanded on his cosmic Christology in Ephesians. Therefore, Ephesians may provide further clarity on how Jewish royal ideology affected Paul's own cosmic Christology.

EPHESIANS 1:3-14

Paul begins Ephesians by focusing on the blessings that God, according to his eternal purposes, has bestowed upon believers "in Christ." Ephesians has an unusually high concentration of Paul's "in Christ" formula. John Allan identifies at least thirty-four instances of this formula in the letter; Son identifies thirty-six instances; and Hoehner identifies thirty-nine potential uses of the formula.[19] A more unique aspect of Paul's use of this formula in Ephesians is the number of times he notes God as the subject of the actions taken "in Christ."[20] Even when the verb appears as passive, God is often the one who initiates the action in Christ.[21] A high concentration of these actions taken "in Christ" are referenced in Paul's opening eulogy (or *berakah*) in Eph 1:3-14.

---

19. Allan, "'In Christ' Formula," 54; Son, *Corporate Elements*, 187-88; and Hoehner, *Ephesians*, 173-74. The instances acknowledged by Allan, Son, and Hoehner occur in Eph 1:1, 3, 4, 7, 10, 11, 12, 13, 15, 20; 2:6, 7, 10, 15, 16, 21, 22; 3:6, 11, 12, 21; 4:1, 17, 21, 30, 32; 5:8; 6:1, 10, 21. Son and Hoehner include the phrase ἐν αὐτῷ in Eph 1:9 (which could be a reference to God) and the expression in Eph 1:6 (ἐν τῷ ἠγαπημένῳ). Hoehner also includes the phrase ἐν αὐτῷ in Eph 6:20 (which could be a reference to the mystery in Eph 6:19) and the expressions συνεζωοποίησεν τῷ Χριστῷ (2:5) and ἐν τῷ αἵματι τοῦ Χριστοῦ (2:13). Given that Deissmann found 164 occurrences of this formula in Paul's letters (excluding Colossians, Ephesians, and the Pastoral epistles), the number of uses of this formula in the small letter of Ephesians is certainly worth noting (Deissmann, *Neutestamentliche Formel*).

20. Son notes various instances throughout the Pauline letters in which a personal subject paired with a verb denotes an action in Christ. He points out four semantic peculiarities with this particular formula: (1) "Paul refers to an activity in Christ without an object." (2) "Paul denotes an activity in Christ with a stated or implied object." (3) "When the verb is used in a passive voice, it indicates an activity done in Christ upon a person." (4) "God is sometimes directly stated as the subject of the activities in Christ." Son notes thirty-five instances where (3) or (4) occur, and eighteen of these occur in Ephesians (Son, *Corporate Elements*, 14-15).

21. Son, *Corporate Elements*, 15.

If God's actions "in Christ" constitute the blessings bestowed upon believers, one needs to understand the primary force behind this prepositional phrase.[22] Specifically, did Paul use the prepositional phrase ἐν Χριστῷ in a locative sense or an instrumental sense? It seems problematic to argue for a pervasive use of either the locative or instrumental sense throughout Ephesians.[23] One may simply suggest that context determines the force of the phrase, but there are many cases where even the context remains uncertain. For this reason, one's own overall understanding of Pauline theology often becomes the primary influencer behind one's classification of the formula.[24] When the phrase is paired with a verb expressing being, the locative sense is clearly dominant. In cases where the phrase is paired with an explicit or implicit verb expressing an action, differentiating between the locative sense and instrumental sense becomes more difficult.[25] This latter formulation appears nine times (Eph 1:3, 4, 6, 9, 10, 11, 12, 13) in Paul's opening eulogy, and God is often the subject of the action performed in Christ (Eph 1:3, 4, 6, 10, 11, 13b). When Paul portrays God as the one who is acting "in Christ," perhaps he intends to communicate both the instrumental and locative sense of the formula.

Paul opens his eulogy with a declaration that God blessed the Ephesian believers "in the heavenlies in Christ" (Eph 1:3). The phrase "in the heavenlies" suggests both the location of believers' spiritual blessings and the location of Christ's dwelling. Believers have blessings in the heavenly places because they have been incorporated into Christ in the place where he now reigns (Eph 1:20).[26] This idea clarifies Paul's statement in

---

22. This is a weakness of Kooten's own interpretation of Ephesians. He gives almost no consideration to the force behind the "in Christ" formula in Eph 1 (Kooten, *Cosmic Christology*, 150–52).

23. In his original study, Deissmann assigned a locative force to the phrase. Further, he suggested that a mystical force undergirds the formula, meaning that believers have an intimate fellowship with the living, spiritual Christ (Deissmann, *Neutestamentliche Formel*, 140). However, Deissmann's argument fails because it mystifies Christ into an impersonal, spiritual force. Allan argues for a "predominantly, if not exclusively . . . instrumental sense" behind the use of the formula in Ephesians (Allan, "'In Christ' Formula," 59). Allan's thesis fails to recognize instances in which the use of the formula could much more easily be considered locative than instrumental (for example, Eph 1:1, 3) and "underestimates the extent to which its use in Ephesians involves incorporation" (Lincoln, *Ephesians*, 21–22). Though Hoehner recognizes that the phrase may sometimes have the idea of instrumentality, he still maintains its locative sense (Hoehner, *Ephesians*, 170–72).

24. See Bouttier, *En Christ*, 29, and Son, *Corporate Elements*, 12.

25. Son, *Corporate Elements*, 13.

26. Best argues that "in Christ" should be taken as a locative like the phrase "in the

Col 3:3 when he refers to the Colossian believers as having their lives hidden in Christ who is enthroned in the heavens. The locative force of the formula also suggests that Paul speaks to Christ's preexistence. God chose believers not only through the agency of Christ, but he also united believers to Christ before the foundation of the world.[27] Such a statement suggests that God presently carried out his purpose through Christ because Christ was personally and temporally part of the eternal plan of God.[28] This concept accords well with Paul's declaration in Colossians concerning Christ's role as the preexistent Creator in Col 1:15–17. While Colossians speaks more broadly concerning Christ's role in creation, Ephesians specifies that God's original creation through Christ involved his plan to incorporate believers in Christ.

One also cannot ignore the instrumental force behind Paul's use of the "in Christ" formula. The ways in which God acts through Christ in Eph 1:3–14 align with Jewish royal traditions where God's ideal king serves as his agent.[29] One may also see several parallels between how Paul uses these royal traditions in Colossians and how he uses them in his opening eulogy in Ephesians. God grants believers spiritual blessings and incorporates them in the place where Christ dwells, but this assertion implies that these blessings can only come through Christ (1:3). Christ serves as the agent by which God chose believers before the world began. Paul specifies that God chose that believers would receive the blessing of adoption "through [διά] Christ" (Eph 1:5).[30] The result is that believers are beneficiaries of God's actions both through the agency of Christ and because they now share their identity with the exalted Christ. As Jipp

---

heavenlies" (Best, *Ephesians*, 114–15). Thielman also suggests the locative sense while giving no consideration to the potential instrumental sense (Thielman, *Ephesians*, 47).

27. Hamerton-Kelly, *Pre-Existence*, 180–82, and Lincoln, *Ephesians*, 22–23.

28. Fee, *Pauline Christology*, 344–45. See also Barth, *Ephesians 1–3*, 109–10. This assertion runs contrary to Thielman, who suggests that the phrase ἐν αὐτῷ functions like the phrase διὰ Ἰησοῦ Χριστοῦ in Eph 1:5. See Thielman, *Ephesians*, 48. This argument could lead one to view ἐν αὐτῷ in v. 4 in an atemporal sense where Paul simply anticipates what God would do "in Christ" on behalf of believers. Fee rightly points out that Paul's use of the word καθώς suggests he is referring to a present reality in v. 3, which is grounded in an antecedent reality mentioned in v. 4.

29. Looking at both Jewish and Greco-Roman thought, Smith argues that God's consistent activity in Christ coheres with the ideal king in antiquity who acted as God's vice-regent (Smith, *Ideal King*, 182–95).

30. Smith argues that the parallelism between the διά phrases and the ἐν phrases suggest that the latter should be read with an instrumental force (Smith, *Ideal King*, 186; see also Talbert, *Ephesians and Colossians*, 44–47; Sellin, *Epheser*, 83–110).

states, "May it be that the formula retains both connotations precisely because when God acts by means of the Messiah, God acts to incorporate the people into the identity and rule of the Messiah?"[31]

Paul declares that Christ, the beloved (ἠγαπημένῳ)[32] of God, serves as the agent by whom God bestows his grace on believers (Eph 1:6). The evidence of this grace is that believers receive redemption and forgiveness through (διά) the blood of Christ (Eph 1:7). The title "beloved" recalls the imagery of the beloved Davidic king (2 Sam 7:18). Paul uses this same christological description in Col 1:13 when describing the transfer of believers from the dominion of darkness into the kingdom of Christ, the "beloved Son." Colossians also views Christ as the agent in/through whom believers receive redemption and forgiveness (Col 1:14). While Ephesians emphasizes that Christ's blood is the means by which believers receive redemption, Colossians presents Christ's blood as accomplishing cosmic reconciliation (Col 1:20) with believers being beneficiaries of this reconciliatory work (Col 1:21–22).

Christ serves as God's agent not just on behalf of believers but on behalf of the whole cosmos. Paul reveals that Christ serves as God's agent by whom he plans to "sum up" (ἀνακεφαλαιώσασθαι) all things.[33] Greek literature commonly uses the word ἀνακεφαλαιόω in reference to the summation of an argument in a speech (Rom 13:9).[34] Paul indicates that this "summing up" happens "in Christ." One should once again note the locative force behind "in Christ" in Eph 1:10. Christ is not only the agent through whom God brings cosmic harmony, but he is also the sphere in which the cosmos finds harmony (see also Col 1:17).[35] Paul clarifies

---

31. Jipp, *Christ Is King*, 199. See also Lincoln, *Ephesians*, 22, and Brannon, *Heavenlies in Ephesians*, 112.

32. Some later manuscripts (D*, F, G, 629) insert υἱῷ αὐτοῦ. The textual support for this insertion is weak and should not be considered part of the original manuscript. See Thielman, *Ephesians*, 55. This later insertion may at least suggest that "beloved" was considered a messianic title (Schlier, *Christus und die Kirche*, 56; Barth, *Ephesians*, 82–83). Others argue that Paul's use of the title reflects the OT designation of God's people as his "beloved." In this case, Christ is God's supreme beloved, and believers are God's beloved by means of their union with Christ (Hoehner, *Ephesians*, 203–4; Thielman, *Ephesians*, 54).

33. Much of the following discussion on the meaning of ἀνακεφαλαιόω is owed to a presentation by Son at the 2019 ETS Annual Meeting (Son, "Christology of Ephesians").

34. Jennifer Maclean conducted a study of over four hundred occurrences of this verb in the TLG and concluded that summation of an argument is its primary meaning (Maclean, "Ephesians and the Problem of Colossians," 51–58).

35. See ch. 4.

in Eph 1:22 that God accomplishes this "summation" by making Christ the head over all things.³⁶ The implication is that God desires to unite all things in the cosmos in Christ. Ephesians 1:10 parallels Paul's declaration in Col 1:20 that Christ serves as God's agent through whom he reconciles the whole cosmos, even though Paul uses the verb ἀποκαταλλάσσω in Col 1:20.³⁷ The concept of "summing up" all things under the headship of Christ implies reconciliation and restoration. In both passages, Paul specifies that the scope of God's reconciliation through Christ includes the heavenly and earthly realms.³⁸

Paul's language points to God's plan to bring everything in the cosmos under the rule of Christ. This declaration presupposes that the cosmos has been thrown into a chaotic state and needs restoration. It is not difficult to conceive that Paul's Adam Christology serves as the presuppositional foundation of Eph 1:10. Adam, as God's first royal agent over creation, brought the creation into disharmony through his failure. Christ, as God's ideal King, becomes the one through whom God once again brings cosmic harmony. As Adam was meant to uphold God's order in creation, Christ now upholds the order of the cosmos in the sphere of his reign. In this way, Christ fulfills the role of the ideal Davidic king who was meant to bring cosmic stability through his reign.

Paul ends his eulogy by focusing on the benefit of God's cosmic work in/through Christ for believers. He reminds the Ephesian believers that God, according to his good will, obtained a people as his own possession in/through Christ (Eph 1:11).³⁹ God brought the Ephesian believers into

36. While the verb ἀνακεφαλαιόω may not specifically mean "to unite under the head," Paul's reference to Christ's headship in Eph 1 and the prominence of this theme in Ephesians suggests that one cannot completely discount the idea of submitting all things under Christ from Eph 1:10 (Son, "Christology of Ephesians").

37. Best argues that the idea of reconciliation should be excluded from Ephesians 1:10 because Paul does not use the verb (ἀποκαταλλάσσω) he used in Colossians 1:20. Rather, he suggests the verb in Eph 1:10 simply conveys the idea of "summing up" and not reconciliation or restoration. See Best, *Ephesians*, 139. Kooten leans on a similar interpretation of the verb in Eph 1:10 (Kooten, *Cosmic Christology*, 151). Best is right to point out the difference in verbs between Col 1:20 and Eph 1:10. However, the concept of "summing up" all things under the headship of Christ implies reconciliation and restoration (Lincoln, *Paradise*, 143). Therefore, even if the nuance in verb usage differs, the ideas presented in Col 1:20 and Eph 1:10 are very similar. The discourse on Christ's exaltation and enthronement over the cosmos in Eph 1:20–23 also suggests that Paul has Christ's headship in view in Eph 1:10.

38. εἴτε τὰ ἐπὶ τῆς γῆς εἴτε τὰ ἐν τοῖς οὐρανοῖς (Colossians 1:20); τὰ ἐπὶ τοῖς οὐρανοῖς καὶ τὰ ἐπὶ τῆς γῆς (Eph 1:10).

39. For this interpretation of ἐκληρώθημεν, see Lincoln, *Ephesians*, 35–36; Barth,

this people in/through Christ (Eph 1:13).[40] Christ then serves as both the agent through whom God forms a people for himself and the sphere in which that new people now exist. Their relationship to Christ means that they are guaranteed an inheritance (Eph 1:14). Ephesians 1:11–14 repeats Paul's declaration in Col 1:12–14 that those who have been transferred into Christ's kingdom now have an inheritance. Ephesians elaborates that the sealing of the Spirit serves as the guarantee of the inheritance believers have received because of God's action in/through Christ his ideal King.

EPHESIANS 1:20–23

Paul clarifies how God worked through Christ his royal agent in Eph 1:20–23. As Col 1:15–20 provides the christological foundation for Paul's argument in Colossians, so Eph 1:20–23 provides the christological foundation for Paul's teaching in Ephesians. Kooten argues that this passage is where Ephesians begins to differ in its cosmic Christology from Colossians. He argues that Colossians presents a "confident cosmology" where the whole cosmos has already been reconciled and put together in Christ as his cosmic body. He suggests that Ephesians argues "that the extension of Christ's influence over the cosmos is still in progress."[41] Kooten argues that Christ's gradual filling of the cosmos in Ephesians derives from Greco-Roman cosmology.[42] However, a closer look at Eph 1:20–23 reveals that (1) the cosmic Christology of the passage does not differ as much from Colossians as Kooten suggests and that (2) one can alternatively discern the cosmic Christology of Eph 1:20–23 through the lens of Jewish royal ideology. Paul's use of Jewish royal ideology is even more apparent in this passage considering his allusions to Ps 110:1 and Ps 8:6.[43]

Ephesians 1–3, 93–94; and Hoehner, *Ephesians*, 226–27. Though believers are the subject of the verb, the use of the passive voice suggests that they are the recipients of the action God initiates. In this way, God is still the subject of the action that has taken place in Christ (Son, *Corporate Elements*, 15).

40. It seems likely that "we" in v. 11 refers to Paul and his fellow Jewish believers while the "you" in v. 13 refers to gentile believers (Barth, *Ephesians*, 92–95). Paul speaks more about the joining of Jews and gentiles into one new people in Eph 2:11–22. The point is that for both Jew and gentile, what God has done for them through Christ and his placement of them in Christ serves as the basis of their identity.

41. Kooten, *Cosmic Christology*, 152.

42. Kooten, *Cosmic Christology*, 157–66.

43. Kooten downplays the significance of these allusions. While he acknowledges that the author's allusion to Ps 8 is due to his borrowing from 1 Cor 15:23–28, he

Given that Paul incorporates a Davidic (Ps 110) and Adamic (Ps 8) royal Psalm in close proximity, Eph 1:20–23 provides a helpful example of how Paul incorporated the Jewish pictures of the Adamic and Davidic king in his cosmic Christology.

Paul explains that the mighty work of God (Eph 1:19) is most clearly exemplified in the resurrection and enthronement of Christ (Eph 1:20). As in Colossians, Paul views Christ's resurrection as the event that secured Christ's rightful place as God's cosmic King (Col 1:18).[44] Paul directly alludes to Ps 110:1, an allusion he also makes in Col 3:1, when he proclaims that Christ has been seated at God's right hand (καθίσας ἐν δεξιᾷ αὐτοῦ).[45] Paul's allusion indicates that Christ fulfills the promise of the ideal Davidic king through his resurrection and subsequent enthronement.[46] The location of Christ's throne "in the heavenlies" (see also Col 3:1)[47] points to the cosmic scope of Christ's reign. It also suggests that though Christ's cosmic kingship is a present reality, it has not yet been fully realized.

The result of Christ's enthronement is that he has been placed far above every competing spiritual power (Eph 1:21). Paul uses similar terminology from his description of Christ's cosmic authority in Colossians (Col 1:16; 2:10) for these spiritual powers in Ephesians:

- πάσης ἀρχῆς καὶ ἐξουσίας καὶ δυνάμεως καὶ κυριότητος καὶ παντὸς ὀνόματος ὀνομαζομένου (Eph 1:21)
- εἴτε θρόνοι εἴτε κυριότητες εἴτε ἀρχαὶ εἴτε ἐξουσίαι (Col 1:16)
- πάσης ἀρχῆς καὶ ἐξουσίας (Col 2:10)
- τὰς ἀρχὰς καὶ τὰς ἐξουσίας (Col 2:15)

suggests that his allusion to Ps 110 is the result of the author borrowing from Col 3:1, not by his familiarity with 1 Cor 15:23–28 (Kooten, *Cosmic Christology*, 155–56n15).

44. See ch. 4.

45. Κάθου ἐκ δεξιῶν μου (Ps 109:1 LXX). The change of the preposition from ἐκ to ἐν is fairly common in passages that do not cite the full psalm (Rom 8:34; Col 3:1; Heb 1:3) (Lincoln, "Use of the OT," 40).

46. Eskola argues that the correlation between resurrection and enthronement in Eph 1:20 reflects a larger pattern in the NT where Christ's resurrection serves as his royal enthronement, meaning that the resurrection and enthronement are the same event (Eskola, *Messiah*, 183–86). While it seems best to maintain some distinction between Christ's resurrection and enthronement, Eskola is right to point out the close association between the two events. See also Brannon, *Heavenlies*, 120–21.

47. Though Paul does not use the phrase ἐν τοῖς ἐπουρανίοις in Col 3:1, he does state that Christ is enthroned at God's right hand in the "above" (τὰ ἄνω ... οὗ ὁ Χριστός ἐστιν).

Christ's position above these cosmic powers presupposes that there are cosmic powers who are hostile to his reign.[48] The opposition that Christ faced is not unlike the opposition faced by God's ideal king in Jewish royal ideology (Pss 2:2–3; 18:32–43; 110:1–2; Dan 7:27; Pss. Sol. 17:30–36; 1 En. 46:4–6). God's exaltation and enthronement of Christ is the means by which God defeats and subjugates these powers.

Paul makes this subjugation more explicit with a direct allusion to Ps 8:6, claiming that God "placed all things under his feet" (πάντα ὑπέταξεν ὑπὸ τοὺς πόδας αὐτοῦ, Eph 1:22).[49] Paul's allusion to Ps 8 places Christ in the role originally given to Adam and demonstrates the way in which Christ both fulfilled and exceeded Adam's original royal function.[50] In both passages, God is the one who subjects the creation under his King.[51] As God subjected his creation under Adam's authority, so now he subjects the whole created cosmos under Christ's authority. Just as God raised Adam from obscurity to kingship, so also did God raise Christ from the lowly state of death to the role of cosmic King. Christ exceeds the original rule of Adam because the scope of his reign includes everything in the spiritual and material realm, not just the creatures in the physical world (Ps 8:7–8).[52] Christ's victory and exaltation over the hostile cosmic powers means that he successfully reversed the effects of Adam's failed reign and regained the dominion that Adam lost (see also Rom 5:12–21; 1 Cor 15:45–48).

A few comments may be made concerning Paul's incorporation of the Adamic and Davidic king into his picture of Christ as the cosmic King.[53] First, Paul's use of these Psalms in Eph 1:20–23 aligns closely

---

48. Jipp, *Christ Is King*, 200. Arnold argues that Paul's list of powers should be understood as evil and angelic due to Paul's allusion to Ps 110:1, which refers to the subjection of the king's enemies (Arnold, *Ephesians*, 52–56; see also Hoehner, *Ephesians*, 279–80). However, even if evil powers are primarily in view, Paul's use of the adjective πᾶς suggests that the scope of Christ's rule includes both good and evil powers and seen and unseen powers (cf. Col 1:16) (Fee, *Pauline Christology*, 353; Baugh, *Ephesians*, 125–27).

49. πάντα ὑπέταξας ὑποκάτω τῶν ποδῶν αὐτοῦ (Ps 8:7 LXX).

50. On the Adamic background of Ps 8, see ch. 2.

51. The use of the preposition ὑπὸ with the accusative brings the act of submission into view (Gese, *Vermächtnis*, 190–91).

52. Hebrews makes a similar application of Ps 8 to Christ (Heb 2:8). See ch. 3.

53. Some scholars suggests that Ephesians merely adapts an early church tradition which combines these two Psalms (Loader, "Christ," 199–217; Hay, *Glory*, 50–51; Lincoln "Use of the OT," 41; Thielman, *Ephesians*, 109). Thorsten Moritz argues that the lack of prominence of Ps 8, especially as compared to Ps 110, suggests that this

with his use of these same two Psalms in 1 Cor 15:24–28.[54] The primary difference is that 1 Cor 15:25 utilizes the second half of Ps 110:1 (θῇ πάντας τοὺς ἐχθροὺς ὑπὸ τοὺς πόδας αὐτοῦ) rather than the first half. Both passages view Christ as fulfilling the promise of the ideal Davidic king through his resurrection and enthronement. Both passages view God as the one who subjects the cosmos under the rule of Christ. First Corinthians 15 does clarify that God would not be subordinated under the rule of Christ (1 Cor 15:27b), but Paul's presentation of God as the one who subordinates the cosmos under Christ implies that God himself is not subordinate to the rule of Christ. Therefore, it seems clear that both 1 Cor 15:24–28 and Eph 1:20–23 use Ps 110 and Ps 8 to present Christ as God's royal vice-regent.[55] Second, the similar themes of enthronement, regal agency, and subjection provide conceptual links by which Paul can connect both Psalms. Third, the differences between the Psalms highlight the way in which Paul views the pictures of the Adamic and Davidic king as complementing each other. Paul utilizes Ps 110:1 to introduce the concept of Christ's Davidic kingship, but he also needs to reference Ps 8 to portray the universality of Christ's rule. Psalm 110:1 refers only to the subjection of the Davidic king's enemies while Ps 8 refers to the subjection of the creation under the Adamic king. Paul uses Ps 110 to introduce Christ's kingly role and incorporates Ps 8 to emphasize the cosmic scope of his kingship.[56] Psalm 8 also complements Ps 110 by adding the motif of reversal. The Davidic picture of Christ demonstrates his exalted state in which all things are subjected to him. However, the Adamic picture demonstrates Christ's work in reversing the effects of Adam's sin upon creation. As a result, Christ has regained what Adam once lost, and the

---

combination of Psalms was a Pauline invention (Moritz, *Profound Mystery*, 13–14; see also Keener, *Eighth Psalm*, 165–67). It is not necessary to assume that Paul merely adopts this combination from an existing exegetical tradition, nor does this solution adequately answer why he connects the two Psalms.

54. While it is possible that Heb 1:13, 2:6–8, and 1 Pet 3:22 may have both Psalms in mind, it is difficult to argue from either text for an intentional combination of both Psalms (Moritz, *Profound Mystery*, 12–13).

55. These passages only differ in that while Ephesians focuses on the present reign of Christ, 1 Corinthians focuses on the future reign of Christ. One can easily account for these differences when considering Paul's reason for writing these two letters. In 1 Cor 15, Paul defends the future resurrection of all believers and utilizes the Psalms to portray Christ's future eschatological reign. In Eph 1:20–23, Paul uses the Psalms to portray the present reality of Christ's reign and his relationship to the church (Eph 1:23) (Gese, *Vermächtnis*, 192). For more on the use of these Psalms in 1 Cor 15, see ch. 3.

56. Mortiz, *Profound Mystery*, 15.

subjection of creation under Adam is once again realized under Christ. By fulfilling the role of the ideal Davidic king, Christ also fulfills the role of the Adamic king.

Paul once again demonstrates how God blesses believers through Christ his ideal King. Paul claims that Christ, as the ruling "head" over the cosmos, has been given to the church to be its ruling "head" (Eph 1:22b). Considering the context of Christ's enthronement, Paul uses the term κεφαλή as a regal metaphor to convey Christ's authority over the cosmos. Paul also transitions from the cosmic implications of Christ's enthronement to the ecclesiological implications of Christ's cosmic kingship. The King who rules the cosmos is the same authority who rules the church. The church, as Christ's body (Eph 1:23a), is the place where Christ's cosmic authority is presently realized. Paul uses κεφαλή in a similar fashion in Colossians to convey both Christ's cosmic kingship and the realization of his authority in the church (Col 1:18, 20). His identification of the church as Christ's body in Ephesians echoes his same declaration in Col 1:18.

This royal background may also clarify Paul's fullness language in Eph 1:23. The church as Christ's fullness (πλήρωμα) indicates the church's full incorporation in Christ.[57] Paul's description of the church as being filled with Christ matches his description of the church in Col 2:10. As those who are joined with Christ, believers now live in the present reality of Christ's kingship and currently benefit from his cosmic rule. The same Christ who has made his rule fully realized in the church also "fills," or rules, all things in the cosmos (τοῦ τὰ πάντα ἐν πᾶσιν πληρουμένου, Eph 1:23).[58] Ephesians 1:23 elaborates on Col 2:10 concerning what it means

---

57. This interpretation suggests that the noun πλήρωμα conveys a passive action. The church is not the one who fills and completes Christ, but Christ is the one who fills the church (Lincoln, *Ephesians*, 73–76; Barth, *Ephesians*, 205–9; Hoehner, 296–99; Thielman, *Ephesians*, 114). For an argument that takes πλήρωμα as active, see Yates, "Re-examination of Ephesians," 149–51.

58. This interpretation takes the participle as a middle voice with an active sense. Some scholars argue that this participle should be considered a passive with God as the understood subject. In this case, the interpretation would be that Christ who fills the church is filled by God. This interpretation is attractive because it would align with Col 1:19 and 2:9 where God's fullness dwells in Christ (Best, *Ephesians*, 185–88; Hoehner, *Ephesians*, 298–99; Thielman, *Ephesians*, 114–15). However, taking the participle as a passive would require that the phrase τὰ πάντα ἐν πᾶσιν be taken adverbially, which seems a bit unnatural. However, taking the participle as a middle voice with an active sense allows one to take the phrase in its natural sense as a direct object (Lincoln, *Ephesians*, 76–77; Jeal, "Strange Style," 129–38; Heil, *Ephesians*, 88–89; Fee, *Pauline Christology*, 354; Baugh, *Ephesians*, 131–32).

for the church to be Christ's fullness. As Christ's fullness, the church serves as the present manifestation of Christ's cosmic reign, a reign that will one day be fully revealed. The church receives blessings that God wishes to bestow through his cosmically enthroned King.[59] This idea aligns with Paul's teaching in Colossians where he looks forward to the full revelation of Christ's cosmic reign (Col 3:3–4).

Kooten argues that Eph 1:22–23 points to the author's belief that Christ's cosmic rule does not yet extend over the whole cosmos. He suggests that since the benefits of Christ's cosmic rule are presently limited to the church, the extension of Christ's rule over the whole cosmos is still in progress. In this way, Kooten argues that Ephesians has corrected Colossians, which presents Christ's cosmic kingship as fully realized.[60] Kooten also argues that Ephesians' identification of the church as Christ's body contradicts Colossians' portrait of the cosmos as Christ's body.[61] Regarding the latter assertion, Kooten's argument fails because he has failed to properly acknowledge Paul's explicit identification of the church as Christ's body in Col 1:18.[62] Regarding the former objection, Kooten's assertion that the present realization of Christ's cosmic rule in the church means that Christ is not yet fully King over the cosmos is a faulty equation. That Christ's cosmic rule only benefits the church in the present does not mean that Christ does not already claim rightful authority over the cosmos. In this regard, Colossians shares a similar view with Ephesians. Both Colossians and Ephesians claim that Christ is currently positioned as the enthroned King over the cosmos (Col 1:18; 2:15; 3:1; Eph 1:20). Both letters claim that the whole cosmos is currently subject to his reign (Col 1:20; 2:10; Eph 1:21–22a). Both letters also suggest that Christ's reign presently benefits the church (Col 1:13–14, 21–22; 2:13–14; Eph 1:3–14, 22; 2:1–10). Both letters imply that though Christ is the current King of the cosmos, his reign has yet to be fully realized (Col 1:20; 3:3–4; Eph 1:23).

---

59. Smith, *Ideal King*, 187.
60. Kooten, *Cosmic Christology*, 156–57.
61. Kooten, *Cosmic Christology*, 157.
62. For more on this point, see ch. 4.

EPHESIANS 2:1-22

Paul elaborates in Eph 2 on the relationship between Christ's cosmic enthronement, believers' deliverance from cosmic powers, and the incorporation of Jews and gentiles into one corporate entity. Each aspect explains the blessings that God bestows upon believers through his royal agent. Ephesians 2 also further vindicates Christ's claim to the throne of God's cosmic King by listing the triumphs that resulted from Christ's enthronement.[63] While Eph 2 gives the implications of Christ's enthronement (Eph 1:20–23) for believers, Paul's digression also gives a more detailed explanation of his teaching in Colossians concerning the church's place in Christ's cosmic kingdom. Paul repeats many of the same Jewish royal themes that he references in Colossians.

Paul explains that God's action in Christ his King on behalf of believers is a cosmic act. In Colossians, Paul explains that for believers to be placed into the kingdom of Christ, God must first deliver them from the "dominion of darkness" (Col 1:13). In Ephesians, Paul details the character of believers' former existence in the dominion of darkness. Formerly, they lived in the state of death within the realm of sin. This description bears a close resemblance to Paul's description of the Colossians believers' former state in Col 2:13:

- ὑμᾶς ὄντας νεκροὺς τοῖς παραπτώμασιν καὶ ταῖς ἁμαρτίαις ὑμῶν (Eph 2:1).[64]
- ὑμᾶς νεκροὺς ὄντας . . . τοῖς παραπτώμασιν (Col 2:13).

Paul explains what it means to walk as those who are dead in the realm of sin. Their behavior and conduct were determined by "a spatio-temporal complex wholly hostile to God."[65] They conducted themselves according to the course of this world (Eph 2:2) and lived under the rule of a malevolent power, "the ruler of the power of the air" (Eph 2:2).[66] This ruler governs the realms hostile to God and leads those who exist in those

---

63. Timothy Gombis rightly points out that "the assertion that Christ has been installed as Cosmic Lord must be vindicated by a display of his credentials as universal sovereign, his triumphs over all competing powers" (Gombis, "Ephesians 2," 407).

64. Hoehner argues that the terms παράπτωμα and ἁμαρτία are synonymous (Hoehner, *Ephesians*, 207–8, 308).

65. Lincoln, *Ephesians*, 410.

66. For more on the identity and function of this figure (probably Satan), see Arnold, *Ephesians*, 59–62.

realms toward disobedience to God.⁶⁷ Because of these influences, they acted in accordance with their wicked flesh in both thought and deed (Eph 2:3; cf. Col 1:21).⁶⁸

Building on his christological assertions in Eph 1:20–23, Paul reveals how God acted through Christ his royal agent to deliver believers from their terrible existence in the dark domain.⁶⁹ Because of God's richness in mercy and great love (Eph 2:4), he raised those who were dead in their sins and brought them to life with Christ (Eph 2:5). Paul's language in Eph 2:5 again bears a striking resemblance to his language concerning God's work in Christ on behalf of believers in Col 2:13:

- καὶ ὄντας ἡμᾶς νεκροὺς τοῖς παραπτώμασιν συνεζωοποίησεν τῷ Χριστῷ (Eph 2:5).
- καὶ ὑμᾶς νεκροὺς ὄντας. . .τοῖς παραπτώμασιν . . .συνεζωοποίησεν ὑμᾶς σὺν αὐτῷ (Col 2:13).

God effectuated believers' transition from death to life through the resurrection and enthronement of Christ.⁷⁰ The implication of their spiritual resurrection is that they have now been enthroned in the heavens "in Christ Jesus" (Eph 2:6).⁷¹ Paul's "in Christ" formula indicates the location of believers' enthronement as well as the means of their enthronement.⁷² The present implication of their enthronement is that they have realized the cosmic authority of Christ, and the future implication is that their eternal destiny is secure.

67. Gombis, "Ephesians 2," 410. In this case, the genitive τοῦ πνεύματος refers to the inward spirit of those who conduct themselves according to the course of this world and acts as a genitive of subordination to the accusative ἄρχοντα. In sum, the ruler of this world governs the inward person of those who live in his realm. Kooten implies that πνεύματος should be considered as in apposition to ἄρχοντα (Kooten, *Cosmic Christology*, 167). The problem with this view is that "a gen. of apposition never involves two personal nouns" (Wallace, *Greek Grammar*, 100n74). For more on this interpretation, see Lincoln, *Ephesians*, 96, and Hoehner, *Ephesians*, 314–15.

68. On the Jewish nature of this characterization of spiritual death, see Yee, *Ethnic Reconciliation*, 45–56.

69. Thomas Allen argues that Eph 1:20–23 provides the "underlying conceptual framework" of Eph 2 (Allen, "Exaltation," 104).

70. Smith, *Ideal King*, 189.

71. It seems that the two verbs συνήγειρεν and συνεκάθισεν in v. 6 give further explanation to the verb συνεζωοποίησεν in v. 5 (Best, *Ephesians*, 218; Brannon, *Heavenlies*, 171n199).

72. Sellin, *Epheser*, 183; Lincoln, *Ephesians*, 105; and Brannon, *Heavenlies*, 171. Hoehner argues that the prepositional phrase is purely locative and points to believers' union with Christ (Hoehner, *Ephesians*, 334–35).

Believers' enthronement in Christ conveys their full incorporation in Christ and their participation in his royal acts. As his royal subjects, believers share in the death, resurrection, and enthronement of their King.[73] Paul's claim that believers' enthronement is in the heavens clarifies both the place of believers in the kingdom of God's "beloved Son" (Col 1:13) and the nature of the believers' "hiddenness" in Christ, who is enthroned at God's right hand (Col 3:3). Paul's claim in Ephesians "is making explicit of what in Col 3:1-3 had only been implicit."[74] Such enthronement implies that believers have a share in Christ's cosmic reign.[75] Believers' enthronement in Christ also implies that God accomplished their enthronement through Christ. Even if the prepositional phrase "in Christ Jesus" is primarily locative, the association between believers' enthronement and God's action in Christ in Eph 1:20 suggests that Christ also serves as the agent through whom God enthrones believers in the heavens. God accomplished this act on behalf of believers "through his great love" (Eph 2:4). God's love is most clearly expressed in what he did through Christ his King.[76] The result is that through Christ, God has inaugurated an act of new creation. This new creation brought about by Christ's resurrection and cosmic enthronement is presently manifested in the lives of those who are now in Christ (Eph 2:10).

Ephesians 2:1-10 shares some common themes with Jewish royal ideology. As, in Jewish thought, the enthronement of the ideal king signaled salvation for those who are oppressed by the wicked (Isa 11:1-9; 42:1-5; 49:1-6; 61:2-4; Pss. Sol. 17; 1 En. 48:4; 53:6), so the enthronement of Christ brings God's gracious salvation to the oppressed who live in the realm ruled by cosmic forces hostile to God. As the enthronement of God's ideal king signaled the reestablishment of God's good rule (Ps 110:4; Isa 9:5-6; 61:2-4; Ezek 37:22, 25), so Christ's enthronement magnifies the gracious act of God on behalf of his creation (Eph 2:8-10). As the Jewish ideal king brings prosperity to those under his reign (Pss 73:3, 15-16; 144:12-14; Isa 11:6-9; Jer 23:6; 33:17), so Christ's enthronement brings new life and new creation to those who are in him. Paul does bring one point of clarification to the Jewish conception of God's ideal king. While Jewish royal ideology suggests that God's ideal king will bring

---

73. Jipp, *Christ Is King*, 201-2. For further discussion on the bond brought about between Christ and believers through exaltation, see Allen, "Exaltation," 103-20.

74. Lincoln, *Ephesians*, 106.

75. Masson, *Ephésiens*, 160-61, and Smith, *Ideal King*, 188.

76. Aletti, *Ephésiens*, 126, and Smith, *Ideal King*, 188.

God's blessings to those under his reign, Paul suggests that these blessings include actual participation in Christ's cosmic reign.[77]

While Paul makes no explicit mention of Adam in this passage, Ephesians does contain some potential implicit references to his Adam Christology in Romans and 1 Corinthians.[78] Paul's allusion to Ps 8 in Eph 1:22 makes it more likely that he had his Adam Christology in mind when writing this passage. Believers' former existence as those who were dead in the realm of sin echoes Paul's statements about the results of Adam's failed reign. As God's first king, Adam failed and introduced the rule of sin and death (1 Cor 15:21a; Rom 5:12, 14, 17, 21). Their former conduct in the dominion ruled by cosmic powers hostile to God (Eph 2:1–3) reflects the conduct of those who follow the pattern of sin that now reigns over them (Rom 5:12, 19). Believers' new existence in Christ echoes Paul's former statements concerning the results of Christ's reign in contrast to Adam's. Believers' union with Christ's resurrection reflects Paul's other arguments regarding resurrection as the cosmic solution to the failed reign of Adam (1 Cor 15:20–22; Rom 5:18, 21).[79] God's gift of grace to believers echoes Paul's suggestion that the establishment of Christ's reign resulted in grace abounding to many (Rom 5:15). Their present enthronement in the heavens (Eph 2:6) suggests that, as those under Adam share in his fate, those who are under the reign of Christ share in Christ's fate (1 Cor 15:49; Rom 5:21, 8:29).[80]

The second part of Paul's digression emphasizes the horizontal dimensions of Christ's cosmic enthronement.[81] Paul views Christ as God's agent who brings peace and creates a new humanity. Paul characterizes the former existence of Ephesian believers without Christ as (1) alienated

---

77. Jipp suggests that by applying Christ's resurrection and enthronement to believers, Paul is "royal-izing the king's subjects" (Jipp, *Christ Is King*, 202; see also Smith, *Ideal King*, 189).

78. See ch. 3.

79. John Coutts argues that the concept of the last Adam lies behind Paul's use of the verb συζωοποιέω (Eph 2:5) (Coutts, "Ephesians and Colossians," 205).

80. Ephesians does emphasize the present reality of believers' enthronement with Christ while Romans and 1 Corinthians emphasize the future reality of believers' destiny with Christ. However, this does not necessitate that one view these passages as contradictory. Rather, the present enthronement of believers in the heavens with Christ ensures the future reality of their reign with Christ. Allen connects this idea to the Qumran community who considered themselves to be heirs of Adam's glory, which would eventually be restored to them (1QS 4:23; 1QH^a 17:15; CD 3:20) (Allen, "Exaltation," 111).

81. Son notes that the focus of Eph 2:11–22 is not on the reconciliation of individual believers to God but on the unity of two groups of people in Christ (Son, "Church," 25).

from Israel,[82] (2) strangers of God's covenant, (3) without hope, and (4) without God (Eph 2:12). Paul reveals that the Ephesian believers have been moved from one locale to another. Rather than being "without Christ," they are now located "in Christ Jesus" (Eph 2:13), a reference to their place in Christ's cosmic kingdom (Eph 2:6).[83] Their entrance into this new locale is made possible by Christ's blood (Eph 2:13).[84] The result is that Christ serves as the agent of peace who unifies Jew and gentile under his cosmic rule.[85] He has brought peace to the two groups that were formerly hostile to one another (Eph 2:14–18). The harmony brought by Christ to the church serves as the present manifestation of the cosmic harmony that God will one day effectuate through Christ. As the one who brings peace, Christ fulfills one of the most important roles assigned to the Jewish ideal king (Pss 72:3–15; 132:15; 144:12–14; Isa 9:6; 11:1–9; Pss. Sol. 17:24, 35; 4Q161 3.18–22).[86]

Paul also presents Christ as God's agent in his new creation activity.[87] Christ destroyed the hostility and enmity between Jews and gentiles so that "he might create in himself one new man" (κτίσῃ ἐν αὐτῷ εἰς ἕνα καινὸν ἄνθρωπον) that consisted of both groups (Eph 2:14–15). Two things in Paul's declaration point to his use of creation imagery. First, Christ is the subject of the verb κτίζω, meaning that Christ serves as

---

82. Paul uses this same verb ἀπαλλοτριόω to describe the alienation of Colossian believers (Col 1:21). He discusses the alienation in broad terms in Colossians, but he specifies the alienation from Israel in Ephesians.

83. Sellin argues that ἐν Χριστῷ Ἰησοῦ is both locative and instrumental (Sellin, *Epheser*, 200–201). While this is possible, Paul's reference to the blood of Christ as the instrument by which the gentiles are brought near suggests that the primary sense of this phrase is the new location of their existence.

84. The prepositional phrase ἐν τῷ αἵματι τοῦ Χριστοῦ presents a clear case in which Paul uses the preposition ἐν in an instrumental sense (Hoehner, *Ephesians*, 363).

85. Smith demonstrates that Greco-Roman thought viewed peacemaking as an essential aspect of great kings (Smith, *Christ Is King*, 211).

86. Joseph Kreitzer argues that Eph 2:14–18 adopts imagery that portrays Jesus as a new Solomon. He notes that while Isa 57:19 may be the primary OT text behind this passage, it evokes the memory of Solomon who was known for ruling over a unified kingdom in a time of peace. The construction of believers into a new temple could also parallel Solomon's construction of the temple (Kreitzer, "Messianic Man," 497–502, 506–7). Whether one can locate this Solomonic imagery, Christ's unifying work does closely reflect the larger Jewish concept that portrays God's ideal king bringing peace and harmony.

87. Moritz suggests that while it is conceivable to see reminiscences of the creation account in this verse, Paul's creation language should be understood through his use of Isa 57:9 (Moritz, *Profound Mystery*, 43).

God's agent in new creation. Paul repeats his view from Colossians that Christ is God's primary creation agent (Col 1:16–18). Second, the "one new man" metaphor recalls Paul's previous reflections on Gen 1 and humanity's original existence and implies a contrast between the "old man" and the "new man." Christ has brought about a new beginning for humanity in his creation. This new beginning involves a new corporate identity defined by Christ,[88] the head of the "new man," and belongs to both Jews and gentiles. The church's new corporate identity is directly tied to Christ's identity. Paul uses this language to speak of the mode of existence that stands in contrast to the mode of existence under the "old man." Whereas the Ephesian believers' existence in the old order was marked by ethnic hostility, their new existence in Christ is marked by ethnic unity.[89] That Christ performed this creation act "in himself" suggests that both Jew and gentile are now defined by their union in Christ and share in his cosmic destiny. This idea is a core characteristic of Paul's Adam Christology in his other letters (Gal 6:14–15; 1 Cor 15:44–49; 2 Cor 5:16–17). Alienation, hostility, and division characterizes the destiny of those under the failed reign of Adam, but oneness characterizes the existence of those under the reign of Christ.

Paul's use of the "one new man" metaphor recalls his old man/new man metaphor in Col 3:9–11, a metaphor which finds its roots in Paul's Adam Christology. Though Paul uses the metaphor for different purposes in the two letters,[90] he remains consistent on the core principles of the metaphor. In both passages, Paul portrays Christ as God's agent in the new creation work.[91] Paul explicitly refers to the "old man" in Colossians, but in Ephesians, the "old man" is implied. However, both passages draw a contrast between believers' former existence in the old order (one which resulted from the failed reign of Adam) to their present existence in the new order ruled by Christ. Both passages imply that believers have been transferred spatially from the old sphere of existence in Adam to

---

88. Son suggests that the "new man" of Eph 2:15 is conceptually related to the "perfect man" in Eph 4:13. This "perfect man" does not refer to a fully mature individual but to Christ Himself. When bringing these two concepts together, Son argues that the "new man denotes primarily Christ and the mode of existence in Christ" (Son, "Church," 26–29).

89. Yee, *Ethnic Reconciliation*, 165–66.

90. The impetus of the metaphor in Col 3 is ethical, but the impetus in Ephesians is ethnic unity.

91. See the discussion on Christ as the "one who creates" in ch. 4.

the new sphere of existence in Christ (see also Col 1:13).[92] Both passages use the old man/new man motif to speak of the christocentric nature of their new existence and refer to the "new man" as Christ's ecclesial body (ἐν ἑνὶ σώματι, Col 3:15; Eph 2:16).[93] In both letters, Paul views this new existence as a direct outcome of Christ's cosmic enthronement. Ephesians 2 does not "neutralize" the cosmological views of Colossians[94] but presents the ecclesial implications of Christ's cosmic rule. The church serves as the present manifestation of the peace and harmony brought by Christ's death (Eph 2:16; cf. Col 1:20) and subsequent enthronement over the whole cosmos. For Paul, Christ's present reconciliation of the cosmos and his reconciliation of Jews and gentiles are not contradictory but complementary concepts. Christ's work to bring peace and create a new humanity vindicates his claim to the cosmic throne.[95]

EPHESIANS 3:8–11

In Eph 3, Paul details the ministry given to him by God. Paul claims insight into the "mystery of Christ," an insight that he shares with the apostles and prophets (Eph 3:2–5). The mystery is the inclusion of the gentiles in God's overall cosmic plan. Specifically, Paul claims that gentiles in Christ are now fellow heirs, members of Christ's body, and partakers of the promise (Eph 3:6). Such a change of fortune was made possible because of their union with Christ (Eph 3:7). God in his grace commissioned Paul to preach this message, which Paul describes as the "unfathomable riches of Christ" (τὸ ἀνεξιχνίαστον πλοῦτος τοῦ Χριστοῦ), to the gentiles (Eph 3:8). At this point, Paul reveals the role of the church in God's overall cosmic plan, a role that is wholly dependent upon the church's union

---

92. Son, "Church," 29.

93. On the ecclesial interpretation of the one body in Eph 2:16, see Son, *Corporate Anthropology*, 95–96.

94. Kooten argues, "It is no longer the cosmos which is said to have been reconciled and made peaceful (Col 1:22) but the formerly conflicting ethnic groups" (Kooten, *Cosmic Christology*, 170).

95. Comparing this passage to divine warrior contexts, Gombis suggests that Christ's work in bringing peace and unifying Jew and gentile functions as part of a list of triumphs (Eph 2:1–16) used to prove Christ's supremacy over all other competing powers (Gombis, "Ephesians 2," 414). Whether or not Gombis is correct that Eph 2 follows the pattern of other divine warrior texts, he is likely correct that one of the functions of Eph 2 is to vindicate Christ's claim to cosmic kingship through his triumphant actions.

with Christ.[96] Paul states that God's final purpose for endowing Paul with his grace is that God might make his "manifold wisdom" (πολυποίκιλος σοφία) known to the cosmic powers. This "wisdom" refers to "the wise divine purpose in the ordering of history."[97] That this wisdom belongs to God "who created all things" (Eph 3:9) suggests that this revelation could be classified as part of God's ongoing creation work. Whereas the cosmic powers are the indirect object of God's revelation, the church serves as the primary means of God's revelation. Paul suggests that as his preaching of the mystery contributes to the formation of the church, God uses the church as the means by which he reveals his cosmic purpose to the cosmic powers. As the Ephesian believers live according to their corporate identity, a unified and multi-ethnic entity joined to Christ the head and positioned in the heavenly realms with Christ, they manifest God's cosmic plan to the spiritual powers.[98] For the cosmic powers that

---

96. There remains significant debate on the reason for Paul's sudden digression in Eph 3. Some suggest that the digression is an irrelevant detour from the overall argument of the letter. It is therefore useless and serves as evidence that Paul was not the true author of the letter (Kitchen, *Ephesians*, 30; Jeal, *Integrating Theology*, 174–75). However, even among those who hold pseudonymous authorship, most scholars suggest more intentionality behind the digression (Bouttier, *Éphésiens*, 133; MacDonald, *Colossians and Ephesians*, 268–72). Others argue that this section serves as a defense of Paul's apostolic credentials and authority (Best, *Ephesians*, 292; Arnold, *Ephesians*, 86). The problem with this view is that there is no obvious polemic against anyone challenging Paul's apostolic authority. Gombis suggests that this section explains how Paul's imprisonment "epitomizes the triumph of God in Christ" (Gombis, "Ephesians 3:2–13," 316). Aaron Sherwood argues that Paul is concerned that his audience would misunderstand his imprisonment and explains how his imprisonment aligned with God's overall plan for him (Sherwood, "Paul's Imprisonment," 97–112).

97. Lincoln, *Ephesians*, 188. Kooten attempts to draw a parallel to Jewish notions of personified Wisdom (Kooten, *Cosmic Christology*, 174), but this parallel does not fit the context of the passage. Paul simply has in view the way God acted in Christ on behalf of the cosmos (Best, *Ephesians*, 323–24; Hoehner, *Ephesians*, 461–62).

98. Arnold, *Ephesians*, 63, and Gombis, "Ephesians 3:2–13," 322. Wink argues that Paul charges the church to preach directly to the cosmic powers (Wink, *Naming the Powers*, 89–96). Kooten argues that this verse suggests that the church needs to convince the cosmic powers of the divine Wisdom so that they would eventually accept Christ's cosmic rule (Kooten, *Cosmic Christology*, 173–74). The church as the means of God's revelation does not necessarily mean the church is responsible to preach God's mystery directly to the cosmic powers. Paul himself assumes an active role in preaching Christ to the gentiles and views himself as responsible for enlightening all people to God's mystery (Eph 3:8–9). The church is included in God's revelatory work not by preaching directly to the cosmic powers but by living according to its new corporate identity.

are hostile to God, the emergence of the church points to the devastating reality of their defeat.[99]

While the church serves as an intermediary agent of God's cosmic plan, Paul reminds his readers that Christ serves as the primary agent in whom God brings about his cosmic purpose (Eph 3:11). Paul reminds the Ephesian believers that God's revelation of his cosmic plan to the cosmic powers through the church was part of his eternal purpose he accomplished in Christ (ἐν τῷ Χριστῷ Ἰησοῦ τῷ κυρίῳ ἡμῶν, Eph 3:11). In the locative sense, Paul's "in Christ" formula indicates that God's purpose was accomplished "in the historical Jesus when he died on the cross."[100] Even if the force of this phrase is primarily locative, the formula is still closely related to the conception of Christ acting as God's royal agent to accomplish his eternal purpose. Paul emphasizes Jesus' regal authority by calling him "Christ" and "Lord." Both terms retain the definite article (ἐν τῷ Χριστῷ Ἰησοῦ τῷ κυρίῳ ἡμῶν, Eph 3:11), which is a departure from Paul's typical practice in Ephesians of dropping the article with the combined name "Christ Jesus" (Eph 1:1, 5; 2:13). By retaining the article, one could argue that Paul emphasizes Jesus' messianic role in assuming the role of God's long-promised king who brought salvation to both Jews and gentiles.[101] As the one who is "our Lord," Paul repeats his idea from Eph 1:21–22 that the one who has been enthroned as "the head" over the cosmos is also "the head" of the church. Therefore, the church's role as a passive agent of God's revelation is a result of its union in Christ and its placement under Christ's kingship. The manifestation of Christ's regal authority over the church reveals to the cosmic powers hostile to God that they are subject to the authority of God's royal agent.

The church's role in Eph 3:9–11 explicates the nature of their "hiddenness" in Christ in Col 3:3–4. While Colossians emphasizes the eschatological implications of the church's existence in Christ, Ephesians further explains the present implications of this existence. While Christ's reign has not yet been fully realized throughout the cosmos, his kingship is presently realized in the church. Further, Paul reveals that the hidden reality of Christ's cosmic authority has been revealed to the cosmic powers that exist in the spiritual realm through the emergence of the church. Contra Kooten,[102] the nature of this revelation is not that the cosmic

---

99. Arnold, *Ephesians*, 64, and Brannon, *Heavenlies*, 184.

100. Hoehner, *Ephesians*, 464.

101. Muddiman, *Ephesians*, 162, and Hoehner, *Ephesians*, 464.

102. Kooten suggests that the church makes the cosmic powers aware that "the

powers would eventually come under the authority of Christ and be filled with Christ but that they have already been defeated and are subject to Christ's cosmic authority. Both letters view the defeat of the cosmic powers by God's cosmic King as a present reality that will eventually be fully realized throughout the whole cosmos. In this sense, Christ fulfills the role of the Jewish ideal king who defeats the powers hostile to God and brings peace to his reign.

EPHESIANS 4:7–16; 5:5

Based upon the work that God has done for the church in Christ, Paul exhorts the Ephesian believers to live in a manner worthy of what God has done. Such a life means living out the oneness that God has brought to the church (Eph 4:1–6). Paul reminds them that they had been enabled to live this life according to the gracious gift of Christ (Eph 4:7). Paul presents a narrative of Christ as the gift-giver using a citation from Ps 68:18 (Eph 4:8–10). Paul's use of this Psalm has proven problematic for many scholars and remains a point of debate.[103] The problem centers on two primary issues: 1) Paul's overall hermeneutic in applying Ps 68 (itself being a psalm of praise to God) to Christ and 2) the change of the action from "receiving" (ἔλαβες, Ps 67:17 LXX) gifts to "giving" gifts (ἔδωκεν, Eph 4:8). A deeper look at Paul's use of Ps 68 reveals that once again Paul casts Christ in the role of cosmic King. Rather than using Adamic or Davidic language, Paul escalates Christ's regal role by explicitly casting Christ in the role of the divine King.

At the outset, this study rejects the notion that Paul merely adopts his use of Ps 68 from either early Jewish traditions or from a Christian tradition prior to his writing of the letter.[104] It is also unnecessary to sug-

---

divine wisdom is capable of permeating the entire cosmos again." The church does this so the cosmic powers might become aware of God's cosmic wisdom and help them accept Christ's cosmic rule so that they might eventually become filled with Christ. Kooten parallels this notion with the Stoic notion of the cosmic city (Kooten, *Cosmic Christology*, 173–79).

103. For a history of discussion regarding this issue, see Ehorn, "Psalm 68(67).19," 96–120.

104. One trend among scholars is to suggest that the author of Ephesians adopts his interpretation from Targum Psalm 68:19, where the verb is altered from "receive" to "give" (Schnackenburg, *Epheser*, 179–80; Best, *Ephesians*, 380–81; Aletti, *Ephésiens*, 215–16; Schwindt, *Weltbild des Epheserbriefes*, 403–22). Others argue that the author of Ephesians was aware of the Targum reading and presented a reactionary dialogue in

gest that Paul simply misquotes or disregards the original context of Ps 68:18 and shapes the imagery to illustrate his point.[105] Paul makes his own unique interpretive contribution to Ps 68[106] by reading it in light of Christ's cosmic work. The psalm celebrates God as the conquering divine warrior who now dwells with his people as their King.[107] Joshua Greever's recent analysis regarding the overall structure of Ps 68 proves helpful here. He argues that the psalm is both retrospective and prospective in orientation. The first half of the psalm recounts God's past victories (Ps 68:1–18), and the second half of the psalm anticipates God's future victories (Ps 68:19–35).[108] Greever demonstrates that both halves of the psalm call for praise to God for his acts (Ps 68:4, 32) and follow the general pattern of victory (Ps 68:7–14, 19–23), ascension (Ps 68:15–18a, 24–27), and temple gifts (Ps 68:18b, 28–31).[109] This general structure suggests that God's past actions on Israel's behalf serve as a pattern for his future actions on Israel's behalf.[110] God's actions in the second half of the psalm both correspond to and escalate his actions in the first half of the psalm. Spatially, the first half emphasizes God's actions on earth, but the second half emphasizes his actions in the heavens.[111] While in the first half God is the one "who rides through the deserts" (Ps 68:4), he is the one "who

---

which he reinterprets the Mosaic interpretation of the Psalm in a christological manner. Further, these scholars see close association between Eph 4:8–10 and Pentecost in Acts 2 (Lindars, *New Testament Apologetic*, 51–59; Lincoln, "Use of the OT," 19–24; Harris, *Descent of Christ*). The problem with these views is (1) the Targum applies this Psalm to Moses while Ephesians makes no obvious reference to Moses, (2) the uncertainty surrounding the date of the Targum Psalms, and (3) regarding the comparison to Pentecost, the equation of Christ with the Spirit (Lunde and Dunne, "Creative and Contextual Use," 99–106; Ehorn, "Psalm 68(67).19," 109–11).

105. This is argued by Fitzmeyer, "Old Testament Quotations," 325. Kooten argues that the author of Ephesians employs this imagery "to illustrate, in a figurative sense, what he meant by Christ filling the cosmos" (Kooten, *Cosmic Christology*, 185–86).

106. Ellis suggested this possibility, and many scholars have argued this point in more recent years (Ellis, *Paul's Use*, 138–39; Hoehner, *Ephesians*, 528–30; Gombis, "Cosmic Lordship," 367–80; Wilder, "Use of Power," 185–200; Lunde and Dunne, "Creative and Contextual Use," 99–117; Greever, "Typological Expectation," 253–79).

107. Gombis, "Cosmic Lordship," 374, and Greever, "Typological Expectation," 257.

108. Greever, "Typological Expectation," 257–59.

109. Greever, "Typological Expectation," 259–60.

110. Greever argues that the first half of Ps 68 alludes to both the victory song in Exodus 15 and the Song of Deborah in Judges 5 (Greever, "Typological Expectations," 261–64). Todd Scacewater makes a similar argument and suggests that early Judaism interpreted Ps 68 along eschatological lines (Scacewater, *Divine Builder in Psalm 68*, 71–117).

111. Greever, "Typological Expectations," 264–70.

rides in the heavens" in the second half (Ps 68:33). In the first half, God's dwelling is on Sinai (Ps 68:17), but in the second half, his dwelling is in the clouds (Ps 68:34). God's defeat of the nations in the first half (Ps 68:6, 12) anticipates the defeat of their gods in the second half (Ps 68:21–23, 30).[112] The gifts he receives from humanity in v. 18 anticipate the gifts he will one day receive from all nations (Ps 68:29).[113] God's receiving of these gifts leads him to give generously to his people (Ps 68:33–35). The implication of this structure is that "God's enthronement on Zion also serves to ground the psalmist's anticipation of these future blessings."[114]

In Eph 4:8–10, Paul presents Christ as the one fulfilling the role of the divine King in Ps 68. Much like Ps 68 views God's work on the earth as a pattern for his work in the cosmos, Paul presents Christ's work on the earth as the grounds for his work in the cosmos. In explaining his citation of Ps 68:18, Paul states that the ascension of Christ implies his initial descension "to the lower parts of the earth" (Eph 4:9- εἰς τὰ κατώτερα [μέρη] τῆς γῆς). While some argue that this phrase references either Hades[115] or to the descent of the Spirit at Pentecost,[116] the more likely reference is to Christ's incarnation.[117] In that case, the genitive τῆς γῆς functions epexegetically to κατώτερα. This view fits the pattern of Ps 68 and suggests that Christ's redemptive work in the physical realm preludes his enthronement over the cosmos in the spiritual realm. It also fits Paul's earlier statement regarding Christ's earthly work, specifically

---

112. Greever, "Typological Expectations," 267–68. Greever argues that the reference to the sea and death in vv. 21–23 refer to cosmic enemies and that the beasts and bulls in v. 30 probably refer to the gods of Egypt.

113. Greever, "Typological Expectations," 268–69. Todd Scacewater argues that the gifts in v. 18 were for the construction of the temple (Scacewater, *Divine Builder*, 46–49). This suggests that the gifts in v. 29 were for the construction of the divine sanctuary.

114. Lunde and Dunne, "Creative and Contextual Use," 107.

115. Bousset, *Kyrios Christos*, 60–68; Arnold, *Ephesians*, 56–58; Bales, "Descent of Christ," 84–100; and Scacewater, *Divine Builder*, 141–47.

116. Some scholars also argue that the descent refers to the descent of Spirit at Pentecost to give spiritual gifts to the church (Caird, "Descent of Christ," 535–45; Lincoln, "Use of the OT," 22–24; Harris, *Descent of Christ*, 171–97). The major problem of this view is that Paul seems to indicate that Christ's descent precedes his ascent, whereas the Pentecost argument would require Christ's ascent to precede his descent.

117. Schnackenburg, *Epheser*, 181; Barth, *Ephesians*, 433–34; Best, *Ephesians*, 384–86; and Heil, *Ephesians*, 173–74. It is possible that this phrase could be a more specific reference to the grave (i.e., Christ's death) (Hoehner, *Ephesians*, 535–36; Gombis, "Cosmic Lordship," 376–78; Fee, *Pauline Christology*, 358; Baugh, *Ephesians*, 327–28). Even if Paul is not specifically referencing the grave, the broader reference to Christ's incarnation encompasses all his earthly work, including his death.

his resurrection, as the grounds of his cosmic enthronement and the affirmation of his cosmic kingship (Eph 1:20–21; cf. Phil 2:6–11).

Christ ascends to his heavenly throne as a victorious warrior. Christ assumes the role of God in Ps 68 by conquering his enemies and taking them as his captives (ἠχμαλώτευσεν αἰχμαλωσίαν, Eph 4:8). By ascribing the role of God to Christ, Paul demonstrates that Christ serves as God's agent through whom he reestablishes order to the cosmos. As Ps 68:18 ties God's ascent to his taking of captives, so Paul ties Christ's ascent to his defeat of the hostile cosmic powers (Eph 4:8; cf. 1:20–22).[118] Spatially, Christ's ascension takes place in the highest of the cosmic realms (Eph 4:10). As Christ is enthroned "far above" (ὑπεράνω) all cosmic powers in Eph 1:20–21, so he also ascends "far above" (ὑπεράνω) the heavenly realms in Eph 4:10. The implication is that Paul has in view Christ's exaltation over all cosmic powers.[119] The purpose of his exaltation is so that Christ "might fill all things." Paul's language hearkens back to his fullness language in Eph 1:23 and refers to the eventual realization of Christ's cosmic authority throughout the entire cosmos.[120] Paul views the eschatological expectations of Ps 68—where God establishes his rule over the whole cosmos—as being fulfilled in Christ.

As the enthroned cosmic King, Christ also acts as God's royal benefactor for his people. Paul alters the text of the psalm to portray Christ as the giver of gifts (ἔδωκεν δόματα, Eph 4:8) rather than the receiver of gifts (ἔλαβες δόματα, Ps 67:19 LXX).[121] Paul does not alter the text simply to make it fit his own argument, but his alteration fits well within the original context of the psalm. The victory and enthronement of God in Ps 68 makes him worthy to receive gifts, but God also empowers his people and shares the spoils of his victory with them (Ps 68:35).[122] In the same way,

118. Scacewater, *Divine Builder*, 131.

119. Gombis, "Cosmic Lordship," 378.

120. This language could also be rooted in OT language regarding God's glory filling the temple. In this case, "all things" refers to an eschatological temple consisting of the new heaven and new earth, and in filling the temple, Christ serves as the temple builder (Scacewater, *Divine Builder*, 24–26, 130–31; Greever, "Typological Expectation," 273).

121. One should note that this alteration is not the only one Paul makes in his citation of the Psalm. He also (1) changes the finite verb ἀνέβης to the participle ἀναβὰς, (2) changes the verbs from second person to third person, (3) changes the singular noun ἀνθρώπῳ and plural noun ἀνθρώποις, (4) leaves out the preposition ἐν, and (5) adds the article τοῖς. However, these other alterations are not as problematic as the change from receiving to giving. For more on these alterations see Hoehner, *Ephesians*, 524–28, and Scacewater, *Divine Builder*, 129–30.

122. Ellis, *Paul's Use*, 138–39; Gombis, "Cosmic Lordship," 374–75; and Wilder,

Christ's victory and enthronement over the powers qualifies him to share the spoils of his victory with the church. By assigning Christ the role of gift-giver, Paul explicitly grants to Christ the role of the divine King who equally shares in the divine prerogatives.[123] Thus, Paul continues to cast Christ as God's regal agent. His role as God's King now includes being the royal benefactor who endows God's people with the spoils of his victory.[124] This role hearkens back to Paul's opening eulogy where he presents Christ as the agent of God's heavenly blessings (Eph 1:3). Christ empowers the church with these gifts so they might grow to full maturity and become like Christ, who is their head (Eph 4:11–16).

From this passage, Christ fulfills the role of the Jewish ideal king in three significant ways. First, as Judaism often portrays the ideal king occupying the heavenly, cosmic throne (Pss 2:4–8; 72:8–11; 89:20–22; 110:1; Dan 7:13–14; 1 En. 45:3; 51:3; 55:4; 61:8; 62:2–3, 5; 69:27, 29), so Paul portrays Christ as occupying the cosmic throne. Paul escalates this concept by suggesting that Christ assumes the role of God in Ps 68 and occupies the divine throne. Second, the descent/ascent pattern reflects the Jewish royal motif in which God's king is elevated from obscurity to kingship (Ps 8:3–8; 2 Sam 7:8–9; Isa 52:13—53:12). Christ descends to lowly humanity and dies, but he resurrects and ascends to the highest of cosmic thrones. Third, Christ's role as royal benefactor reflects Jewish royal ideological texts that present God's ideal king as the one who brings prosperity and God's blessings to his subjects (Ps 132:15; 144:12–14; Isa 53:12; Pss. Sol. 17:43).

Paul's description of Christ's cosmic victory and enthronement in Eph 4:8–10 also parallels his description of Christ's cosmic victory in Col 2:15. In Col 2:15, Christ serves as God's royal agent through whom he brings about the defeat of the hostile cosmic powers. Christ's cosmic triumph comes because of his work on the cross (Col 2:14). Through Christ, God disarms the hostile cosmic powers and triumphs over them. God

---

"Use of Power," 197–98. Since Paul wished to emphasize Christ's role as gift giver, one may wonder why Paul did not cite Ps 68:35 instead of Ps 68:18. Wilder points out that Ps 68:18 succinctly brings together the themes of exaltation, subjugation, and gift-giving, all of which are important themes in Ephesians.

123. Fee, *Pauline Christology*, 359.

124. Jonathan M. Lunde and John Anthony Dunne rightly note that Paul's switch of referent from YHWH to Christ "assumes a christological mediation of Yahweh's actions" (Lunde and Dunne, "Creative and Contextual Use," 111–12). Smith demonstrates that the king's role as the one who bestows divine benefits to his people is a well-attested motif in Greco-Roman and Jewish royal ideologies (Smith, *Ideal King*, 218–21).

bestows honor upon Christ through this cosmic triumph and reveals Christ to be his ideal King.[125] In Eph 4:8–10, Christ assumes the role of YHWH in Ps 68 by triumphing over the hostile cosmic powers and by taking his place on the cosmic, divine throne.[126] This cosmic triumph and enthronement could only occur after Christ's earthly death and resurrection. His work on the earth gives him the rightful claim to the cosmic throne. Paul also adds that the implication of this cosmic triumph and enthronement results in Christ's assuming the regal role of gift giver. While Colossians does refer to the "gifts" of redemption and reconciliation that have been bestowed upon believers through Christ (Col 1:14, 21–22), Eph 4 refers specifically to Christ's giving of gifts that are for the explicit purpose of building up the church (Eph 4:11–16).

Paul continues the escalation of Christ's role to divine kingship in Eph 5:5. After exhorting the Ephesian believers to live according to the principles of the new man and not the principles of the old man (Eph 4:17—5:4), Paul reminds them that those who are part of the old cosmic order (characterized by the pagan gentiles) will have no place in the kingdom belonging to both Christ and God (ἐν τῇ βασιλείᾳ τοῦ Χριστοῦ καὶ θεοῦ, Eph 5:5).[127] This verse is the only time the phrase "the kingdom of Christ and God" appears in the NT. In his other writings, Paul mostly associates the kingdom with God (Gal 5:21; 1 Cor 4:20, 15:50; Rom 14:17; Col 4:11); but in Colossians, he associates the kingdom with the "beloved Son" (Col 1:13). Even though Paul's phrasing in this passage is unique,

---

125. See ch. 4.

126. While God is the subject of Col 2:15 with Christ being the agent (see ch. 4), Eph 4:8–10 focuses specifically on Christ as the subject. However, as the context of Ephesians indicates, Christ carries out his actions as God's royal agent. Both Colossians and Ephesians expound upon the royal agency of Christ.

127. Barth accepts a textual variant that reads Χριστοῦ τοῦ θεοῦ (1739*, vgms), which he translates "the kingdom of God's Messiah" (Barth, *Ephesians*, 564–65). The textual evidence for this reading is lacking, which makes the possibility that it was the original reading unlikely. Another possibility is that the anarthrous noun θεοῦ stands in apposition to the articular noun τοῦ Χριστοῦ. This interpretation applies the Granville-Sharp rule where the articular noun and anarthrous noun are joined by a copulative καί with the second noun further describing the first noun. In this case, this phrase could be used to defend Christ's deity and would be translated "the kingdom of Christ, who is God." This possibility is unlikely for two reasons. First, the noun θεός is often used without an article, especially in cases where it appears as a genitive with βασιλεία (1 Cor 6:9, 10; 15:50; Gal 5:21). Second, the article before Christ is likely used to denote his proper title. For more on the grammatical possibilities of this passage, see Harris, *Jesus as God*, 261–63; Hoehner, *Ephesians*, 661–62; Smith, *Ideal King*, 193–94; and Lopez, "Paul's Vice List," 205–6.

the idea that, for Paul, the kingdom belongs to both Christ and God is not unique to this passage (see 1 Cor 15:24–28). The order in which Paul puts these nouns in Eph 5:5 does indicate an emphasis on the rule of Christ,[128] but he does not view Christ and God as having two separate kingdoms. Instead, Paul views the rule of Christ, God's royal agent, as the fullest expression of the kingdom of God.[129] The fact that those who are part of the old cosmic order have no inheritance in the kingdom of God and Christ reemphasizes Paul's point in Eph 4:7–16 that Christ serves as God's royal benefactor.

Ephesians 5:5 parallels Paul's assertion in Col 1:13. Both passages present Christ as God's royal agent who presently rules over the cosmos. Both passages also make mention of an inheritance. Ephesians 5:5 presents a negative statement regarding the inheritance. Those who are a part of the old, corrupt cosmic order and live according to it will not receive the kingdom inheritance. Paul's assertion that these people will not receive it implies that there are people who will receive the inheritance. Colossians 1:13 presents the positive statement regarding the inheritance. Paul states that those who receive the inheritance are the ones whom God delivered from the old, corrupt cosmic order and transferred into Christ's kingdom (Col 1:12–13). The point of both passages remains the same: the only way to receive the inheritance of God's kingdom is through submission to the rule of Christ, God's royal benefactor.

SUMMARY AND CONCLUSION

Jewish royal ideology once again provides a helpful framework for understanding Paul's cosmic Christology in Ephesians. Rather than critique or correct the views of Colossians, the cosmic Christology of Ephesians complements the cosmic Christology of Colossians and expands on many of its regal themes. The way both Colossians and Ephesians utilize Jewish royal language and themes to cast Christ as the cosmic King demonstrates their complementary nature. Like the writing in Colossians, Paul uses both Davidic and Adamic themes in Ephesians to frame Christ's cosmic enthronement and kingly function. Paul characterizes Christ's enthronement and function as the fulfillment of the ideal Davidic King in Jewish royal ideology. His use of the "in Christ" formula reveals Christ as

---

128. Fee, *Pauline Christology*, 351.
129. Sellin, *Epheser*, 399, and Smith, *Ideal King*, 193–94.

the sphere and agent of God's action, meaning that God brings about his cosmic purpose through Christ's cosmic enthronement and rule. Christ's enthronement comes about as a result of his incarnation, death, and resurrection. Christ adopted the obscure status that originally characterized David and Adam, and, like them, he is exalted to kingship. As God's royal agent, Christ conquers and subdues the hostile cosmic powers, brings peace and prosperity to those under his reign, enthrones believers in the heavens, serves as the royal benefactor for those in his kingdom, and brings about a new cosmic order. These functions repeat the characterization of the Jewish ideal king and of Christ's rule in Colossians.

Paul also repeats some Adamic themes in Ephesians that he uses in Colossians. By viewing Christ as the Adamic King, Paul elevates the Davidic kingship to cosmic proportions. As Adam had all things put under his feet at creation, so now God has put all things under Christ's feet. The submission of the cosmic powers under Christ's feet shows that Christ exceeds the original reign of Adam and reverses the negative effects of his failed reign, making Christ's kingship the ideal antitype to the reign of Adam. Ephesians further details existence in the "dominion of darkness" (Col 1:13), specifically that this dominion is totally hostile to God and that those who live in it are under the rule of a malevolent cosmic being. Paul's description fits well with his Adam Christology in his other letters where he views Adam's failure as God's first king as introducing the rule of cosmic powers hostile to God. Paul uses the old man / new man contrast to characterize the new existence that believers have under Christ's reign. As Adam stood at the head of the original creation, so Christ stands at the head of new creation, but he exceeds Adam in serving as God's agent in new creation.

Ephesians reflects and further explains the eschatological and ecclesial implications of Christ's cosmic kingship in Colossians. Like Colossians, Ephesians presents the whole cosmos as currently subject to the reign of the Christ but also anticipates the full realization of Christ's reign. Paul escalates the role of the Jewish ideal king by casting Christ in the role of divine King and suggests that the eschatological expectations of divine rule are fulfilled in Christ. One could argue that Ephesians puts more emphasis on the eschatological implications of Christ's reign, but this does not necessitate an argument for conflicting cosmic Christologies. While both letters view believers as the present beneficiaries of Christ's cosmic kingship, Paul elaborates in Ephesians on the relationship between the present manifestation of Christ's reign over the church and the future manifestation of Christ's reign over the cosmos. While Paul speaks of believers' "hiddenness" in Christ in Colossians, he explains in Ephesians that this state involves present enthronement in the heavens. Paul also elevates the Jewish royal motif where God's ideal king brings prosperity to those under his reign to argue that believers presently participate in Christ's cosmic reign. The present oneness of the church serves as the present manifestation of the cosmic harmony that will be effectuated through Christ's reign. For this reason, the church presently enjoys the spoils of Christ's cosmic enthronement. The church can also have confidence in its fight against the hostile cosmic powers because these powers are presently subject to the cosmic rule of Christ (Eph 6:10–17).

6

Conclusion

THIS STUDY ENDEAVORED TO investigate how Paul framed his cosmic Christology in Colossians and Ephesians and how he conceived of Christ's relationship to the cosmos in light of his Jewish background. The objective was to determine whether Jewish royal ideology, specifically the Adamic and Davidic king, provides the necessary linguistic and conceptual framework through which Paul could have conceived of Christ as the cosmic Lord. This study was deemed necessary because previous arguments suggesting the cosmic Christology of Colossians and Ephesians reflect either Greco-Roman cosmology or Jewish Wisdom traditions are unsatisfactory. Instead, this study contends that Jewish royal ideology provides valuable insight for understanding the cosmic Christology of Colossians and Ephesians.

THE ROYAL BACKDROP

This study began with an exploration of Jewish royal ideology as presented in the OT and early Jewish literature. Jewish royal ideology represents the belief that God desires to enact his rule over the creation and cosmos through his ideal king. The enthronement of this king brings about the restoration of God's people and the cosmic order. Jewish royal ideology presents the Adamic and Davidic king as the embodiment of God's ideal king. First, Judaism presents the Adamic king as both a positive and negative figure. Positively, God brought Adam from a position of obscurity to a place of honor within the created order. God appointed Adam as his royal representative over creation and commissioned him to exercise his good rule over creation. Adam's royal commissioning meant that he was to be the agent through whom creation would experience the benefits of God's rule. Negatively, Adam's failure to steward God's good rule over creation corrupted the cosmic order and introduced the rule of cosmic powers hostile to God's rule.

Second, Jewish royal ideology views the ideal Davidic king as the primary figure through whom God will restore his good rule over his people, creation, and the cosmos. This king both embodies many aspects of Adam's kingship and serves as a solution to the failed reign of Adam. Like God did with Adam, he elevated the Davidic king from a position of obscurity to kingship. Jewish royal ideology sometimes presents this king as a transcendent being and even as a preexistent figure. As one enthroned by God, the ideal Davidic king rules under the authority of God and possesses a unique relationship with God that is often described in terms of divine sonship. As God's royal agent, the ideal Davidic king reflects and restores God's good rule. Jewish royal ideology views the reign of the ideal Davidic king as extending over all the nations and, at times, over cosmic forces. God invites his ideal king to join with him in the battle against hostile cosmic forces so he might restore peace and harmony through his royal agent. The enthronement of the ideal Davidic king signals judgment on the wicked and blessings for the righteous. Whereas Adam's failure resulted in cosmic chaos, God's enthronement of the ideal Davidic king reestablishes cosmic harmony.

This study continued by examining how the Gospels, Paul's undisputed letters, and other parts of the NT built on these Jewish royal themes. The Gospels make clear that Jesus fulfills many expectations of the Jewish ideal king. He is ascribed a divine and Davidic lineage, which establishes his credentials as God's ideal King who claims authority over the cosmos (Mark 12:35–37; Matt 22:41–46; Luke 1:26–27). His enthronement and eventual parousia signal the reestablishment of God's cosmic rule (Mark 14:61–65; Matt 26:63–65; Luke 22:67–71). Jesus claims to have a share in the divine throne and to have authority to command angels (Mark 8:38, 13:24–27; Matt 16:27–28, 24:29–31; Luke 9:26–27, 21:25–28; John 18:36–37). He assumes the role of God's ideal King in bringing judgment on the wicked, hostile cosmic forces and vindication for God's people (Matt 19:28, 25:34–46; Luke 22:28–30).

Paul pushes Jewish royal ideology forward in his undisputed letters. Paul views Christ's role as messianic King from David (Rom 1:3–4) as fulfilling God's original intent of subduing the creation under Adam. Paul views Christ's reign as the antitype of Adam's reign. Paul sets Christ and Adam at the head of two cosmic orders (Rom 5:12–21). Adam's failure introduced the reign of cosmic powers hostile to God and led to creation's demise. Paul viewed Adam's failure as a cosmic problem that required a cosmic solution. Christ assumes and exceeds the role of Adam and reverses the effects of Adam's failed reign (Rom 5:15–21; 1 Cor 15:21–22, 27). Paul presents Christ's enthronement as the event which liberates the creation and cosmos from the reign of the hostile cosmic powers and reintroduces the reign of God over the cosmos (1 Cor 15:24–28; Rom 8:19–23). Paul's description of Christ's regal role mirrors the Jewish portrait of the ideal Davidic king. Like the ideal Davidic king, Christ is enthroned by God, is brought from obscurity to kingship, and is God's royal agent through whom he defeats and subjects the hostile cosmic powers (1 Cor 15:23–28; Phil 2:10–11). Christ's enthronement as God's ideal King signals judgment for the wicked and vindication for the righteous (1 Thess 4:13—5:9). Paul also views Christ's kingship as exceeding the Jewish ideal king. Whereas Jewish royal ideology hints at the preexistence of God's ideal king, Paul identifies Christ with God and views his preexistent, divine nature as essential to his claim to the cosmic throne (1 Cor 8:5–6; Phil 2:6). Where Jewish royal ideology presents the ideal king as being given authority over creation, Paul argues that Christ's authority rightfully belongs to him as one who bears the divine image (2 Cor 4:5) and as God's agent in both old and new creation (Gal 6:15; 1 Cor 8:6b; 2 Cor 5:16–17; Phil 3:20–21). Paul also argues that Christ's enthronement comes as a result of his death and resurrection, which serves as the revelation of how God's ideal King would reclaim cosmic authority (Rom 8:31–39; Phil 2:8–11). Given the importance of this royal ideology in Paul's and the NT's portrait of Christ, this study suggested that this royal framework may prove helpful in explaining the cosmic Christology of Colossians and Ephesians.

THE COSMIC KING IN COLOSSIANS AND EPHESIANS

Paul repeats and expands upon Jewish royal ideological themes in Colossians and Ephesians. Paul uses Adamic and Davidic language and

CONCLUSION

themes in his portrait of Christ as supreme King over the cosmos. This Jewish royal backdrop of the letters suggests that the cosmic Christology of Colossians and Ephesians complement each other. Paul implies the existence of two dominions in the cosmos in both letters. Paul's contrast between the dominion of darkness and Christ's kingdom (Col 1:12–13; Eph 2:1–10) echoes his previous Adam-Christ statements in which the failed reign of Adam ushered in the rule of hostile, cosmic powers. The existence of this dark dominion (which Paul describes in Eph 2:1–3 as the result of Adam's failure) serves as the presuppositional foundation by which Paul sees the need for God to reconcile and bring all things in the cosmos under the headship of Christ (Col 1:19–20; Eph 1:10).

Paul places Christ in the role of Adam in Colossians by calling him "the image of the invisible God" (Col 1:15; cf. Gen 1:26–27) and in Ephesians with an allusion to Adam's original position in creation in Ps 8:6 (Eph 1:22). As Adam was God's royal representative to creation, so Christ, in his incarnation, became God's visible, royal representative to the cosmos. Paul presents Christ as superior to Adam by asserting that Christ preexisted creation (Eph 1:3–4) and served as God's agent in creation (Col 1:16). His status as Creator proves his power to overcome the hostile cosmic powers that rule as the result of Adam's failed reign. Whereas Adam's failure plunged creation into chaos, Christ's reign restores and maintains cosmic order (Col 1:17; Eph 1:10). Christ's authority over these cosmic powers exceeds the authority originally given to Adam. Whereas God subjected the creation under Adam's rule, God subjects the cosmos under Christ's rule (Eph 1:20–22). Paul's use of the old man / new man motif (Col 3:9–10; Eph 2:15) is another implicit reference to Adam and draws a contrast between the old existence in Adam and the new existence in Christ. The "one new man" points to Christ's work in reversing the effects of Adam's reign to form a new humanity that would operate under his kingship and perpetuate the rule of God throughout the cosmos.

Paul presents Christ's function as the Adamic antitype as a fulfillment of the ideal Davidic king. Paul attributes to Christ the titles "beloved son" (Col 1:13, Eph 1:6) and "firstborn" (Col 1:15, 18), both of which were attributed to the Davidic king in Jewish royal ideology. Christ fulfills the father-son relationship that God promised to have with his king (Eph 4:13). Christ is both the "firstborn of creation" and the "firstborn of the dead," meaning that Christ is the rightful King of the original creation and of the new creation order. Paul also calls him the κεφαλή and the ἀρχή (Col 1:18), both titles with regal connotations. As the Jewish ideal king was sometimes presented as a transcendent ruler, Paul presents the transcendent nature of Christ's reign. Paul asserts that Christ is presently seated "above" at God's right hand "in the heavenlies" (Col 3:1; Eph 1:20b), a place which was reserved for the Jewish ideal king (Ps 110:1). Paul also views Christ fulfilling the functions typically attributed to the ideal Davidic king. He is the agent through whom God liberates his people from the oppressive reign of the hostile cosmic powers (Col 1:12–14; Eph 1:7, 2:4–10). He joins with God in his battle against the cosmic powers, and his enthronement signals the defeat of these powers (Col 2:14–15, Eph 1:20–22). As a result, Christ serves as God's agent who brings peace to the cosmos and under whom God unites and restores the cosmos (Col 1:20, Eph 1:22). As the Jewish ideal king brought prosperity to those under his reign, Christ serves as God's royal benefactor who grants a heavenly inheritance to his people, which includes life, salvation, redemption, peace, access to the Father, empowerment by the Spirit, and participation in Christ's reign (Col 1:12, 21–22; 2:12–14; Eph 1:3–14; 2:4–10, 13–22; 4:8–13; 5:5).

Paul pushes Jewish royal ideology forward in Colossians and Ephesians in a few ways. First, he draws a connection between Adamic and Davidic kingship and clarifies the importance of Christ's fulfilling both roles. Paul's connection between the Adamic and Davidic king is most evident in his combination of Ps 110:1 (a Davidic Psalm) and Ps 8:6 (an Adamic Psalm) in Eph 1:20–23. Christ's fulfillment of Davidic kingship was necessary to undo the effects of Adam's failed reign and to regain the dominion that Adam lost. On the other hand, Christ's role as the Adamic King expands the scope of the Davidic king's reign to a cosmic level. By placing Christ in the role of the Adamic-Davidic King, Paul views Christ as not only the hope of restoration for God's people but also as the hope of restoration for the whole cosmic order. Second, while Jewish royal ideology sometimes presents the ideal king as a unique, transcendent figure, Paul argues that Christ is equal with the divine. Christ bears the divine fullness in himself (Col 1:19, Eph 1:23), which means he possesses the glory and honor necessary to claim the cosmic throne. His father-son relationship with God is not one that is given to him but one that he has always possessed. His function as the preexistent agent in creation and his continued work as the agent of God's ongoing creation project evidences his divine character (Eph 2:10, 15). Christ claims authority over the cosmos because he is the Creator and goal of the cosmos (Col

1:15–17; Eph 1:9–10, 20–23; 3:11). Paul further elevates the picture of the Jewish ideal king by using Ps 68 to identify explicitly Christ with the divine King (Eph 4:8–10), making Christ's rule the fullest expression of God's kingdom (Eph 5:5). Third, the way Christ achieves his cosmic victory and enthronement is something unexpected in Jewish royal ideology. While Jewish royal ideology does suggest that God raises his king from obscurity to kingship, the revelation of Christ gives this motif new light. Rather than military conquest, Christ achieves his cosmic victory and enthronement through his incarnation, death, and resurrection (Col 1:18, 2:13–15; Eph 1:20, 4:8–10). Christ's death and resurrection serve as the revelation and validation of his right to the divine cosmic throne.

While Christ presently reigns over the cosmos, Paul views the church as the present manifestation of Christ's reign. God places believers under the reign of Christ, resulting in their becoming the present beneficiaries of Christ's cosmic reconciliatory work (Col 1:13–14, 21–22). As the enthroned cosmic King, Christ presently rules over the church (Col 1:18a) and negates any reason the church would have for fearing the hostile cosmic powers. While Paul states in Colossians that the church is filled with Christ (Col 2:10), he clarifies in Ephesians that the church, as Christ's fullness, is the present manifestation of Christ's cosmic reign (Eph 1:23). Through the unity of Jew and gentile in Christ, the church presently manifests the cosmic harmony brought by Christ's reign (Eph 2:14–16). As Christ's body, the church participates in Christ's cosmic rule and reflects the ethics of Christ's kingdom over the ethics of the old, fallen kingdom. In so doing, the church perpetuates the rule of God and Christ his King throughout the cosmos (Col 3:9–11). Believers' "hiddenness" in Christ suggests that while Christ's reign is presently realized in the church, it will eventually be fully revealed throughout the cosmos (Col 3:3–4). In Ephesians, Paul clarifies that believers' "hiddenness" in Christ involves present enthronement in the heavens (Eph 2:6), where Christ is currently enthroned. Believers' union with Christ and enthronement in the heavens reveal to the hostile cosmic powers in the spiritual realm that they have been defeated and are under Christ's cosmic authority (Eph 3:10–11). As Christ's body and the present manifestation of his cosmic authority, Christ empowers the church to participate in his cosmic rule and to reflect the ethics of his kingdom over the ethics of the old, fallen kingdom (Col 3:9–11, Eph 4:8–16). In so doing, the church perpetuates the rule of God and Christ his King throughout the cosmos.

IMPLICATIONS AND FURTHER POINTS OF STUDY

The results of this study have a few implications for the study of Colossians and Ephesians. First, the way both Colossians and Ephesians use Jewish royal ideology demonstrates that these letters complement rather than contradict each other. Colossians and Ephesians both utilize Adamic and Davidic motifs in their portrait of cosmic Christ and share many of the same royal themes. In some cases, one letter will provide more explanation on a royal motif that was mentioned in the other letter. For example, Colossians mentions that believers are "hidden with Christ," but Ephesians explains the nature of the believers' hiddenness with Christ. Therefore, this study suggests a complementary rather than a contradictory portrait of Colossians and Ephesians.

Second, this study provides a potential alternative to previous explanations on the background of the Christology in Colossians and Ephesians. One does not need to make strained connections to personified Wisdom to explain Christ's role in the created order. One also does not need to regard the cosmic aspects of the letters' Christology as an outgrowth of complex interactions with Greco-Roman cosmologies. This study contends that Jewish royal ideology provides a crucial link to how the letters relate Christ to God, to the cosmos, and to the church. Jewish royal ideology provided Paul with the linguistic and conceptual resources needed to define and develop his own thoughts on Christ's identity and function within the Godhead. The development of Jewish royal ideological themes in the christological portrait of Colossians and Ephesians demonstrates that Paul neither "copied and pasted" Jewish royal ideology, nor did he completely abandon his own Jewish background. Rather, Paul's belief in the risen Christ made him an innovator of Jewish royal ideological themes. Paul developed Jewish royal ideology with his explicit connection between the Adamic and Davidic king via Christ's kingship. Previous studies on Christ's kingship tend to focus on his role as Jewish Messiah, but Christ's role as the last Adam is an important aspect of Paul's royal portrait. Paul's other innovations of Jewish royal ideology include Christ's agency in creation as a necessary qualification of his cosmic kingship and Christ's death and resurrection as the means by which he is enthroned as God's ideal King. The use of Jewish royal ideology does not mean that Jewish Wisdom or Greco-Roman categories are completely absent from the cosmic Christology of Colossians and Ephesians, but it does suggest that these categories may not provide the same explanatory power as Jewish royal ideology.

Third, Paul's use of royal ideology in Colossians and Ephesians illustrates one of the ways by which Paul articulated Christ's divine status. Jewish royal ideology viewed the ideal king as having a vital role in reestablishing God's good rule over creation. Paul sees Christ as the one who fulfills this regal role. The cosmic scope of Christ's rule suggests that Christ is not just a subordinate agent through whom God exercises his rule, but Christ's cosmic, heavenly throne suggests he shares coequally with God's cosmic reign. In this way, Paul does not break away from Judaism, but he elevates Jewish royal agency categories. Paul viewed Christ's resurrection as the event that signaled Christ's cosmic enthronement and elevated his kingship to a cosmic scale. Christ's resurrection not only validated his present claim to the cosmic throne, but it also affirmed that the throne of God's ideal King rightfully belonged to Christ from before the creation of the cosmos. For Paul, Christ's resurrection served as the revelation of his identity as the divine, cosmic King.

Fourth, Christ's position as the rightful cosmic King is foundational to Paul's understanding of Christ's function in God's work in creation and redemption. Christ serves as the royal agent through whom God brings about his creative and redemptive purpose. In Jewish royal ideology, the enthronement of God's ideal king serves as the event that will reestablish God's good rule over the cosmos. Christ uniquely fulfills this role because he served as God's agent in establishing the original created order. For Paul, Christ's agency in creation is essential to his agency in the new creation. It is not necessarily novel to view Christ's lordship as the lens through which he views creation and redemption. However, this study pushes this concept forward by showing how Paul articulates Christ's lordship in Adamic and Davidic terms in Colossians and Ephesians. Christ fulfills the role of the ideal Davidic king, reverses the cosmic damage caused by the failure of the Adamic king, and fulfills God's original purpose to rule over his created order through his good king.

Fifth, Paul's use of Jewish royal ideology also helps explain the link between Christ's cosmic function and his ecclesial function in Colossians and Ephesians. Christ's kingship over the cosmos qualifies him as the rightful head over the church. While both letters affirm Christ's current position as the cosmic King, they also recognize that Christ's rule has yet to be fully realized. The church serves as the present manifestation of Christ's cosmic rule. The church's present reconciliation to God and its unity in Christ presently demonstrates the eventual full reconciliation of the cosmos under Christ's reign. As a corporate entity joined to Christ as his body / one new man, Christ's identity as cosmic King has significant implications for the church's identity. The church has been granted a royal identity as those who share in Christ's enthronement. The church is the present recipient of the spoils of Christ's cosmic victory. The church presently participates in Christ's reign and perpetuates his good rule.

One potential consequence of this study is that it affirms the likelihood that Paul was indeed the author of Colossians and Ephesians. While this study does not necessarily aim to prove Pauline authorship, the way in which Colossians and Ephesians use Adamic and Davidic themes does not differ much from the way Paul uses these themes in his undisputed letters. The hesitancy of scholars to accept Colossians and Ephesians into the Pauline corpus possibly hinders one's ability to develop a full understanding of Paul's own cosmic Christology. Rather than viewing the unique aspects of the Christology in Colossians and Ephesians as separate from or contradictory to Paul, scholarship could be better served to view the Christology of Colossians and Ephesians as complementary to Paul's undisputed letters. At the very least, even if one is not convinced of Pauline authorship, this study shows that Colossians and Ephesians fit very well within the Pauline school of thought.

If these conclusions prove convincing, this study may lead to other avenues of study within Colossians and Ephesians. Since this study focused primarily on how Paul used Jewish royal ideology to articulate his cosmic Christology in Colossians and Ephesians, others may provide more focused studies on how Paul uses Jewish royal ideology in each of his letters. While this study does suggest some ways in which Christ's royal identity forms the identity of the church in Colossians and Ephesians, other studies could explore this idea further. Others may explore the church's cosmic role as it awaits the full revelation of Christ's cosmic reign. Other studies may simply expand upon and improve the arguments made in this study.

Overall, this study has attempted to demonstrate that Jewish royal ideology serves as a useful tool for explaining how Paul articulated his cosmic Christology in Colossians and Ephesians. As God's King, Christ fulfills and exceeds the expectations of the Jewish ideal king. He also exceeds the kingship of Adam and restores the cosmic harmony that was disrupted because of Adam's failed reign. The reality of Christ's cosmic kingship gave the churches at Colossae and Ephesus purpose in the present as they perpetuated Christ's good rule and hope for the future as they awaited the full realization of Christ's cosmic reign. As the church finds its identity in its union to Christ, the cosmos finds restoration under the reign of Christ, God's ideal cosmic King.

Bibliography

Adams, Edward. *Constructing the World: A Study in Paul's Cosmological Language.* New York: T&T Clark, 2000.

———. "Paul's Story of God and Creation: The Story of How God Fulfills His Purposes in Creation." In *Narrative Dynamics in Paul: A Critical Assessment,* edited by Bruce W. Longenecker, 19–43. Louisville: Westminster John Knox, 2002.

Alexander, T. Desmond. "Messianic Ideology in the Book of Genesis." In *The Lord's Anointed: Interpretation of Old Testament Messianic Texts,* edited by Philip E. Satterthwaite et al., 19–39. Grand Rapids: Baker, 1995.

———. "Royal Expectations in Genesis to Kings: Their Importance for Biblical Theology." *TynBul* 49 (1998) 191–212.

Aletti, Jean-Noël. *Colossiens 1,15–20: Genre et exégèse du texte; Fonction de la thématique sapientielle.* Rome: Biblical Institute, 1981.

———. *Saint Paul: Epitre aux Colossiens; Introduction, traduction et commentaire.* Paris: J. Gabalda, 1993.

———. *Saint Paul: Epître aux Éphésiens.* Paris: Gabalda, 2001.

Allan, John A. "The 'in Christ' Formula in Ephesians." *NTS* 5 (1958) 54–62.

Allen, Thomas. "Exaltation and Solidarity with Christ: Ephesians 1.20 and 2.6." *JSNT* 28 (1986) 103–20.

Arnold, Clinton. *Ephesians: Power and Magic; The Concept of Power in Ephesians in Light of Its Historical Setting.* New York: Cambridge University Press, 1989.

———. "Jesus Christ: 'Head' of the Church (Colossians and Ephesians)." In *Jesus of Nazareth: Lord and Christ; Essays on the Historical Jesus and New Testament Christology,* edited by Joel B. Green and Max Turner, 346–66. Grand Rapids: Eerdmans, 1994.

———. *The Colossian Syncretism: The Interface between Christianity and Folk Belief at Colossae.* Tübingen: Mohr Siebeck, 1995.

Avemarie, Friedrich. "Image of God and Image of Christ: Developments in Pauline and Ancient Jewish Anthropology." In *The Dead Sea Scrolls and Pauline Literature,* edited by Jean-Sebastien Rey, 209–36. Leiden: Brill, 2014.

Baker, David L. "Typology and the Christian Use of the Old Testament." In *The Right Doctrine from the Wrong Texts: Essays on the Use of the Old Testament in the New,* edited by G. K. Beale, 313–30. Grand Rapids: Baker, 1994.

Balchin, J. F. "Colossians 1:15–20: An Early Christian Hymn? An Argument from Style." *VE* 15 (1985) 65–93.

Bales, William. "The Descent of Christ in Ephesians 4:9." *CBQ* 72 (2010) 84–100.
Barr, James. *Biblical Faith and Natural Theology*. The Gifford Lectures, 1991. Oxford: Clarendon, 1993.
Barrett, C. K. *From First Adam to Last: A Study in Pauline Theology*. New York: Scribner, 1962.
———. *The Acts of the Apostles: Preliminary Introduction and Commentary on Acts I–XIV*. ICC 1. Edinburgh: T&T Clark, 1994.
Barth, Markus. *Ephesians: Introduction, Translation and Commentary on Chapters 1–3*. AB 34. New York: Doubleday, 1974.
Barth, Markus, and Helmut Blanke. *Colossians*. Translated by Astrid B. Beck. AB 34B. New York: Doubleday, 1994.
Barthel, Jörg. *Prophetenwort und Geschichte. Die Jesajaüberlieferung in Jes 6–8 und 28–31*. Tübingen: Mohr Siebeck, 1997.
Barthelemy, Dominique. *Critique textuelle de l'Ancien Testament*. Göttingen: Vandenhoeck & Ruprecht, 1986.
Batto, Bernard F. "The Divine Sovereign: The Image of God in the Priestly Creation Account." In *David and Zion: Biblical Studies in Honor of J. J. M. Roberts*, edited by Bernard F. Batto and Kathryn L. Roberts, 143–86. Winona Lake, IN: Eisenbrauns, 2004.
Bauckham, Richard. *Jesus and the God of Israel: God Crucified and Other Studies on the New Testament's Christology of Divine Identity*. Grand Rapids: Eerdmans, 2009.
———. "The Throne of God and the Worship of Jesus." In *The Jewish Roots of Christological Monotheism: Papers from the St. Andrews Conference on the Historical Origins of the Worship of Jesus*, edited by Carey C. Newman et al., 43–69. Leiden: Brill, 1999.
Baugh, S. M. *Ephesians*. EEC. Bellingham, WA: Lexham, 2016.
Beale, Gregory K. *Colossians and Philemon*. BECNT. Grand Rapids: Baker Academic, 2019.
———. *Handbook on the New Testament Use of the Old Testament: Exegesis and Interpretation*. Grand Rapids: Baker, 2012.
———. *The Temple and the Church's Mission: A Biblical Theology of the Dwelling Place of God*. Downers Grove, IL: InterVarsity, 2004.
Beetham, Christopher A. *Echoes of Scripture in the Letter of Paul to Colossians*. Leiden: Brill, 2008.
Beker, J. C. *Paul's Apocalyptic Gospel*. Philadelphia: Fortress, 1982.
———. *Paul the Apostle: The Triumph of God in Life and Thought*. Philadelphia: Fortress, 1980.
Beskow, Per. *Rex Gloriae: The Kingship of Christ in the Early Church*. Translated by Eric J. Sharpe. Eugene, OR: Wipf and Stock, 2014.
Best, Ernest. *A Critical and Exegetical Commentary on Ephesians*. ICC. Edinburgh: T&T Clark, 1998.
———. "Ephesians 1.1 Again." In *Paul and Paulinism: Essays in Honor of C. K. Barrett*, edited by Morna D. Hooker and S. G. Wilson, 273–79. London: SPCK, 1982.
———. "Who Used Whom? The Relationship of Ephesians and Colossians." *NTS* 43 (1997) 72–96.
Bevere, Allan R. *Sharing in the Inheritance: Identity and Moral Life in Colossians*. London: Sheffield Academic, 2003.

Beyerle, Stefan. "Der mit den Wolken des Himmels kommt." In *Gottessohn und Menschensohn*, edited by Dieter Sänger, 1–52. Neukirchen-Vluyn: Neukirchener, 2004.

Bird, Michael F. *Colossians and Philemon*. NCC. Eugene, OR: Cascade, 2009.

———, ed. *How God Became Jesus: The Real Origins of Belief in Jesus' Divine Nature—A Response to Bart Ehrman*. Grand Rapids: Zondervan, 2014.

Bird, Phyllis A. "'Male and Female He Created Them': Gen 1:27b in the Context of the Priestly Account of Creation." *HTR* 74 (April 1981) 129–59.

Blanchette, Oliva A. "Does the 'Cheirographon' of Col 2.14 Represent Christ Himself?" *CBQ* 23 (1961) 306–12.

Blenkinsopp, Jospeh. *Isaiah 40–55*. AB 19A. New York: Doubleday, 2000.

Block, Daniel I. "Bringing Back David: Ezekiel's Messianic Hope." In *The Lord's Anointed: Interpretation of Old Testament Messianic Texts*, edited by Philip E. Satterthwaite et al., 167–88. Grand Rapids: Baker, 1995.

———. "My Servant David: Ancient Israel's Vision of the Messiah." In *Israel's Messiah in the Bible and the Dead Sea Scrolls*, edited by Richard S. Hess and M. Daniel Carroll, 17–56. Grand Rapids: Baker Academic, 2003.

Bock, Darrell L. *Acts*. BECNT. Grand Rapids: Baker Academic, 2007.

———. "Blasphemy and the Jewish Examination of Jesus." *BBR* 17 (2007) 53–114.

Bockmuehl, Markus. Review of *Cosmic Christology in Paul and the Pauline School: Colossians and Ephesians in the Context of Greco-Roman Cosmology*, by George van Kooten. *Bib* 86 (2005) 443–44.

Bogaert, Pierre. *Apocalypse de Baruch: Introduction, traduction du syriaque et commentaire*. Paris: du Cerfs, 1969.

Borgen, Peder. "Observations on the Targumic Character of the Prologue of John." *NTS* 16 (1970) 288–95.

Böttrich, Christfried. "Konturen des 'Menschensohnes' in äthHen 37–71." In *Gottessohn und Menschensohn: Exegetische Studien zu zwei Paradigmen biblischer Intertextualität*, edited by Dieter Sänger, 53–90. Neukirchen-Vluyn: Neukirchener Verlag, 2004.

Bousset, Wilhelm. *Kyrios Christos: A History of the Belief in Christ from the Beginnings of Christianity to Irenaeus*. Translated by John E. Steely. Nashville: Abingdon, 1970.

Bouttier, Michel. *En Christ: Etude d'exegese et de theologie Pauliennes*. Paris: Presses Universitaires de France, 1962.

———. *L'épître de Saint Paul aux Éphésiens*. Geneva: Labor et Fides, 1991.

Brandenburger, Egon. *Adam und Christus: Exegetisch-religionsgeschichtliche Untersuchung zu Röm. 5, 12–21 (1.Kor 15)*. Neukirchen: Kreis Moers, 1962.

Brannon, M. Jeff. *The Heavenlies in Ephesians: A Lexical, Exegetical, and Conceptual Analysis*. New York: T&T Clark, 2011.

Brooke, George. "Kingship and Messianism in the Dead Sea Scrolls." In *King and Messiah in Israel and the Ancient Near East: Proceedings of the Oxford Old Testament Seminar*, edited by John Day, 434–55. Sheffield: Sheffield Academic, 1998.

Brown, Jeanine K. "Creation's Renewal in the Gospel of John." *CBQ* 72 (2010) 275–90.

Brown, Raymond E. *The Gospel according to John (i–xii)*. AB 29. Garden City, NY: Doubleday, 1970.

Bruce, F. F. *1 and 2 Corinthians*. NCBC. Grand Rapids: Eerdmans, 1980.

———. *1 and 2 Thessalonians*. WBC 45. Waco, TX: Word, 1982.

———. "Colossians Problems III: The Colossian Heresy." *BSac* 141 (1984) 195–208.

———. *The Epistles to the Colossians, to Philemon, and to the Ephesians*. NICNT. Grand Rapids: Eerdmans, 1984.

———. *The Epistle to the Galatians: A Commentary on the Greek Text*. NIGTC. Grand Rapids: Eerdmans, 1982.

Brucker, Ralph. *'Christushymnen' oder 'Epideiktisched Passagen'? Studien zum Stilwechsel im Neuen Testament und seiner Umwelt*. Göttingen: Vandenhoeck & Ruprecht, 1997.

Brueggemann, Walter. "From Dust to Kingship." *ZAW* 84 (1972) 1–18.

———. *The Message of the Psalms: A Theological Commentary*. AOTS. Minneapolis: Augsburg, 1984.

Buchanan, Wesley. *To the Hebrews*. AB. New York: Doubleday, 1972.

Bultmann, Rudolf. *Theology of the New Testament*. Vol 2. London: SCM, 1955.

Burney, C. F. "Christ as the APXH of Creation (Prov. viii 22, Col i 15–18, Rev iii 14)." *JTS* 27 (1926) 160–77.

Busse, Ulrich. "Metaphorik und Rhetorik im Johannesevangelium: Das Bildfeld vom König." In *Imagery of the Gospel of John*, edited by J. Frey et al., 279–318. Tübingen: Mohr Siebeck, 2006.

Caird, G. B. "The Descent of Christ in Eph 4,7–11." In *Studia Evangelica* II, edited by Frank L. Cross, 535–45. Berlin: Akademie, 1964.

Canavan, Rosemary. *Clothing the Body of Christ at Colossae: A Visual Construction of Identity*. Tübingen: Mohr Siebeck, 2012.

Capes, David B. *The Divine Christ: Paul, the Lord Jesus, and the Scriptures of Israel*. Grand Rapids: Baker, 2018.

Carr, Wesley. *Angels and Principalities: The Background, Meaning, and Development of the Pauline Phrase HAI ARCHAI KAI EXOUSIAI*. Cambridge: Cambridge University Press, 1981.

Casey, Maurice. *Son of Man: The Interpretation and Influence of Daniel 7*. London: SPCK, 1993.

Charlesworth, James H. "From Jewish Messianology to Christian Christology." In *Judaisms and Their Messiahs at the Turn of the Christian Era*, edited by Jacob Neusner et al., 225–64. Cambridge: Cambridge University Press, 1987.

Chester, Andrew. "Jewish Messianic Expectations and Mediatorial Figures and Pauline Christology." In *Paulus und Antike Judentum*, edited by Martin Hengel and Ulrich Heckel, 17–89. Tübingen: Mohr Siebeck, 1991.

———. *Messiah and Exaltation: Jewish Messianic and Visionary Traditions and New Testament Christology*. Tübingen: Mohr Siebeck, 2007.

Childs, Brevard. "Psalm 8 in the Context of Christian Canon." *Int* 23 (1969) 20–31.

Clines, David J. A. "Humanity as the Image of God." In *On the Way to Postmodern: Old Testament Essays*, edited by David J. A. Clines, 447–97. Sheffield: Sheffield Academic, 1998.

Collins, Adela Yarbro. "Psalms, Philippians 2:6–11, and the Origins of Christology." *BibInt* 11 (2003) 361–72.

———. "The Worship of Jesus and the Imperial Cult." In *The Jewish Roots of Christological Monotheism: Papers from the St. Andrews Conference on the Historical Origins of the Worship of Jesus*, edited by Carey C. Newman et al., 234–57. Leiden: Brill, 1999.

Collins, Adela Yarbro, and John J. Collins. *King and Messiah as Son of God: Divine, Human, and Angelic Messianic Figures in Biblical and Related Literature*. Grand Rapids: Eerdmans, 2008.

Collins, C. John. "Colossians 1,17 'Hold Together': A Co-opted Term." *Bib* 95 (2014) 64–87.

———. "Galatians 3:16: What Kind of Exegete Was Paul?" *TynBul* 54 (2003) 75–86.

———. *Genesis 1–4: A Linguistic, Literary, and Theological Commentary*. Philipsburg, NJ: P&R, 2006.

Collins, John J. *Daniel: A Commentary on the Book of Daniel*. Hermeneia. Minneapolis: Fortress, 1993.

———. *The Apocalyptic Imagination: An Introduction to Jewish Apocalyptic Literature*. Grand Rapids: Eerdmans, 1998.

———. *The Scepter and the Star: Messianism in Light of the Dead Sea Scrolls*. 2nd ed. Grand Rapids: Eerdmans, 2010.

Compton, Jared. *Psalm 110 and the Logic of Hebrews*. London: T&T Clark, 2015.

Condra, Ed. *Salvation for the Righteous Revealed: Jesus Amid Covenantal and Messianic Expectations in Second Temple Judaism*. Boston: Brill, 2002.

Copenhaver, Adam. *Reconstructing the Historical Background of Paul's Rhetoric in the Letter to the Colossians*. London: T&T Clark, 2018.

Coutts, John. "The Relationship of Ephesians and Colossians." *NTS* 4 (1958) 201–7.

Cox, Ronald. *By the Same Word: Creation and Salvation in Hellenistic Judaism and Early Christianity*. Berlin: De Gruyter, 2007.

Craigie, Peter C. *Psalms 1–50*. WBC 19. Waco, TX: Word, 1983.

Cranfield, C. E. B. *A Critical and Exegetical Commentary on the Epistle to the Romans: Romans I–VIII*. Vol 1. ICC. Edinburgh: T&T Clark, 1975.

Creach, Jerome F. D. *The Destiny of the Righteous in the Psalms*. St Louis: Chalice, 2008.

Crouch, Carly L. "Made in the Image of God: The Creation of אדם, the Commissioning of the King and the Chaoskampf of YHWH." *JANER* 16 (2016) 1–21.

———. *War and Ethics in the Ancient Near East: Military Violence in Light of Cosmology and History*. Berlin: De Gruyter, 2009.

Cullmann, Oscar. *The Christology of the New Testament*. Translated by Shirley C. Guthrie and Charles A. M. Hall. 1959. Reprint, Waco, TX: Baylor University Press, 2018.

Curtis, Edward Mason. "Man as the Image of God in Genesis in the Light of Ancient Near Eastern Parallels." PhD diss., University of Pennsylvania, 1984. ProQuest (8422896).

Daly-Denton, Margaret. *David in the Fourth Gospel: The Johannine Reception of the Psalms*. Leiden: Brill, 1999.

Davies, W. D. *Paul and Rabbinic Judaism: Some Rabbinic Elements in Pauline Theology*. 2nd ed. London: SPCK, 1955.

———. "The Jewish Sources of Matthew's Messianism." In *The Messiah: Developments in Earliest Judaism and Christianity*, edited by James H. Charlesworth, 494–511. Minneapolis: Fortress, 1992.

Davidson, Robert. "Covenant Ideology in Ancient Israel." In *The World of Ancient Israel: Sociological, Anthropological, and Political Perspectives*, edited by Ronald E. Clements, 323–47. Cambridge: Cambridge University Press, 1989.

Day, John. *God's Conflict with the Dragon and the Sea*. Cambridge: Cambridge University Press, 1985.

De Boer, Martinus C. "Paul and Jewish Apocalyptic Eschatology." In *Apocalyptic and the New Testament: Essays in Honor of J. Louis Martyn*, edited by Joel Marcus and Marion L. Soards, 169–90. Sheffield: Sheffield Academic, 1989.

———. *Paul, Theologian of God's Apocalypse: Essays on Paul and Apocalyptic*. Eugene, OR: Cascade, 2020.

———. *The Defeat of Death: Apocalyptic Eschatology in 1 Corinthians 15 and Romans 5*. Sheffield: JSOT, 1988.

Deichgräber, Reinhard. *Gotteshymnus und Christushymnus in der frühen Christenheit: Untersuchungen zur Form, Sprache und Stil der frühchristlichen Hymnen*. Göttingen: Vandenhoeck & Ruprecht, 1967.

Deissmann, Adolf. *Die Neutestamentliche Formel "in Christo Jesus."* Marburg: N. G. Elwert'sche Verlagsbuchhandlung, 1892.

Demaris, Richard E. *The Colossian Controversy: Wisdom in Dispute at Colossae*. Sheffield: JSOT, 1994.

Dianzon, Bernardita. "Adam Language in Genesis and Early Judaism: A Survey." *Landas* 22 (2008) 1–33.

Docherty, Susan E. *The Use of the Old Testament in Hebrews: A Case in Early Jewish Bible Interpretation*. Tübingen: Mohr Siebeck, 2009.

Dodd, C. H. *The Interpretation of the Fourth Gospel*. Cambridge: Cambridge University Press, 1953.

Dübbers, Michael. *Christologie und Existenz im Kolosserbrief: Exegetische und semantische Untersuchungen zur Intention des Kolosserbriefes*. Tübingen: Mohr Siebeck, 2005.

Duguid, Iain. "Messianic Themes in Zechariah 9–14." In *The Lord's Anointed: Interpretation of Messianic Old Testament Texts*, edited by Philip E. Satterthwaite et al., 265–80. Grand Rapids: Baker, 1995.

Dunn, James D. G. *Christology in the Making: A New Testament Inquiry into the Origins of the Doctrine of the Incarnation*. Philadelphia: Westminster, 1980.

———. "Jesus—Flesh and Spirit: An Exposition of Romans 1:3–4." *JTS* 24 (1973) 40–68.

———. *Romans 1–8*. WBC 38A. Dallas: Word, 1988.

———. *Romans 9–16*. WBC 38B. Dallas: Word, 1988.

———. *The Epistles to Colossians and to Philemon: A Commentary on the Greek Text*. NIGTC. Grand Rapids: Eerdmans, 1996.

———. "The Human Face of God: God and the Christology of the New Testament." In *One God, One People, One Future: Essays in Honor of NT Wright*, edited by John Anthony Dunne and Eric Lewellen, 72–85. Minneapolis: Fortress, 2018.

———. *The Theology of Paul the Apostle*. Grand Rapids: Eerdmans, 1998.

Dunne, John Anthony. "The Regal Status of Christ in the Colossian Christ Hymn: A Reevaluation of the Influence of Wisdom Traditions." *TrinJ* 32 (2011) 3–18.

Dupont, Jacques. *Gnosis: La connaissance religieuse dans les épîtres de Saint Paul*. 2nd ed. Louvain: E. Nauwlaerts, 1960.

Eaton, J. H. *Kingship and Psalms*. London: SCM, 1976.

Ehorn, Seth M. "The Use of Psalm 68(67).19 in Ephesians 4:8: A History of Research." *CurBR* 12 (2013) 96–120.

Ellingworth, Paul. *The Epistle to the Hebrews: A Commentary on the Greek Text*. NIGTC. Grand Rapids: Eerdmans, 1993.

Ellis, E. Earle. "Deity-Christology in Mark 14:58." In *Jesus of Nazareth: Lord and Christ; Essays on the Historical Jesus and New Testament Christology*, edited by Joel B. Green and Max Turner, 192–203. Eugene, OR: Wipf and Stock, 1999.

———. *Paul's Use of the Old Testament*. 1957. Reprint, Grand Rapids: Eerdmans, 1991.

Eskola, Timo. *Messiah and the Throne: Jewish Merkabah Mysticism and Early Christian Discourse*. Tübingen: Mohr Siebeck, 2001.

Evans, Craig. "Diarchic Messianism in the Dead Sea Scrolls and the Messianism of Jesus of Nazareth." In *The Dead Sea Scrolls Fifty Years after Their Discovery: Proceedings of the Jerusalem Congress, July 20–25*, edited by Lawrence W. Schiffman et al., 558–67. Jerusalem: Israel Exploration Society, 2000.

———. *Matthew*. CBC. Cambridge: Cambridge University Press, 2012.

———. "Qumran's Messiah: How Important Is He?" In *Religion in the Dead Sea Scrolls*, edited by John J. Collins and Robert A. Kugler, 135–49. Grand Rapids: Eerdmans, 2000.

Fabricatore, Daniel J. *Form of God, Form of a Servant: An Examination of the Greek Noun μορφή in Philippians 2:6–7*. Lanham, MD: University Press of America, 2010.

Fantin, Joseph D. *The Lord of the Entire World: Lord Jesus, a Challenge to Lord Caesar*. Sheffield: Sheffield Phoenix, 2011.

Fee, Gordon. "Old Testament Intertextuality in Colossians: Reflections on Pauline Christology and Gentile Inclusion in God's Story." In *History and Exegesis: New Testament Essays in Honor of Dr. E. Earle Ellis for his 80th Birthday*, edited by Sang-Won (Aaron) Son, 201–21. New York: T&T Clark, 2006.

———. *Pauline Christology: An Exegetical-Theological Study*. Peabody, MA: Hendrickson, 2007.

———. "Wisdom Christology in Paul: A Dissenting View." In *To What End Exegesis? Essays in Textual, Exegetical, and Theological*, 351–75. Grand Rapids: Eerdmans, 2001.

Ferda, Tucker S. "Naming the Messiah: A Contribution to the 4Q246 'Son of God' Debate." *DSD* 21 (2014) 150–75.

Fishbane, Michael. *Biblical Interpretation in Ancient Israel*. New York: Clarendon, 1985.

Fitzmeyer, Joseph A. *First Corinthians: A New Translation with Introduction and Commentary*. AB 32. New Haven: Yale University Press, 2008.

———. "The Use of Explicit Old Testament Quotations in Qumran Literature and in the New Testament." *NTS* 7 (2009) 297–333.

Fossum, Jarl. *The Image of the Invisible God: Essays on the Influence of Jewish Mysticism on Early Christology*. Göttingen: Vandenhoeck & Ruprecht, 1995.

Fowl, Stephen E. *The Story of Christ in the Ethics of Paul: An Analysis of the Function of the Hymnic Material in the Paulin Corpus*. Sheffield: Sheffield Academic, 1990.

France, R. T. *The Gospel of Mark: A Commentary on the Greek Text*. NIGTC. Grand Rapids: Eerdmans, 2002.

Fuchs, E. *Die Freiheit des Glaubens: Römer 5–8 ausgelegt*. Munich: Kaiser, 1949.

Fuller, Reginald H. *The Foundations of New Testament Christology*. New York: Scribner, 1965.

Garland, David E. *A Theology of Mark's Gospel: Good News about Jesus the Messiah, the Son of God*. Grand Rapids: Zondervan, 2015.

Gathercole, Simon J. *The Preexistent Son: Recovering the Christologies of Matthew, Mark, and Luke*. Grand Rapids: Eerdmans, 2006.

Gaventa, Beverly Roberts. *Apocalyptic Paul: Cosmos and Anthropos in Romans 5–8*. Waco, TX: Baylor University Press, 2013

———. "Neither Height nor Depth: Discerning the Cosmology of Romans." *SJT* 64 (2011) 265–78.

———. "The Cosmic Power of Sin in Paul's Letter to the Romans: Toward a Widescreen Edition." *Int* 58 (2004) 229–40.

Geddert, Timothy J. "The Implied YHWH Christology of Mark's Gospel: Mark's Challenge to the Reader to 'Connect the Dots.'" *BBR* 25 (2015) 325–40.

Gese, Michael. *Das Vermächtnis des Apostels: Die Rezeption der paulinischen Theologie im Epheserbrief.* Tübingen: Mohr Siebeck, 1997.

Gibbs, John C. *Creation and Redemption: A Study in Pauline Theology.* Leiden: Brill, 1971.

Goppelt, Leonhard. *Typos: The Typological Interpretation of the Old Testament.* Translated by Donald H. Madvig. Grand Rapids: Eerdmans, 1982.

Gordley, Matthew E. *New Testament Christological Hymns: Exploring Texts, Contexts, and Significance.* Downers Grove, IL: IVP Academic, 2018.

———. *The Colossian Hymn in Context: An Exegesis in Light of Jewish and Greco-Roman Hymnic and Epistolary Conventions.* Tübingen: Mohr Siebeck, 2007.

Goldingay, John. *Daniel.* Rev. ed. WBC 30. Grand Rapids: Zondervan, 2019.

Gombis, Timothy. "Ephesians 2 as a Narrative of Divine Warfare." *JSNT* 26 (2004) 403–18.

———. "Ephesians 3:2–13: Pointless Digression or Epitome of the Triumph of God in Christ?" *WTJ* 66 (2004) 313–23.

———. "Cosmic Lordship and Divine Gift-Giving: Psalm 68 in Ephesians 4:8." *NovT* (2005) 367–80.

Greever, Joshua M. "The Typological Expectation of Psalm 68 and Its Application in Ephesians 4:8." *TynBul* 71 (2020) 253–79.

Grenz, Stanley J. "Jesus as the Imago Dei: Image-of-God Christology and the Non-linear Linearity of Theology." *JETS* 47 (2004) 617–28.

———. "The Social God and the Relational Self." In *Trinitarian Soundings in Systematic Theology*, edited by P. L. Metzger, 87–100. New York: T&T Clark, 2005.

Gundry, Robert H. "A Brief Note on 'Hellenistic Formal Receptions and Paul's Use of απαντησις in 1 Thessalonians 4:17.'" *BBR* 6 (1996) 39–41.

Gunkel, Hermann. *Ausgewählte Psalmen.* Göttingen: Vandenhoeck & Ruprecht, 1911.

Gupta, Nijay K. "Behold the Word of Christ: A Geological Reading of Colossians." *CTR* 1 (2013) 21–43.

———. *Colossians.* SHBC. Macon: Smyth & Helwys, 2013.

Hagner, Donald. "Paul's Christology and Jewish Monotheism." In *Perspectives on Christology: Essays in Honor of Paul K. Jewett*, edited by Marguerite Shuster and Richard Muller, 19–38. Grand Rapids: Zondervan, 1991.

Hahn, Ferdinand. *Christologische Hoheitstitel: Ihre Geschichte im frühen Christentum.* Göttingen: Vandenhoeck & Ruprecht, 1963.

Hahne, Harry Alan. *The Corruption and Redemption of Creation: Nature in Romans 8.19–22 and Jewish Apocalyptic Literature.* London: T&T Clark, 2006.

Hamerton-Kelly, R. G. *Pre-existence, Wisdom, and the Son of Man: A Study of the Idea of Pre-existence in the New Testament.* Cambridge: Cambridge University Press, 1973.

Hamilton, Victor P. *The Book of Genesis 1–17.* NICOT. Grand Rapids: Eerdmans, 1990.

Harris, Murray J. *Colossians and Philemon.* EGGNT. Grand Rapids: Eerdmans, 1991.

———. *Jesus as God: The New Testament Use of Theos in Reference to Jesus.* Grand Rapids: Baker, 1992.

———. *The Second Epistle to the Corinthians: Commentary on the Greek Text.* NIGTC. Grand Rapids: Eerdmans, 2005.

Harris, W. Hall. *The Descent of Christ: Ephesians 4:7–11 and Traditional Hebrew Imagery*. New York: Brill, 1996.
Hawthorne, Gerald F. *Philippians*. WBC 43. Waco, TX: Word, 1983.
Hay, David M. *Glory at the Right Hand: Psalm 110 in Early Christianity*. Nashville: Abingdon, 1973.
Hays, Richard B. *Echoes of Scripture in the Gospels*. Waco, TX: Baylor University Press, 2018.
———. *Echoes of Scripture in the Letters of Paul*. New Haven: Yale University Press, 1989.
———. *The Faith of Jesus Christ: The Narrative Substructure of Galatians 3:1—4:11*. Grand Rapids: Eerdmans, 2002.
Heath, Jane. "'You Say That I Am a King' (John 18.37)." *JSNT* 34 (2012) 232–53.
Hehn, Johannes. "Zum Terminus 'Bild Gottes.'" In *Festschrift Eduard Sachau zum siebzigsten Geburtstage*, edited by Gotthold Weil, 36–52. Berlin: Georg Reimer, 1915.
Heil, John Paul. *Colossians: Encouragement to Walk in All Wisdom as Holy Ones in Christ*. Atlanta: Society of Biblical Literature, 2010.
———. *Ephesians: Empowerment to Walk in Love for the Unity of All in Christ*. Atlanta: Society of Biblical Literature, 2007.
Helyer, Larry R. "Cosmic Christology and Col 1:15–20." *JETS* 37 (1994) 235–46.
Hengel, Martin. *Studies in Early Christology*. Edinburgh: T&T Clark, 1995.
———. *The Son of God: The Origin of Christology and the History of Jewish-Hellenistic Religion*. London: SCM, 1976.
Henrichs-Tarasenkova, Nina. *Luke's Christology of Divine Identity*. London: T&T Clark, 2015.
Hewitt, J. Thomas. "Ancient Messiah Discourse and Paul's Expression ἄχρις οὗ ἔλθῃ τὸ σπέρμα in Galatians 3:19." *NTS* 65 (2019) 398–411.
Hoehner, Harold. *Ephesians: An Exegetical Commentary*. Grand Rapids: Baker Academic, 2002.
Holladay, Carl R. "What David Saw: Messianic Exegesis in Acts 2." *SCJ* 19 (2016) 95–108.
Holtzmann, Heinrich J. *Kritik der Epheser- und Kolosserbriefe: Auf Grund einer Analyse ihres Verwandtschaftsverhältnisses*. Leipzig: Wilhelm Engelmann, 1872.
Hooker, Morna D. *From Adam to Christ: Essays on Paul*. Cambridge: Cambridge University Press, 1990.
———. *The Gospel according to Saint Mark*. BNTC. London: Continuum, 1991.
———. *The Son of Man in Mark: A Study of the Background of the Term "Son of Man" and Its Use in St. Mark's Gospel*. London: SPCK, 1967.
Hoover, R. W. "The HARPAGMOS Enigma: A Philological Solution." *HTR* 64 (1971) 95–119.
Horbury, William. *Jewish Messianism and the Cult of Christ*. London: SCM, 1998.
Horrell, David G. "A New Perspective on Paul? Rereading Paul in a Time of Ecological Crisis." *JSNT* 33 (2010) 3–30.
Horsley, Richard A. "The Background of the Confessional Formula in 1 Kor 8.6." *ZNW* 69 (1978) 130–35.
Hoskins, Paul M. *Jesus as the Fulfillment of the Temple in the Gospel of John*. Eugene, OR: Wipf & Stock, 2007.
Hubbard, Moyer V. *New Creation in Paul's Letters and Thought*. Cambridge: Cambridge University Press, 2002.

Hugenberger, Gordon P. "The Servant of the Lord in the 'Servant Songs' of Isaiah: A Second Moses." In *The Lord's Anointed: Interpretation of Old Testament Messianic Texts*, edited by Philip E. Satterthwaite et al., 105–40. Grand Rapids: Baker, 1995.

Hurst, L. D. "Did Qumran Expect Two Messiahs?" *BBR* 9 (1999) 157–80.

Hurtado, Larry. *Ancient Jewish Monotheism and Early Christian Jesus-Devotion: The Context and Character of Christological Faith*. Waco, TX: Baylor University Press, 2017.

———. *Lord Jesus Christ: Devotion to Jesus in Earliest Christianity*. Grand Rapids: Eerdmans, 2003.

———. *Mark*. NIBCNT. Peabody, MA: Hendrickson, 1989.

———. *One God, One Lord: Early Christian Devotion and Ancient Jewish Monotheism*. 3rd ed. New York: T&T Clark, 2015.

Hutter, Manfred. "Adam als Gartner und Konig (Gen 2,8. 15)." *BZ* 30 (1986) 258–62.

Ibrahim, Najib. *Gesu Cristo Signore dell'universo: La dimension Cristologica della lettera ai Colossesi*. Jerusalem: Franciscan Printing, 2007.

Jackson, T. Ryan. *New Creation in Paul's Letters: A Study of the Historical and Social Setting of a Pauline Concept*. Tübingen: Mohr Siebeck, 2010.

Jeal, Roy R. "A Strange Style of Expression: Ephesians 1:23." *FilNeot* 10 (1997) 129–38.

———. *Integrating Theology and Ethics in Ephesians: The Ethos of Communication*. New York: Mellen, 2000.

———. "Starting Before the Beginning: Precreation Discourse in Colossians." *R&T* 18 (2011) 287–310.

Jewett, Robert. "The Redaction and Use of an Early Christian Confession in Romans 1:3–4." In *The Living Text: Essays in Honor of Ernest W. Saunders*, edited by Dennis E. Groh and Robert Jewett, 99–122. New York: University Press of America, 1985.

Jipp, Joshua W. *Christ Is King: Paul's Royal Ideology*. Minneapolis: Fortress, 2015.

Johansson, Daniel. "*Kyrios* in the Gospel of Mark." *JSNT* 33 (2010) 101–24.

Jonsson, Gunnlaugur A. *The Image of God: Genesis 1:26–28 in a Century of Old Testament Research*. Stockholm: Almqvist & Wiksell, 1988.

Joyce, Paul M. "King and Messiah in Ezekiel." In *King and Messiah in Israel and the Ancient Near East: Proceedings of the Oxford Old Testament Seminar*, edited by John Day, 323–37. Sheffield: Sheffield Academic, 1998.

Juel, Donald H. "The Origin of Mark's Christology." In *The Messiah: Developments in Earliest Judaism and Christianity*, edited by James H. Charlesworth, 449–60. Minneapolis: Fortress, 1992.

Juel, Donald H., and N. A. Dahl, eds. *Jesus the Christ: The Historical Origins of Christological Doctrine*. Minneapolis: Fortress, 1991.

Käsemann, Ernst. "A Primitive Christian Baptismal Liturgy." In *Essays on New Testament Themes*, translated by W. J. Montague, 149–68. London: SCM, 1964.

———. *New Testament Questions for Today*. Translated by W. J. Montague. Philadelphia: Fortress, 1969

Keener, Craig S. *Acts: An Exegetical Commentary*. Vol 1. Grand Rapids: Baker Academic, 2012.

Keener, Hubert James. *A Canonical Exegesis of the Eighth Psalm: YHWH's Maintenance of the Created Order through Divine Intervention*. Winona Lake, IN: Eisenbrauns, 2013.

Keith, Chris. "Jesus the Galilean in the Gospel of John: The Significance of Earthly Origins in the Fourth Gospel." In *Portraits of Jesus in the Fourth Gospel*, edited by Crag R. Koester, 45–60. London: T&T Clark, 2019.

Kehl, Nikolaus. *Der Christushymnus im Kolosserbrief: Eine motivgeschichtliche Untersuchung zu Kol 1,12–20*. Stuttgart: Verlag Katholisches Bibelwerk, 1967.
Kim, Kyu Seop. "The Meaning of ΧΕΙΡΟΓΡΑΦΟΝ in Colossians Revisited." *TynBul* 68 (2017) 223–39.
Kim, Seyoon. *The Origin of Paul's Gospel*. 2nd ed. Tübingen: J. C. B. Mohr, 1984.
———. *The "Son of Man" as the Son of God*. Tübingen: J. C. B. Mohr, 1983. Repr., Eugene: Wipf & Stock, 2011.
Kingsbury, Jack D. *The Christology of Mark's Gospel*. Philadelphia: Fortress, 1983.
Kirk, J. R. Daniel. *Unlocking Romans: Resurrection and the Justification of God*. Grand Rapids: Eerdmans, 2008.
Kitchen, Martin. *Ephesians*. NTR. London: Routledge, 1994.
Kline, Meredith G. *Kingdom Prologue: Genesis Foundations for a Covenantal Worldview*. Eugene, OR: Wipf & Stock, 2006.
Kooten, Geurt Hendrik van. *Cosmic Christology in Paul and the Pauline School: Colossians and Ephesians in the Context of Greco-Roman Cosmology, with a New Synopsis of the Greek Texts*. Tübingen: Mohr Siebeck, 2003.
———. *Paul's Anthropology in Context: The Image of God, Assimilation to God, and Tripartite Man in Ancient Judaism, Ancient Philosophy, and Early Christianity*. Tübingen: Mohr Siebeck, 2008.
Kraftchick, Steven J. "Paul's use of Creation Themes: A Test of Romans 1–8." *ExAud* 3 (1987) 72–87.
Kraus, Hans-Joachim. *Psalms 1–59*. Translated by Hilton C. Oswald. Minneapolis: Fortress, 1993.
———. *Theology of the Psalms*. Translated by Keith Crim. Minneapolis: Augsburg, 1986.
Krecidlo, Janusz. "The Reconciliation of the World through the Blood of Christ's Cross as the Completion of the Work of Creation (Col 1:15–20)." *VV* 39 (2021) 1133–57.
Kreitzer, L. Joseph. "The Messianic Man of Peace as Temple Builder: Solomonic Imagery in Ephesians 2:13–22." In *Temple and Worship in Biblical Israel*, edited by John Day, 484–512. Edinburgh: T&T Clark, 2005.
Kügler, Joachim. *Der andere König: Religionsgeschichtliche Perspektiven auf die Christologie des Johannesevangeliums*. Stuttgart: Katholisches Bibelwerk, 1999.
Kvalbein, Hans. "The Kingdom of God and the Kingship of Christ in the Fourth Gospel." In *Neotestamentica et Philonica: Studies in Honor of Peder Borgen*, edited by David E. Aune et al., 215–32. Leiden: Brill, 2003.
Kvanvig, Helge. "The Son of Man in the Parables of Enoch." In *Enoch and the Messiah Son of Man: Revisiting the Book of Parables*, edited by Gabriele Boccaccini, 179–215. Grand Rapids: Eerdmans, 2007.
Laato, Antii. *A Star Is Rising: The Historical Development of the Old Testament Royal Ideology and the Rise of the Jewish Messianic Expectations*. Atlanta: Scholars, 1997.
———. *Josiah and David Redivivus: The Historical Josiah and the Messianic Expectations of Exilic and Postexilic Times*. Stockholm: Almqvist & Wiksell, 1992.
Lacocque, André. *The Book of Daniel*. Translated by David Pellauer. Louisville: Westminster John Knox, 1979.
Lee, Dorothy. "Christological Identity and Authority in the Gospel of Mark." *Phron* 33 (2018) 1–19.
Lee, Howard Clark. "Christology in Mark's Gospel." *Judaisms and Their Messiahs at the Turn of the Christian Era*, edited by Jacob Neusner et al., 189–208. Cambridge: Cambridge University Press, 1987.

Lee, Sang Myeng. *The Cosmic Drama of Salvation: A Study of Paul's Undisputed Writings from Anthropological and Cosmological Perspectives*. Tübingen: Mohr Siebeck, 2010.

Leese, J. Johnson. *Christ, Creation and the Cosmic Goal of Redemption: A Study of Pauline Creation Theology as Read by Irenaeus and Applied to Ecotheology*. London: T&T Clark, 2018.

LeFebvre, Michael. "Adam Reigns in Eden: Genesis and the Origins of Kingship." *BET* 5 (2018) 25–57.

Leppä, Outi. *The Making of Colossians: A Study on the Formation and Purpose of a Deutero-Pauline Letter*. Göttingen: Vandenhoeck & Ruprecht, 2003.

Levenson, Jon D. *Creation and the Persistence of Evil: The Jewish Drama of Divine Omnipotence*. San Francisco: Harper & Row, 1988.

Levison, John R. "2 Apoc. Bar. 48:42—52:7 and the Apocalpytic Dimension of Colossians 3:1–6." *JBL* 108 (1989) 93–108.

———. *Portraits of Adam in Early Judaism: From Sirach to 2 Baruch*. Sheffield: JSOT, 1987.

Lewis, Gladys S., et al., eds. *The Jewish Roots of Christological Monotheism: Papers from the St. Andrews Conference on the Historical Origins of the Worship of Jesus*. Leiden: Brill, 1999.

Lightfoot, Joseph B. *Colossians*. 2nd ed. Grand Rapids: Zondervan, 1977.

———. "The Colossian Heresy." In *Conflict at Colossae: A Problem in the Interpretation of Early Christianity Illustrated by Selected Modern Studies*, edited by F. O. Francis and Wayne A. Meeks, 13–59. Missoula, MT: Society for Biblical Literature and Scholars, 1975.

Lincoln, Andrew T. *Ephesians*. WBC 42. Dallas: Word, 1990.

———. *Paradise Now and Not Yet: Studies in the Role of Heavenly Dimension in Paul's Thought with Special Reference to His Eschatology*. Grand Rapids: Baker, 1981.

———. "The Use of the OT in Ephesians." *JSNT* 14 (1982) 16–57.

Lindars, Barbabas. *New Testament Apologetic: The Doctrinal Significance of the Old Testament Quotations*. London: SCM, 1961.

Lindemann, Andreas. "Paulus und die Korinthische Eschatologie: Zur These von einer 'Entwicklung' im Paulinischen Denken." *NTS* 37 (1991) 373–99.

Lioy, Dan. "New Creation Theology in 2 Corinthians 5:11—6:2." *Conspectus* 17 (2014) 53–87.

———. "Paul's Apocalyptic Interpretation of Reality: A Case Study Analysis of Ephesians 1:15–23." *Conspectus* 19 (2015) 27–64.

Loader, W. R. G. "Christ at the Right Hand—Ps. cx.1 in the New Testament." *NTS* 24 (1978) 199–217.

Lohmeyer, Ernst. *Die Briefe an die Philipper, an die Kolosser und an Philemon: Nach dem Handexemplar des Verfassers durchgesehne Ausgabe*. Göttingen: Vandenhoeck & Ruprecht, 1964.

Lohse, Eduard. *Colossians and Philemon*. Translated by William R. Poehlmann and Robert J. Karris. Hermeneia. Philadelphia: Fortress, 1971.

Lopez, Rene. "Paul's Vice List in Ephesians 5:3–5." *BSac* 169 (2012) 203–18.

Lövestam, Evald. "Die Davidssohnsfrage." *SEÅ* 27 (1962) 72–82.

Lucass, Shirley. *The Concept of the Messiah in the Scriptures of Judaism and Christianity*. London: T&T Clark, 2011.

Lunde, Jonathan M., and John Anthony Dunne. "Paul's Creative and Contextual Use of Psalm 68 in Ephesians 4:8." *WTJ* 74 (2012) 99–117.
Macaskill, Grant. "Union(s) with Christ: Colossians 1:15–20." *ExAud* 33 (2017) 92–107.
MacDonald, Margaret Y. *Colossians and Ephesians*. SP 17. Collegeville, MN: Liturgical, 2000.
Mainville, Odette. "Le messianisme de Jésus. Le rapport annonce/accomplissement entre Lc 1,35 et Ac 2,33." In *The Unity of Luke–Acts*, edited by J. Verheyden, 313–27. Leuven: Leuven University Press, 1999.
Manns, Frédéric. "Col. 1,15–20: Midrash chrétien de Gen 1,1." *RevScRel* 53 (1979) 100–110.
Maronde, Christopher A. "'You Are My Beloved Son': The Foundations of a 'Son of God' Christology in the Second Psalm." *CTQ* 85 (2021) 313–39.
Marshall, I. Howard. *The Gospel of Luke: A Commentary on the Greek Text*. NIGTC. Exeter: Paternoster, 1978.
———. *The Origins of New Testament Christology*. Downers Grove, IL: InterVarsity, 1976.
Martin, Ralph. "The Christology of the Prison Epistles." In *Contours of Christology in the New Testament*, edited by Richard Longenecker, 201–17. Grand Rapids: Eerdmans, 2005.
Martin, Troy W. *By Philosophy and Empty Deceit: Colossians as Response to Cynic Critique*. Sheffield: JSOT, 1996.
Martyn, J. Louis. *Theological Issues in the Letters of Paul*. Nashville: Abingdon, 1997.
Mason, Rex. "The Messiah in the Postexilic Old Testament Literature." In *King and Messiah in Israel and the Ancient Near East: Proceedings of the Oxford Old Testament Seminar*, edited by John Day, 338–64. Sheffield: Sheffield Academic, 1998.
Masson, Charles. *L'épître de Saint Paul aux Colossiens*. Neuchâtel: Delachaux et Niestlé, 1950.
———. *L'épître de Saint Paul aux Éphésiens*. Paris: Delachaux & Niestlé, 1953.
Matera, Frank. *New Testament Christology*. Louisville: Westminster John Knox, 1999.
Mays, James L. *Psalms*. IBC. Louisville: Westminster John Knox, 2011.
McCarthy, John. "Le Christ cosmique et l'âge de l'écologie: Une lecture de Col 1,15–20." *NRTh* 116 (1994) 27–47.
McCaulley, Esau. *Sharing the Son's Inheritance: Davidic Messianism and Paul's Worldwide Interpretation of the Abrahamic Land Promise in Galatians*. London: T&T Clark, 2019.
McDonough, Sean M. *Christ as Creator: Origins of a New Testament Doctrine*. Oxford: Oxford University Press, 2009.
McDowell, Catherine L. *The Image of God in the Garden of Eden: The Creation of Humankind in Genesis 2:5—3:24 in Light of the Mīs Pî Pīt Pî and Wpt-r Rituals of Mesopotamia and Ancient Egypt*. Winona Lake, IN: Eisenbrauns, 2015.
Mell, Ulrich. *Neue Schöpfung: Eine Traditionsgeschichtliche und exegetische Studie zu einem soteriologischen Grundsatz Paulinischer Theologie*. Berlin: De Gruyter, 1989.
Merkel, Helmut. "Der Epheserbrief in der neueren exegetischen Diskussion." In ANRW 25.4.3212–20. Part 2, *Principat*, 25.4. Edited by Wolfgang Haase. New York: de Gruyter, 1989.
Merklein, Helmut. *Das Kirchliche Amt nach dem Epheserbrief*. München: Kösel-Verlag, 1973.

Middleton, J. R. *The Liberating Image: The Imago Dei in Genesis 1*. Grand Rapids: Brazos, 2005.

Mitton, Leslie. *The Epistle to the Ephesians: Its Authorship, Origin, and Purpose*. Oxford: Clarendon, 1951.

Moltmann, Jürgen. *The Way of Jesus Christ: Christology in Messianic Dimensions*. San Francisco: HarperCollins, 1990.

Monzani, Paolo. "'Au dire des hommes, qui est le Fils de l'homme?' (Mt 16,13): Etude narrative de l'expression 'le fils de l'homme' dans les évangiles synoptiques." *NRTh* 143 (2021) 376–92.

Moo, Douglas. *The Letters to the Colossians and to Philemon*. PNTC. Grand Rapids: Eerdmans, 2008.

———. "'The Type of the One to Come': Adam in Paul's Theology." *TrinJ* 40 (2019) 145–64.

Moritz, Thorsten. *A Profound Mystery: The Use of the Old Testament in Ephesians*. Leiden: Brill, 1996.

Mosca, Paul G. "Ugarit and Daniel 7: A Missing Link." *Bib* 67 (1986) 496–517.

Moscicke, Hans. "The Final Judgement as Ritual Purgation of the Cosmos: The Influence of Scapegoat Traditions on Matt 25.31–46." *NTS* 67 (2021) 241–59.

Morissette, Rodolphe. "La citation du Psaume VIII, 7b dans I Corinthians XV, 27a." *ScEs* 24 (1972) 313–42.

Motyer, J. Alec. *The Prophecy of Isaiah: Introduction and Commentary*. Downers Grove, IL: InterVarsity, 1993.

Moule, C. F. D. *The Epistles of Paul the Apostle to the Colossians and to Philemon*. CGTC. New York: Cambridge University Press, 1968.

Mowinckel, Sigmund. *He That Cometh: The Messiah Concept in the Old Testament and Later Judaism*. Translated by G. W. Anderson. Grand Rapids: Eerdmans, 2005.

———. *The Psalms in Israel's Worship*. Translated by D. R. Ap-Thomas. Sheffield: JSOT, 1967.

Muddiman, John. *The Epistle to the Ephesians*. BNTC. London: Continuum, 2001.

Müller, Karlheinz. "Der Menschensohn im Danielzyklus." In *Jesus und der Menschensohn: für Anton Vögtle*, edited by Rudolf Pesch and Rudolf Schnackenburg, 37–80. Freiburg im Breisgau: Herder, 1975.

Murphy-O'Connor, Jerome. "I Cor 8:6, Cosmology or Soteriology." *RB* 85 (1978) 253–67.

———. *Keys to First Corinthians: Revisiting the Major Issues*. Oxford: Oxford University Press, 2009.

Murray, Robert. *The Cosmic Covenant: Biblical Themes of Justice, Peace, and the Integrity of Creation*. London: Sheed & Ward, 1992.

Myers, Alicia D. "Jesus the Son of God in John's Gospel: The Life-Making Logos." In *Portraits of Jesus in the Fourth Gospel*, edited by Crag R. Koester, 141–56. London: T&T Clark, 2019.

Nickelsburg, George W. E. *Resurrection, Immortality and Eternal Life in Intertestamental Judaism*. Cambridge: Harvard University Press, 1972.

Niskanen, Paul. "The Poetics of Adam: The Creation of אדם in the Image of אלהים." *JBL* 128 (2009) 417–36.

Njeri, George. "Surprise on the Day of Judgment in Matthew 25:31–46 and The Book of the Watchers." *Neot* 54 (2020) 87–104.

Nolland, John. *The Gospel of Matthew: A Commentary on the Greek Text*. NIGTC. Grand Rapids: Eerdmans, 2005.

Northcutt, Christopher S. "'King of Kings' in Other Words: Colossians 1:15a as a Designation of Authority Rather Than Revelation." *TynBul* 69 (2018) 205–24.

Novenson, Matthew V. *Christ among the Messiahs: Christ Language in Paul and Messiah Language in Ancient Judaism*. Oxford: Oxford University Press, 2012.

Oakes, Peter. "Re-mapping the Universe: Paul and the Emperor in 1 Thessalonians and Philippians." *JSNT* 27 (2005) 301–22.

O'Brien, P. T. *Introductory Thanksgivings in the Letters of Paul*. Leiden: Brill, 1977.

Oropeza, B. J. "New Covenant Knowledge in an Earthenware Jar: Intertextual Reconfigurations or Jeremiah in 2 Corinthians 1:21–22, 3:2–11, and 4:7." *BBR* 28 (2018) 405–24.

Otto, Eberhard. "Der Mensch als Geschöpf und Bild Gottes in Ägypten." In *Probleme biblischer Theologie*, edited by H. W. Wolff, 334–48. Munich: Kaiser, 1971.

Painter, John. "Rereading Genesis in the Prologue of John." In *Neotestamentica et Philonica: Studies in Honor of Peder Borgen*, edited by David E. Aune et al., 179–201. Boston: Brill, 2003.

Pao, David. *Colossians and Philemon*. ZECNT. Grand Rapids: Zondervan, 2012.

Peppard, Michael. *The Son of God in the Roman World: Divine Sonship in Its Social and Political Context*. Oxford: Oxford University Press, 2011.

Peterson, Erik. "Die Einholung des Kyrios." *ZST* 7 (1929) 682–702.

Pizzuto, Vincent A. *A Cosmic Leap of Faith: An Authorial, Structural, and Theological Investigation of the Cosmic Christology in Col 1:15–20*. Leuven: Peeters, 2006.

Pomykala, Kenneth. *The Davidic Dynasty Tradition in Early Judaism: Its History and Significance for Messianism*. Atlanta: Scholars, 1995.

Porter, Stanley E., and Kent D. Clarke. "Canonical-Critical Perspective and the Relationship of Colossians and Ephesians." *Bib* 78 (1997) 57–86.

Puech, Emile. "Le fils de Dieu, le fils du Très-Haut, messie rol en 4Q246." In *Le jugement dans l'un et l'autre testament: Melanges offert à Raymond Kuntzmann*, edited by Oliver Artus, 271–86. Paris: Cerf, 2004.

Quek, Tze-Ming. "A Text Critical Study of John 1:34." *NTS* 55 (2009) 22–34.

Rad, Gerhard von. *Old Testament Theology*. Vol 1. Translated by D. M. G. Stalker. Lund: Oliver & Boyd, 1962.

Reichenbach, Bruce R. "Genesis 1 as a Theological-Political Narrative of Kingdom Establishment." *BBR* 13 (2003) 47–69.

Reumann, John. *Philippians: A New Translation with Introduction and Commentary*. AB 33B. New Haven: Yale University Press, 2008.

Ridderbos, Herman N. *Paul: An Outline of His Theology*. Grand Rapids: Eerdmans, 1975.

Roberge, Michel. "Jean 1,51 et l'annonce de la glorification du Fils de l'homme." *LTP* 74 (2018) 193–217.

Roberts, J. J. M. "The Enthronement of Yhwh and David: The Abiding Theological Significance of the Kingship Language of the Psalms." *CBQ* 64 (2002) 675–86.

Robinson, John A. T. *The Body: A Study in Pauline Theology*. London: SCM, 1952.

Romanov, Andrey. "Through One Lord Only: Theological Interpretation of the Meaning of διά in 1 Cor 8,6." *Bib* 96 (2015) 391–415.

———. "Εἷς κύριος and ἡμεῖς in 1 Corinthians 8:6: An Investigation of the First Person Plural in Light of the Lordship of Jesus Christ." *Neot* 49 (2015) 47–74.

Roon, A. van. *The Authenticity of Ephesians*. Leiden: Brill, 1975.

Ross, Allen P. *A Commentary on the Psalms: 1–41*. Vol 1. Grand Rapids: Kregel Academic, 2011.

Rowland, Christopher. "John 1:51, Jewish Apocalyptic and Targumic Tradition." *NTS* 30 (1984) 498–507.

———. *The Open Heaven: A Study of Apocalyptic in Judaism and Early Christianity*. London: SPCK, 1982.

Ruppert, Lothar. *Genesis: Ein Kritischer und Theologischer Kommentar*. Vol 1. Würzburg: Echter Verlag, 1992.

Santmire, H. P. "So That He Might Fill All Things: Comprehending the Cosmic Love of Christ." *Di* 42 (2003) 257–78.

Sappington, Thomas J. *Revelation and Redemption at Colossae*. Sheffield: Sheffield Academic, 1991.

Sasson, Victor. "The Language of Rebellion in Psalm 2 and the Plaster Texts from Deir 'Alla." *AUSS* 24 (1986) 147–54.

Scacewater, Todd. *The Divine Builder in Psalm 68: Jewish and Pauline Tradition*. London: T&T Clark, 2020.

Schibler, Daniel. "Messianism and Messianic Prophecy in Isaiah 1–12 and 28–33." In *The Lord's Anointed: Interpretation of Old Testament Messianic Texts*, edited by Philip E. Satterthwaite et al., 87–104. Eugene, OR: Wipf & Stock, 1995.

Schlatter, Adolf. *Romans: The Righteousness of God*. Peabody, MA: Hendrickson, 1995.

Schlier, Heinrich. *Christus und die Kirche im Epheserbrief*. Tübingen: Mohr Siebeck, 1930.

———. *Der Brief an die Epheser: Ein Kommentar*. Düsseldorf: Patmos-Verlag, 1962.

Schmid, Josef. *Der Epheserbrief des Apostels Paulus*. Freiburg: Herder, 1928.

Schmidt, Werner H. *Die Schöpfungsgeschichte der Priesterschrift: Zur Überlieferungsgeschichte von Genesis 1,1–2, 4a und 2,4b–3, 24*. Neukirchen-Vluyn: Neukirchener-Verlag, 1967.

Schnackenburg, Rudolf. *Der Brief an die Epheser*. Neukirchen-Vluyn: Neukirchener-Verlag, 1982.

———. *Jesus in the Gospels: A Biblical Christology*. Translated by O. C. Dean Jr. Louisville: Westminster John Knox, 1995.

Schreiber, Stefan. *Gesalbter und König: Titel und Konzeptionen der Königlichen Gesalbtenerwartung in Frühjüdischen und Urchristlichen Schriften*. Beihefte zur Zeitschrift für die Neutestamentliche Wissenschaft und die Kunde der älteren Kirche. New York: De Gruyter, 2000.

Schüle, Andreas. *Der Prolog der Hebräischen Bibel: Der Literar und Theologiegeschichtle Diskurs der Urgeschichte (Genesis 1–11)*. Zürich: Theologischer Verlag Zürich, 2006.

———. "Made in the 'Image of God': The Concepts of Divine Images in Gen 1–3." *ZAW* 117 (2005) 1–20.

Schultz, Richard. "The King in the Book of Isaiah." In *The Lord's Anointed: Interpretation of Old Testament Messianic Texts*, edited by Philip E. Satterthwaite et al., 141–66. Grand Rapids: Baker, 1995.

Schweitzer, Albert. *The Mysticism of Paul the Apostle*. Translated by William Montgomery. New York: Holt, 1931.

Schweizer, Eduard. *Neotestamentica: Deutsche und Englische Aufsätze, 1951–63*. Zürich: Zwingli Verlag, 1963.

———. "Slaves of the Elements and Worshippers of Angels: Gal. 4.3, 9 and Col. 2.8, 18, 20." *JBL* 107 (1988) 455–68.

———. *The Letter to the Colossians*. Translated by Andrew Chester. London: SPCK, 1982.
Schwindt, Rainer. *Das Weltbild des Epheserbriefes: Eine religionsgeschichtlich-exegetische Studie*. Tubingen: Mohr Siebeck, 2002.
Scott, James M. *Adoption as Sons of God: An Exegetical Investigation into the Background of ΥΙΟΘΕΣΙΑ in the Pauline Corpus*. Tübingen: Mohr Siebeck, 1992.
Scroggs, Robin. *The Last Adam: A Study in Pauline Theology*. Philadelphia: Fortress, 1966.
Sellin, Gerhard. *Der Brief an die Epheser*. 9th ed. Kritisch-exegetischer Kommentar über das Neue Testament. Göttingen: Vandenhoeck & Ruprecht, 2008.
Sherwood, Aaron. "Paul's Imprisonment as the Glory of the Ethnē: A Discourse Analysis of Ephesians 3:1–13." *BBR* 22 (2012) 97–112.
Shogren, Gary. "Presently Entering the Kingdom of Christ: The Background and Purpose of Col 1:12–14." *JETS* 31 (1988) 173–80.
Siliezar, Carlos Raul Sosa. *Creation Imagery in the Gospel of John*. London: T&T Clark, 2015.
Smith, Ian K. *Heavenly Perspective: A Study of the Apostle Paul's Response to a Jewish Mystical Movement at Colossae*. London: T&T Clark, 2006.
Smith, Julien. *Christ the Ideal King: Cultural Context, Rhetorical Strategy, and the Power of Divine Monarchy in Ephesians*. Tübingen: Mohr Siebeck, 2011.
Soden, John. "From the Dust: Creating Adam in Historical Context." *BSac* 172 (2015) 45–66.
Son, Sang-Won. *Corporate Elements of Pauline Anthropology: A Study of Selected Terms, Idioms, and Concepts in Light of Paul's Usage and Background*. Rome: Editrice Pontificio Istituto Biblico, 2001.
———. "The Church as 'One New Man': Ecclesiology and Anthropology in Ephesians." *SwJT* 52 (2009) 18–31.
———. "The Christology of Ephesians: Exploring Its Cosmic Dimension." Paper presented at the ETS Annual Meeting. San Diego, November 2019.
Starbuck, Scott R. A. *Court Oracles in the Psalms: The So-Called Royal Psalms in Their Ancient Near Eastern Context*. Atlanta: Society of Biblical Literature, 1999.
Steenberg, M. C. *Irenaeus on Creation: The Cosmic Christ and the Saga of Redemption*. Leiden: Brill, 2008.
Sterling, Gregory E. "Prepositional Metaphysics in Jewish Wisdom Speculation and Early Christian Liturgical Texts." *SPhilo* 9 (1997) 219–38.
Stettler, Christian. *Der Kolosserhymnus: Untersuchungen zu Form, traditionsgeschichtlichem Hintergrund und Aussage von Kol 1,15–20*. Tübingen: Mohr Siebeck, 2000.
Strack, H. L., and G. Stemberger, *Introduction to the Talmud and Midrash*. Translated by Markus Bockmuehl. Edinburgh: T&T Clark, 1991.
Strauss, Mark. *The Davidic Messiah in Luke–Acts: The Promise and Its Fulfillment in Lukan Christology*. Sheffield: Sheffield Academic, 1995.
Stuckenbruck, Loren T. "Messianic Ideas in the Apocalyptic and Related Literature of Early Judaism." In *The Messiah in the Old and New Testaments*, edited by Stanley E. Porter, 90–113. Grand Rapids: Eerdmans, 2007.
Sumney, Jerry L. *Colossians: A Commentary*. NTL. Louisville: Westminster John Knox, 2008.

———. "Writing 'in the Image' of Scripture: The Form and Function of References to Scripture in Colossians." In *Paul and Scripture: Extending the Conversation*, edited by Christopher D. Stanley, 185–229. Atlanta: SBL, 2012.

Talbert, Charles. *Ephesians and Colossians*. Paidea. Grand Rapids: Baker Academic, 2007.

———. *The Development of Christology during the First Hundred Years, and Other Essays on Early Christian Christology*. Leiden: Brill, 2011.

Thielman, Frank. *Ephesians*. BECNT. Grand Rapids: Baker Academic, 2010.

Thiselton, Anthony C. *The First Epistle to the Corinthians: A Commentary on the Greek Text*. NIGTC. Grand Rapids: Eerdmans, 2000.

Thrall, Margaret. *2 Corinthians 1–7*. ICC. New York: T&T Clark, 1994.

Tilling, Chris. *Paul's Divine Christology*. Tübingen: Mohr Siebeck, 2012.

Trainor, Michael. "The Cosmic Christology of Colossians 1:15–20 in the Light of Contemporary Ecological Issues." *ABR* 53 (2005) 54–69.

Tuckett, Christopher M. *Christology and the New Testament: Jesus and His Earliest Followers*. Louisville: Westminster John Knox, 2001.

Turner, Max. *Power from on High: The Spirit in Israel's Restoration and Witness in Luke-Acts*. Sheffield: Sheffield Academic, 1996.

———. "The Spirit of Christ and Christology." In *Christ the Lord: Studies in Christology Presented to Donald Guthrie*, edited by H. H. Rowden. Leicester: Inter-Varsity, 1982.

Urassa, Wenceslaus Mkeni. *Psalm 8 and Its Christological Re-interpretations in New Testament Context*. Frankfurt: Peter Lang, 1998.

Van der Watt, Jan. "The Spatial Dynamics of Jesus as King of Israel in the Gospel According to John." *HvTSt* 72 (2016) 1–7.

Vanderkam, James. "Righteous One, Messiah, Chosen One, and Son of Man in *1 Enoch* 37–71." In *The Messiah: Developments in Earliest Judaism and Christianity*, edited by James H. Charlesworth, 169–91. Minneapolis: Fortress, 1992.

Vollenweider, Samuel. "Der 'Raub' der Gottgleichheit: Ein Religionsgeschichtlicher Vorschlag zu Phil 2.6(–11)." *NTS* 45 (1999) 413–33.

Vries, Pieter de. "The Identity of Him Who Is like a Son of Man in Daniel 7:13–14." *JESOT* 6 (2020) 11–13.

Vriezen, T. C. "La creation de l'homme d'apres l'image de Dieu." *OtSt* 2 (1943) 87–105.

Waddell, James. *The Messiah: A Comparative Study of the Enochic Son of Man and the Pauline Kyrios*. New York: T&T Clark, 2011.

Wallace, Daniel. *Greek Grammar beyond the Basics: An Exegetical Syntax of the New Testament*. Grand Rapids: Zondervan, 1996.

Walton, John. "The Imagery of the Substitute King Ritual in Isaiah's Fourth Servant Song." *JBL* 122 (2003) 734–43.

Watts, Joseph D. W. *Isaiah 34–66*. WBC 25. Waco, TX: Word, 1987.

Weinfeld, Moshe. *Social Justice in Ancient Israel and in the Ancient Near East*. Minneapolis: Fortress, 1995.

Wenham, Gordan J. *Genesis 1–15*. WBC 1. Waco, TX: Word, 1987.

———. "Sanctuary Symbolism in the Garden of Eden Story." In *Proceedings of the Ninth World Congress of Jewish Studies*, 19–25. Jerusalem: World Union of Jewish Studies, 1986.

Westermann, Claus. *Creation*. Minneapolis: Fortress, 1974.

———. *Genesis 1–11*. Translated by John J. Scullion. CC. Minneapolis: Fortress, 1994.

Weymouth, Richard J. "The Christ-Story of Philippians 2:6–11: Narrative Shape and Paraenetic Purpose in Paul's Letter to Philippi." PhD diss., University of Otago, 2015. https://ourarchive.otago.ac.nz/esploro/outputs/doctoral/The-Christ-Story-of-Philippians-26-11-Narrative/9926481775701891/filesAndLinks?index=0.

Whitelam, Keith W. "Israelite Kingship: The Royal Ideology and Its Opponents." In *The World of Ancient Israel: Sociological, Anthropological, and Political Perspectives*, edited by Ronald E. Clements, 119–40. Cambridge: Cambridge University Press, 1989.

Whitsett, Christopher G. "Son of God, Seed of David: Paul's Messianic Exegesis in Romans 1:3–4." *JBL* 119 (2000) 661–81.

Wifall, Walter R. "Gen 3:15: A Protevangelium?" *CBQ* 36 (1974) 361–65.

Wildberger, Hans. "Das Abbild Gottes, Gen 1:26–30." *TZ* 21 (1965) 245–59.

Wilder, William N. "The Use (or Abuse) of Power in High Places: Gifts Given and Received in Isaiah, Psalm 68, and Ephesians 4:8." *BBR* 20 (2010) 185–200.

Wilfong, Marsha. "Human Creation in Canonical Context: Gen 1:26–31 and Beyond." In *God Who Creates: Essays in Honor of W. Sibley Towner*, edited by William P. Brown and S. Dean McBride Jr., 42–52. Grand Rapids: Eerdmans, 2000.

Wilson, Walter. *The Hope of Glory: Education and Exhortation in the Epistle to the Colossians*. Leiden: Brill, 1997.

Windisch, Hans. "Die göttliche Weisheit der Jüden und die Paulinische Christologie." In *Neutestamentliche Studien: Georg Heinrici zu seinem 70. Geburtstag*, edited by H. Windisch, 220–34. Leipzig: Hinrichs, 1914.

Wink, Walter. *Naming the Powers: The Language of Power in the New Testament*. Philadelphia: Fortress, 1984.

Witherington, Ben, III. *Conflict and Community in Corinth: A Socio-rhetorical Commentary on 1 and 2 Corinthians*. Grand Rapids: Eerdmans, 1995.

———. *Jesus the Sage: The Pilgrimage of Wisdom*. Minneapolis: Fortress, 1994.

———. *Paul's Letter to the Philippians: A Socio-rhetorical Commentary*. Grand Rapids: Eerdmans, 2011.

Wolter, Michael. *Der Brief an die Kolosser: Der Brief an Philemon*. Gütersloh: Gütersloher Verlaghaus, 1993.

Wright, N. T. *Colossians and Philemon*. TNTC. Grand Rapids: Eerdmans, 1986.

———. *The Climax of the Covenant: Christ and the Law in Pauline Theology*. Edinburgh: T&T Clark, 1991.

———. "Poetry and Theology in Colossians 1:15–20." *NTS* 36 (1990) 444–68.

———. *Paul and the Faithfulness of God*. Minneapolis: Fortress, 2013.

Wright, N. T., and Michael F. Bird. *The New Testament and Its World: An Introduction to the History, Literature, and Theology of the First Christians*. Grand Rapids: Zondervan, 2019.

Wright, Arthur M., Jr. "Disarming the Rulers and Authorities: Reading Colossians in Its Roman Imperial Context." *RevExp* 116 (2019) 446–57.

Wyatt, Nicholas. "A Royal Garden: The Ideology of Eden." *SJOT* 28 (2014) 1–35.

Yamauchi, Edwin M. "Some Alleged Evidences for Pre-Christian Gnosticism." In *New Dimensions of New Testament Study*, edited by Richard N. Longenecker and Merrill Chapin Tenney, 46–70. Grand Rapids: Zondervan, 1974.

Yates, Roy. "A Re-examination of Ephesians 1:23." *ExpTim* 83 (1972) 146–51.

———. "Colossians 2:15: Christ Triumphant." *NTS* 37 (1991) 573–91.

———. "The Christian Way of Life: The Paraenetic Material in Colossians 3:1—4:6." *EvQ* 63 (1991) 241–51.

Yee, Tet-Lim N. *Jews, Gentiles and Ethnic Reconciliation: Paul's Jewish Identity and Ephesians*. New York: Cambridge University Press, 2005.

Ziegler, Philip G. "The Love of God Is a Sovereign Thing: The Witness of Romans 8:31–39 and the Royal Office of Jesus Christ." In *Apocalyptic Paul: Cosmos and Anthropos in Romans 5–8*, edited by Beverly Roberts Gaventa, 111–30. Waco, TX: Baylor University Press, 2013.